the **SOUND ON SOUND** book of

home
recording
made easy

professional recordings on a demo budget

p a u l   w h i t e

Also available by Paul White from Sanctuary Publishing

Creative Recording I – Effects & Processors
Creative Recording II – Microphones, Acoustics, Soundproofing & Monitoring
MIDI For The Technophobe
Live Sound For The Recording Musician
Recording & Production Techniques
Music Technology – A Survivor's Guide
Desktop Digital Studio

The BASIC series

basic DIGITAL RECORDING
basic EFFECTS & PROCESSORS
basic HOME STUDIO DESIGN
basic LIVE SOUND
basic MASTERING
basic MICROPHONES
basic MIDI
basic MIXERS
basic MIXING TECHNIQUES
basic MULTITRACKING

contents

introduction

Home multitrack recording has revolutionised music by enabling anyone with musical ideas to record and mix their own compositions without the need to hire expensive studios. The other major revolutions in music making are MIDI and sequencing, which provide the musician with access to a vast range of sounds, both realistic and abstract. The technology that makes all of this possible is now affordable enough for almost anyone to get involved with it, yet the quality of the end result can rival or even exceed what was possible in top studios just a couple of decades ago. Used properly, even the simplest home-recording set-up can produce unbelievably good results; but, as with all technology, you have to understand how to use it properly if you're to get the best out of it.

Traditionally, home recording has involved recording onto tape, but now we have the choice of analogue or digital tape and tapeless recording onto computer disk. However, the majority of the computer-based systems aim to emulate, as closely as possible, an analogue tape-based environment, so the majority of this book describes the traditional tape-based method of working, although digital tape and tapeless systems are also discussed in some detail. Once you're familiar with the traditional processes involved in recording, you'll find they translate quite easily to the more modern tapeless platforms.

At the time that this book was revised, in the summer of 2000, commercial production of analogue open-reel multitrack machines had ceased completely in the project-studio arena, although some basic cassette multitrackers were still in production – professional two-inch, 24-track machines were being produced only in small numbers by specialist manufacturers. Nevertheless, it appears that used analogue open-reel tape machines – particularly those that use the half-inch, 16-track format – are both common and relatively inexpensive. Despite the advances in digital technology, there are still many musicians who feel that analogue tape produces a more musical sound, so don't feel that you have to go with the flow and choose digital equipment in order to obtain good results.

The purpose of this book is to help you make the most of home recording by taking you through the whole recording and mixing process. You don't have to be particularly technical to use recording equipment, any more than you need to know all about photography to use an automatic camera, but as with all practical subjects there are right ways and wrong ways to do things, as well as useful shortcuts to be learned. I've had many years' experience in recording, and I've taken pains to strip away much of the jargon and mystique that surrounds the subject to help explain the whole recording and mixing process in a straightforward, non-technical way.

You can only fully master recording by actually doing it, which is why this book takes a very practical approach and is comprehensively illustrated with easy-to-follow diagrams. No matter whether you're working with a simple cassette deck and two mics or with a full multitrack recording studio, this book will help you to produce more professional results. More than two decades of experience are concentrated in these pages, making *Home Recording Made Easy* one of the most useful studio accessories you'll ever own.

chapter 1

home recording

When home multitrack recording first became financially practical, little more than 20 years ago, the available equipment was very basic and relatively expensive. For example, a four-track, open-reel tape machine plus a small mixer cost about the same as a high-powered computer-based system capable of recording 24 or more tracks of audio, MIDI sequencing and mixing does today. Furthermore, the choice of affordable effects back in those pioneering days was limited to little more than spring reverb and analogue delay pedals or tape-loop echo units, whereas a modern computer-based system can offer a huge choice of sophisticated studio effects and even "virtual" synthesisers and samplers without the need for any additional hardware, other than a suitable soundcard.

Technology is always evolving, and the rate of evolution has increased dramatically over the past few decades. As is usually the case during times of rapid change, the older technology runs alongside the new, and as each new innovation appears we have to take the time to understand it and learn how to use it effectively. In fact, the only limits to the evolution of technology in the future may be the rate at which we humans can adapt to use it.

In the case of recording, large-format analogue tape machines are still used in many professional studios, but there are no new analogue multitrack machines currently being built for the project-studio market (with the exception of entry-level cassette multitrackers). The last "great" project-studio analogue recorders were the Tascam and Fostex 24-track, one-inch machines and 16-track, half-inch machines. Many feel that the demise of these machines was brought about prematurely, as they had been refined to a very high level of sophistication and were capable of challenging professional large-format machines for the sound quality they produced. Analogue machines have the advantage of being easy to use, although the number of moving parts they use makes them more expensive to build than their tapeless counterparts. Musicians also found themselves increasingly attracted to the sophisticated editing facilities that digital systems offer, while with analogue tape the razor blade and splicing block remain the only editing tools available to the user.

digital recording options

The first successor to the analogue tape machine was the so-called MDM (Modular Digital Multitrack) recorder, and the eight-track Alesis ADAT was the first to capture the imagination of the project-studio user. Although MDMs offer little more scope in the way of editing than analogue systems, with these machines there's no need to make splice edits, as audio tracks can be copied between two machines in the digital domain, thus avoiding the loss in quality that always occurs when analogue tapes are copied. By offsetting the time locations of the two recorders (something that can be done to single-sample accuracy), sections of audio can be copied to different locations, making it possible to copy one good chorus or rhythm part to numerous locations within the same song, for example.

Today there are huge numbers of MDMs in both project and professional studios around the world. Their appeal lies in the fact that the hardware is affordable, the recording media (which is usually some type of video cassette) is cheap and their basic operation is almost exactly the same as a conventional analogue tape machine. Furthermore, multiple machines can be "locked" together to provide more recording tracks. At the same time, stereo DAT (Digital Audio Tape) machines took over from analogue mastering machines – they were cheaper, the technical specs looked attractive (ie they were very quiet and didn't need to employ noise-reduction systems) and, by using two machines, digital back-up copies could be made in the digital domain with no loss in quality.

a tapeless future

Nevertheless, everyone accepts that digital tape is an interim technology, and many users now prefer to go the tapeless route. Tapeless recording is much more flexible and sophisticated than tape-based recording, which means that the user has more to learn in order to use a system effectively and archiving recordings is no longer a matter of putting a box of tapes onto the shelf. However, the sheer power and affordability of modern systems – especially those based around desktop computers – often makes the extra effort worthwhile. Ultimately, though, your choice of recording system is largely dictated by your budget, the type of recording you wish to do and the way in which you prefer to work.

This book looks at the various types of recording systems on the market today and examines the strengths and weaknesses of each. In fact, few people choose to adopt just one approach – more often they'll put together a hybrid system containing some new technology and some less so. For example, few of those who've decided to set up computer-based studios will use the computer to do absolutely everything; more often than not, some external synthesiser, sampler or drum machine modules will also be used, and this normally means that a small mixer will be needed to combine the audio output from the computer system with the audio outputs from these external instruments. MIDI has become so deeply embedded in the way that we make recordings that few people work without it. (Don't worry if it's new to you, though, as this book includes a crash course in MIDI to help you get started.)

the analogue legacy

You may ask – with some justification – why so much emphasis is placed on analogue recording so early on in the book, given that it's yesterday's technology. The reasons are two-fold. Firstly, most people take their first steps into recording via a cassette multitracker. While these don't produce the most professional results, they're compact, affordable and easy to use. More importantly, they can help you to learn the basics of recording, and you can then carry this knowledge and experience forward and apply it to whatever recording platform you decide to use next.

Secondly (and equally importantly), the majority of digital systems emulate the key aspects of an analogue tape machine's user interface in order to make the user feel comfortable. For example, both hardware and software recorders tend to organise their recordings into tracks; there are Record buttons for each track; there are tape-style Stop, Play, Pause and Fast-wind transport buttons; and so on. Even more reliance is placed on analogue ergonomics when it comes to mixing, as both digital hardware and software mixers tend to mimic the user interface of a traditional analogue console in both control layout and signal routing. If you learn how an analogue mixing console works, you'll have little trouble figuring out a digital console; but if you approach a digital console with no prior knowledge, you may find yourself facing a dauntingly steep learning curve.

Furthermore, even in computer-based systems, analogue components – such as mixing consoles and external mic pre-amps – are still widely used, and so you need to know about both analogue and digital equipment in order to use a typical recording system effectively. I feel that it will be many years before digital microphones, digital pre-amps and digital monitoring systems become standard equipment in project-studio circles.

what is home recording?

In the context of this book, home recording means making music recordings that sound as much like commercial records as possible by using affordable equipment in a home environment. Naturally, everyone's definition of affordable will be different, so at one end of the scale there are techniques for recording live performances straight to a stereo tape machine or MiniDisc recorder, while at the other extreme we have a cutting-edge computer-based recording studio capable of producing professional-sounding CDs. Many of the techniques described in this book may be applied wherever you find yourself on this scale, and the aim is to provide an easily digested overview of the equipment involved and the techniques needed to coax the best results out of that equipment. *Home Recording Made Easy* also serves as a starting point from which you can easily access the other books in this series, so if you find yourself needing to know more about mixers, MIDI, mic techniques, desktop studio systems or more advanced production techniques, you'll find everything you need in these books, written in the same approachable style. A full list of complementary titles is detailed at the front of this book.

chapter 2

basic concepts

While the aim of this book is to make recording your own music as hands-on and non-technical as possible, there are certain operational principles that must be understood in order to operate recording and mixing equipment effectively. I've tried to keep this chapter as simple as possible, but please take the time to read it at least once before progressing to the rest of the book.

While it's possible to record music onto analogue tape, digital tape, hard disk or removable magnetic and magneto-optical computer media, analogue cassette-based systems are still the easiest to understand, and the majority of tapeless systems make a deliberate attempt to emulate a traditional "tape" way of working in order to place the user in as familiar a working environment as possible. To explain the underlying process of multitrack recording, I've made a conscious decision to stick with the old "analogue tape" model used in cassette multitrackers, but digital alternatives will be covered in a later chapter.

The main point of multitrack recording is that it enables recorded compositions to be built up one part at a time rather than everything having to be played, mixed and recorded in one go. This makes it particularly attractive to the solo musician working at home, who may want to play many or all of the musical parts himself.

A conventional analogue tape machine, such as a cassette deck, employs a record head, which converts the incoming music waveform into an alternating magnetic field. This field is what transfers the magnetic information from the head onto the magnetic tape. When the tape is played back, the magnetic message now stored on the tape is read by a playback head and then amplified to reproduce the original electrical signal. Of course, the exact physics is a little more complicated than that, but it isn't necessary to know precisely how a tape machine works before you can use it any more than you need to know how a telephone works to call your friends on one.

tape tracks

Magnetic tape is really just a flexible strip made from a durable, non-magnetic material coated with a layer of specially formulated oxide particles that are able to retain magnetic information. The simplest form of recorder is the single-track or mono machine, which writes the magnetic information as a single, invisible stripe along the length of the tape.

Because tape is designed to be re-usable, an erase head is positioned just in front of the record head so that, when you make a recording, the erase head wipes the tape just before it arrives at the record head. If you think of the magnetic recording as being the magnetic equivalent of pictures drawn in sand, the erase head effectively shakes the sand until it's level again by applying a high-frequency magnetic field to the tape. Another way of looking at it is that the erase process randomises the magnetic information on the tape, effectively removing any recognisable signal that may once have been stored there.

Stereo recorders actually make two different recordings side by side along the tape in the form of two parallel tracks. One track feeds the left loudspeaker of a stereo system and the other feeds the right-hand speaker. A stereo record head is really just two heads in one – one to record the left-hand signal and one to record the right. Similarly, the playback head is also two heads in one.

cassette tapes

With a compact cassette, you turn it over once it's got to the end, which lets you record more music "on the other side". This isn't actually recorded on the other side of the tape (the terminology is a throwback to vinyl records, which did have two sides), but rather the two recordings are on the same side, running in opposite directions. If you could see the individual tracks, you'd see something like a two-lane motorway with side one being represented by two lanes running in one direction and side two by two lanes running in the other. This is made clearer by the diagram in Figure 2.1, which shows how the tracks are recorded on a stereo compact cassette.

The figure also shows how the tracks are arranged in a four-track multitrack recorder. Note that the track layout is the same, except that they're now all recorded in the same direction and are all played back at the same time. This means that you can't turn the tape over – it's only used in one direction. It's also important to understand that there's no difference between a mono, a stereo or a multitrack tape cassette. Recording tape is a

Figure 2.1a: Track layout on a stereo cassette

Figure 2.1b: Track layout on a multitracker

single strip of flexible plastic coated on one side with magnetic material. The tracks themselves are created by the record head in the tape machine.

multitrack recorders

Multitrack works on the same principle as stereo, but instead of being able to record only two tracks at once (right and left) you can record, four, eight, 16 or even more tracks, depending on the choice of machine, although eight tracks is the current maximum for cassette-based systems. These tracks may be recorded all at once, a few at once or all independently, depending on how you want to work. You could either record a live performance and then mix it afterwards or build up your composition an instrument at a time. In practice, most people record the first few tracks all at once and then add extra instruments and vocals afterwards in a process known as *overdubbing*. The main point is that you can work whichever way you feel most comfortable.

Being able to build up a recording in layers offers several advantages – for example, one musician can play or sing many different parts in the same piece of music and then, when the recording is finished, the levels of the different tracks can be balanced and panned to give the perfect mix. Even when all musicians are playing together, multitrack provides the ability to record each instrument and voice separately, allowing the relative balance and tone of the various instruments to be adjusted during mixing.

overdubbing

After the first tracks have been recorded, you need some way of hearing these play back while you overdub new parts. For example, if your band has just played the bass, drums and rhythm guitar part to a song, you need to hear this while singing the lead vocal or playing the guitar solo. Listening to a signal being played back on a tape machine is known as *monitoring*, and when recording overdubs this is generally done using headphones to prevent the previously recorded sound spilling back into the microphone.

tape monitoring

On early multitrack machines, different heads were used for recording and playback, and this led to timing problems when overdubbing because the record head was several centimetres further along the tape than the replay head, resulting in a delay of a fraction of a second between the recorded and replayed sound. Complicated switching systems were devised to get around the problem. Today, all cassette multitrackers and virtually all modern semi-pro open-reel multitrack recorders use the same head for both recording and playback, which neatly avoids the problem. Figure 2.2 shows the delay problem associated with older multitrack machines and also the simpler modern system, which uses a combined play/record head.

A single tape track can be used to record only a mono signal, so stereo signals need to be recorded onto two tracks, which must then be panned right and left in the mix to recreate the original stereo image. In many instances, signals are recorded in mono and then positioned across the soundstage during the mix using pan controls. For example, there's little point in recording a lead vocal in stereo. Although there are some advantages to be obtained from recording some instruments in true stereo, the limited number of tracks available from a cassette multitracker makes stereo recording something of a luxury.

punch in/punch out

The concept of multitracking basically involves recording different tracks at different times and then mixing these tracks to stereo so that the result can be recorded onto a conventional stereo tape machine. However, few people make flawless recordings, and so, before you can mix, you'll need some way of being able to fix any mistakes or wrong notes that you may have recorded. The process by which small parts of a recording are replaced with new sections is known as *punching in*.

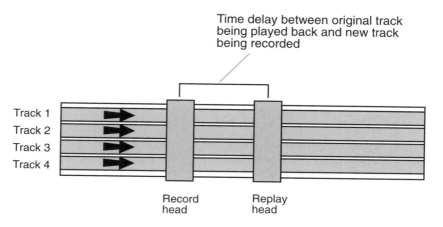

Figure 2.2a: Separate record and replay heads

Figure 2.2b: Combined record and playback head

Imagine that you've recorded a vocal part on track one but one word turns out to be sung flat. You don't have to sing the whole song again; you simply start the tape a few seconds before the mistake, sing along with what's already recorded and then, at the right moment, put the machine into Record (just on the vocal track!) without stopping the tape. At the end of the new section – ideally between words or phrases – you punch out of record again and you have your repair.

Punching in is very simple, but you need to punch in and out during a slight pause or the repair won't necessarily be seamless. Why? Because there's always an overlap in the old and new recorded material at the punch-in point, due to the physical distance between the erase head and the record head. When you punch in, the erase head will turn on, but the short section of tape between the two heads still contains previously recorded material, because it passed the erase head before it came on. Consequently, as new material is recorded, it will overlap the old material by the time it takes the tape to move from the erase head to the record head.

When you punch out, there will be a slight gap, as the short section of tape between the erase head and the record head will already have been erased and nothing new will have been recorded onto it. This might only last a quarter of a second or so, but if it happens in the middle of a sound, rather than during a pause, you'll almost certainly be able to hear it.

So, how do you execute a punch-in? Many multitrack machines allow you to punch in by first setting the track (or tracks) in question into Record Ready mode by using the individual track Record Ready buttons. The punch-in is then executed by putting the machine into Play and then holding down the Play button while pushing down the Record button at the punch-in point. You can punch out again by hitting Stop or, sometimes, by hitting Play. Another system is to put the machine into Record with no tracks selected as Ready and then use the Record Ready buttons themselves to drop in and out. Some recorders also let you use a footswitch for punching in, which is perfect for musicians working on their own. Consult your multitrack manual to find out how your machine handles punching in and out.

auto monitoring

Before the drop in, the existing recording is monitored, preferably via headphones, which means that you can sing or play along to get the feel of the piece. When you punch in to record, the monitoring automatically changes from playing what was originally on the track to the new part that you're recording, and when you punch out of record again the monitoring goes back to playing the recording from tape. Any tracks not set to Record will continue to play normally during a punch-in.

Because most tape machines can handle the monitor switching automatically when you punch in or out, you always hear the right thing in your headphones, which means that you can concentrate on your performance rather than on technicalities.

When recording pop music, it sometimes helps to make the punch-in and punch-out points coincide with a drum beat so as to hide any slight discontinuities which might occur at the edit points. Even if you find suitable gaps to punch in and out, you might find that the sustain of the instrument is still audible at the edit points, and without a beat to disguise it there's a chance that you might hear the edit. Similarly, it's important to start playing before the punch-in point, because the act of punching in may record over the sustain of a note that was playing beforehand. By playing the same notes as the original part before the punch-in point, any sustained notes will be duplicated, making the edit less obvious.

bouncing

At first, having four or even eight tracks to record on seems wonderful, but very soon you'll find that you want to record more parts than you have tracks. The way around this is called *bouncing* – the process of mixing together two or more already recorded tracks and re-recording the result onto a spare track. If you're working with four-track, the most you can do in one go is to record three tracks and then bounce them onto the fourth, which leaves the first three tracks free to be used for new recordings, a process shown in Figure 2.3. All home recording equipment uses the same tape head for recording and playback, so the bounced recording is always in perfect sync with the original tracks. It's very important to check the quality of a bounced mix, because there's no going back once you've wiped over the original tracks.

If you really need to stretch the capacity of your recorder, most multitrack machines will allow you to add one part live as you're bouncing, so you could,

Figure 2.3: Bouncing tracks

Mixer

Record/replay head

Tracks 1-3 are in Play mode

Track 1
Track 2
Track 3

Track 4 is in Record mode

Track 4

Tracks 1, 2 and 3 are combined in the mixer and then recorded back onto track 4. This is known as *track bouncing.* After bouncing, tracks 1, 2 and 3 are free for re-use for example, play a synth part live while bouncing your drum machine, rhythm guitar and bass parts onto a single track, giving you a total of four parts on one track. Those working with other musicians can also record two or more parts at once on the same track, but you won't be able to change the balance of these two parts afterwards.

Digital recorders handle recording and overdubbing in a similar way as analogue machines, but they're invariably designed to provide seamless punch-ins and -outs, which means that it's possible to make an edit in the middle of a continuous sound without producing clicks, gaps or overlaps. The usual means of avoiding clicks is by recording a short crossfade at the edit point, usually of around 10ms or so in length.

Because digital recorders have no record and playback heads in the traditional sense (even though a hard drive has its own record and play heads), there is no equivalent of switching between monitoring from the record head and the play head, as is possible on analogue systems. However, there is another mechanism that causes unwanted monitoring delay, known as *latency*. In simple terms, this is a short but sometimes audible delay between a signal being fed into a digital audio system and the same signal appearing at the outputs. As a rule, latency is only an issue in computer-based systems, and both its causes and solutions will be discussed later in the book.

the ten-track bounce

Using a four-track machine and adding one "live" part every time you bounce means that a solo musician can get ten different parts onto tape without ever having bounced any sound more than once. The so-called ten-track bounce works like this:

- Record tracks 1, 2 and 3;

- Bounce tracks 1, 2 and 3 to track 4 while adding a new "live" part. If you make a mistake recording the live part, you'll have to go back to the start. You can't punch in successfully while working this way, so choose an easy part;

- Check that track 4 sounds exactly the way you want it to – you're about to burn your bridges behind you;

- Record new parts over tracks 1 and 2, then bounce these to track 3, again adding another new live part;

- Again, check the result;

- Record over track 1 and bounce to track 2 while adding another live part;

- Check the result;

- Finally, record your last part back over track 1. Now you're ready to mix.

limitations of bouncing

When you bounce two or more tracks together, you're actually making a copy of your original recording onto a new tape track, and every time you copy a recording you lose a little quality – the noise level increases and the overall clarity tends to suffer, too. Even with a good machine, if you bounce more than once you should expect to notice a drop in sound quality. The best quality will be maintained if you record at the optimum level, and you should always use the meters on the recorder to help you get it right. I'll be talking a lot more about levels later in the book, as poor level matching is responsible for most of the problems concerning sound quality that occur in home recording.

Using a standard four-track machine, you don't have enough tracks to bounce everything in stereo, so what you tend to end up with is four separate mono submixes on the four tracks, which you have to pan in the final mix the best way you can. A little forward planning can go a long way in making the best of this limitation, and a useful tip is to try to keep all of your bass and rhythm sounds together so that you can pan them to the centre of the mix. Solos, sound effects and backing vocals can then be panned to other places in the mix to create the illusion of a wide stereo recording. Stereo effects help with this enormously, as we'll find out later.

Bouncing signals on a digital system generally results in less signal degradation than it does on an analogue system, but some degradation always takes place, whether the mixer is analogue or digital. Ultimately, you have to trust your ears to inform you what sounds acceptable and what doesn't, whichever type of system you use.

In computer-based systems, bouncing isn't necessary for jobs such as compiling a perfect vocal track from the best sections of several different takes. By cutting, copying, pasting and moving material, all of the needed elements can be combined in a single track without the original audio data having to be changed in any way.

As most computer-based systems offer at least 16 tracks of audio recording, and often two or three times this number, bouncing to save on tracks becomes less of an issue. Nevertheless, track bouncing may still be necessary to conserve computing power when software-based plug-in effects are being used. For example, a number of audio tracks – each using different real-time plug-in effects – may be bounced to a single stereo pair, making the effects permanent parts of the new recording. This frees up the computing power that was being used to create those effects, which can now be used for other purposes.

what to bounce?

It's a fact that some sounds take more kindly to being bounced than others, and it's also true that a sound that will eventually end up right in the background can usually be bounced without compromising the final product. In contrast, bouncing a lead part destined to be high in the mix will expose any weaknesses. Bright or percussive sounds tend to suffer the most from bouncing, so try not to bounce your drums or lead vocal parts if at all possible.

Once you've gained a little experience with your machine, you'll probably get familiar with the way that sounds change when bounced, and you may be able to compensate to some extent by adding a little high EQ as you bounce to make up for the drop in brightness that bouncing invariably entails.

recording levels

I mentioned earlier that recording levels are vitally important; if you record at too low a level, your recording will be noisier (with more hiss) than it should be, whereas if you record at too high a level the sound will become distorted as the magnetic coating on the tape becomes saturated. Check the meters on your tape machine when recording and then make a test recording to make sure that everything sounds OK. For most material, the level meters should go just a little way into the red on the loudest parts of your music, but the absolute level varies from one machine to another and from one brand of tape to another. You'll also find that some types of sound show up distortion more than others; vocals and overdrive-style electric guitar can generally be recorded fairly hot before you hear any distortion, while predominantly high-frequency sounds – like bells or cymbals – may distort well before the meters go into the red. For this reason, it's very important to make a few test recordings to see how your individual machine copes with different types of sound. Ultimately, all that matters is the sound, so listen first and then, if the result is OK, make a note of the meter readings for future reference. I know that keeping a notebook isn't very trendy, but unless you have a perfect memory, it's the best way of keeping a record of your settings.

trust the meters?

Short or peaky sounds, such as drums, often produce misleading meter readings on mechanical VU meters, because the meter mechanism isn't fast enough to respond accurately to very short sounds. In fact, a mechanical VU meter really shows you the average sound level as perceived by the human ear. With experience, you get used to what meter reading to expect with what type of sound, but most modern machines use bar-graph meters, which are less likely to be misinterpreted. Bar-graph meters are faster, and so more accurately represent the peak signal level, but you still need to run some tests to find the best levels. Of course, your setting may change if you use a different brand of tape, so it's best to find a brand you're happy with and then stick with it. Most cassette multitrack recorders are designed to use Type II or chrome-type tape, and it's false economy to use anything less than the best-quality tape.

tape speed

You may have noticed that some cassette multitrack machines run at the same speed as a hi-fi cassette deck, whereas others run at twice the speed. As a general rule, the faster the tape speed, the lower the tape noise and the better the high-frequency response, so you can expect better recordings from a double-speed machine. The downside is that your recording time is cut in half. Because multitrack work only uses the tape in one direction, a C60 will last for 30 minutes at normal speed or 15 minutes at double speed. A good tip is to avoid recording anything on the first or last 15 seconds of the tape; if there's a problem with the tape winding evenly onto the hub, this is where it's most likely to cause problems with sound quality.

varispeed

All modern multitrack recorders are fitted with a variable tape-speed control known as either Varispeed or Pitch. The range is only a few per cent, but it's enough to push the pitch of a recording up or down by more than a semitone, which is very useful if you're trying to overdub a piano or some other instrument that isn't at concert pitch. You simply use the Varispeed control to "tune" your recording to the piano, record the piano part and then put the speed back to normal. Varispeed is also useful for helping out singers who can't quite make the high notes – you just slow down the tape a little and try again!

tape noise reduction

Semi-pro analogue tape recorders need to use some form of noise-reduction system, because without it the level of background tape hiss is likely to become obtrusive during passages where the recording isn't loud enough to mask it. Noise-reduction systems provide an effective means of increasing the available dynamic range by reducing the subjective level of tape hiss during quiet passages.

To understand how systems such as Dolby work, it helps to know a little about what went before. There is a very old (but still valid) technique called pre-emphasis/de-emphasis, which entails applying a high-frequency boost to signals during recording and then applying an equal degree of high-frequency cut during playback. This restores the programme material to its original state, but the top cut reduces the level of any high-frequency hiss caused by the tape itself.

Although simple pre- and de-emphasis is rarely used on its own to counter tape hiss, it illustrates very well that noise reduction comprises two stages – the encoding stage, which is applied during recording, and the decoding stage, where the exact opposite treatment is applied during playback. If the same noise-reduction system isn't used both during recording and playback, the programme material's balance of tonal and dynamic accuracy will be compromised.

Tape machines are factory-adjusted for a specific brand and type of tape, and using any other brand is likely to result in a level difference on playback that may upset your noise-reduction system. If you want to use a type of tape not recommended for your machine, get the machine set up specifically for your choice of tape.

You don't have to know how noise reduction works as long as you appreciate that, if you make a recording with noise reduction, you have to play it back using the same type of noise reduction. You also have to appreciate that such noise-reduction systems only help to reduce tape hiss – they don't have any effect on hiss that's recorded as part of your original signal. However, if you'd like to know a little more about the various noise-reduction systems available, read the next section.

dbx

The majority of Tascam Portastudios – including the 488 – use the dbx system, which provides very high levels of noise reduction by combining high-frequency pre-emphasis with 2:1 compression. (If you don't know what compression is yet, check out Chapter 8 on "Effects And Processors".) On replay, a 1:2 expansion (the opposite of compression) is used, along with de-emphasis, resulting in a maximum of 30dB of noise reduction. If noise-reduction systems were judged solely on how much hiss they avoided, dbx would be an outright winner, but in reality all noise-reduction systems cause some side-effects.

Using such a high degree of compression means that the replay signal from the tape machine must match the recorded signal very accurately, both in terms of level and frequency response. That's because the compressor/expander system magnifies level errors in such a way that a 2dB error in the tape machine becomes a 4dB error after decoding. In theory, this implies that the machines best able to benefit from dbx are those that are so good that they don't need it.

To get around this shortcoming, there are actually two different dbx formats: Type 1 for professional use and Type 2 for domestic sound equipment. Type 2 is used in cassette multitrack machines, where the degree of noise reduction is traded off against a greater tolerance to machine and tape errors.

Dbx works by dramatically increasing the level of quiet signals being recorded to tape, with a view to overpowering the tape hiss with brute force. The expansion process on replay reverses the processing and returns the signal to normal, but sometimes it's still possible to hear hiss in the presence of low-frequency sounds where there is no top end present to mask the hiss. A solo bass guitar or deep bass synth may be accompanied by noise which decays as the notes decay, and there is little that you can do about this other than optimise recording levels (and perhaps use some EQ when mixing), although in the context of a complete mix it's rarely a problem, provided that recordings are made on good-quality tape.

When using dbx, it's also important that the recording level shouldn't be driven up into the red but should instead peak at around or just below 0VU. If you push more level onto tape, the tape saturation will cause audible decoding errors, resulting in a dull or squashed sound. In any event, dbx is so effective in reducing noise that you don't need to push your tape to the limit.

Dolby A

Dolby is still the best-known noise-reduction system, and Dolby A has been around for almost three decades, although it's only ever used in professional recording machines. In recent years, Dolby SR has taken over as the preferred professional noise-reduction system.

Dolby B

Dolby B is the most popular version for use in domestic hi-fi cassette machines. Unlike dbx, Dolby B only comes into action when the signal falls below a certain threshold level, where the signal is no longer loud enough to mask the noise. Because hiss is most audible at higher frequencies, Dolby B treats high frequencies differently from low frequencies, and as such it has a lot in common with pre-emphasis/de-emphasis. However, the frequency above which boost is applied during recording varies according to the spectral content of the programme material, and because high-level signals that are loud enough to mask the tape noise aren't treated at all there are fewer audible side-effects. Only the vulnerable low-level signals are subjected to high-frequency boost. Dolby B is quite a well-behaved system, but it can achieve only a modest 10dB of noise reduction.

It's essential that any recorder using Dolby B is lined up to give an accurate playback level; otherwise, the decoding part of the system will come into action at the wrong threshold value. Dolby B is often accused of sounding dull on domestic hi-fi cassette decks, but I suspect that this is largely due to poor machine alignment or a failure both to record and to play back using Dolby B.

Dolby C

Fostex use Dolby C noise reduction for the majority of their cassette multitrackers and open-reel machines, although they have made Dolby B and Dolby S models, too. Dolby C works in a similar way to Dolby B but includes anti-saturation circuitry to prevent high-frequency tape saturation when top boost is being applied to already bright signals. By helping prevent tape saturation, decoding errors are reduced.

As well as being a more tolerant system than Dolby B, Dolby C provides up to 20dB of noise reduction. Playing a Dolby B-encoded tape back via Dolby C sounds tonally incorrect, but at least it's usually listenable.

Dolby SR

Dolby SR is Dolby's flagship noise-reduction system, and was introduced to give the analogue recorder a longer lease of life in the face of competition from digital machines. Up to 25dB of noise reduction is possible with minimal side-effects, but Dolby SR is both technically complicated and very costly. Dolby SR attempts to ensure that the maximum possible energy is recorded in all frequency bands at all times using ten filters, some with fixed frequency bands and others that vary to cover different parts of the audio spectrum depending on the programme material. Anti-saturation circuits are included to prevent high-frequency tape overload.

Dolby SR enables analogue recordings to sound cleaner and more transparent than the best digital recordings, and it's reasonably tolerant of level errors and changes in tape speed. Dolby SR is unlikely ever to find its way into semi-pro recording equipment, but the newer Dolby S system offers some of the benefits of SR without the high cost.

Dolby S

Dolby S is strictly a semi-pro/consumer system, but it's related to Dolby SR, which is why SR was discussed first. Even so, it would be wrong to think of Dolby S as a low-cost version of SR, because in most respects it's more similar to Dolby C, with some of the filter technology from SR added. Dolby S sounds more natural than either Dolby B or C, but although it's much cheaper than SR it still costs significantly more than Dolby B or C.

If you don't fully understand the technicalities, at least you'll now know what noise reduction can do for you and also that, in order to benefit from it, the recording has to be both recorded and played back with the noise reduction switched on. Although all noise-reduction systems introduce side-effects of varying degrees, these are generally minor compared with the level of background hiss that would be present if noise reduction weren't used.

notes on tape care

Good-quality recording starts with good-quality tape, but unless that tape is stored carefully, it could start to deteriorate, putting your precious recordings at risk. Tape should be stored in a dust-free environment (a sealed plastic bag is fine), out of direct sunlight and at a steady room temperature. Because tape is a magnetic medium, it should also be kept well away from magnetic fields, such as those generated by loudspeakers, VDU power supplies and so on.

Never leave tapes in the car or close to radiators, as direct sunlight and heat can greatly shorten the life of recording tape. Avoid damp or dusty atmospheres, and always ensure that your tape machine is clean, especially before making important recordings.

gain structure

On an artistic level, the concept of gain structure is pretty boring, but it's the key to making the best recordings of which your equipment is capable. Failure to pay attention to this vital subject will seriously compromise the quality of your recordings, and even professional equipment will perform extremely poorly if the rules explained here aren't followed.

The human ear can hear sounds ranging in level from the dropping of a pin to nearby thunder. Even the very best recording equipment fails to match the dynamic range of the human ear. In music, we never need to go to these extremes – our quietest sounds are rather louder than dropping pins, while the loudest sounds fall well short of the power of thunder. This leaves us with a more realistic dynamic range, which electronic equipment can cope with, if used properly; but even so, this still involves signal levels varying from just a few microvolts up to around 20 volts.

At the start of any audio chain is the microphone, and once the signal has left the microphone it's electronically amplified to bring it up to line level and then passed through a complex chain of circuitry – which may include mixers, equalisers, amplifiers, effects units and routing systems – before being recorded onto the master tape.

electrical noise

Each piece of circuitry along the way adds a little more noise to the signal due to the thermally induced random movement of electrons, but a well-designed circuit need add only a small amount of noise. While real-life sound signals are always changing in level, the level of noise is essentially constant, so it's evident that, if you feed a very low-level audio signal into a circuit, the ratio of noise to wanted signal is going to be worse than if you feed in a strong signal.

The obvious way to minimise the percentage of noise added to a signal is to make sure that the signal is at as high a level as possible, but there is also a limit to how high a signal level can be before it overloads the circuit it's passing through. Overloading causes the circuitry to clip the extremes of the incoming waveform, causing audible distortion. Figure 2.4 shows a signal being clipped.

To avoid the twin evils of noise and clipping distortion, it's important to use the highest signal level possible while still leaving a little safety margin so that any unexpected peaks can pass through without being distorted. If you look at the VU meters on an analogue tape recorder, you'll see that the optimum operating level is the 0VU mark. The safety headroom is how far you can push the level beyond this point before you hear distortion. Figure 2.5 shows a realistic signal level with enough safety margin to accommodate unexpected signal peaks.

analogue and digital distortion

Most analogue circuits (and analogue tape, for that matter) don't suddenly clip when the level gets too high but, instead, the amount of distortion increases until all of the headroom is used up, and then clipping occurs. That's why the record level meters on an analogue tape recorder can occasionally be driven past the 0VU mark, up into the red. Distortion increases progressively as the signal level exceeds 0VU, but it's normally possible to go several decibels "into the red" before the distortion is severe enough to become audible.

Digital circuits (and digital tape), on the other hand, have no safety margin or area of progressive distortion beyond 0VU, only clipping. For this reason, the

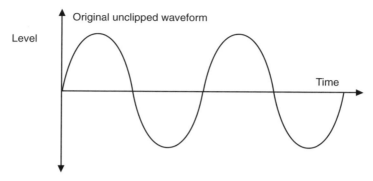

Level

Original unclipped waveform

Time

Figure 2.4: Effect of signal clipping

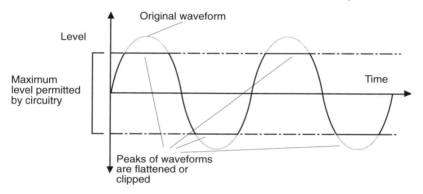

Level

Original waveform

Maximum
level permitted
by circuitry

Time

Peaks of waveforms
are flattened or
clipped

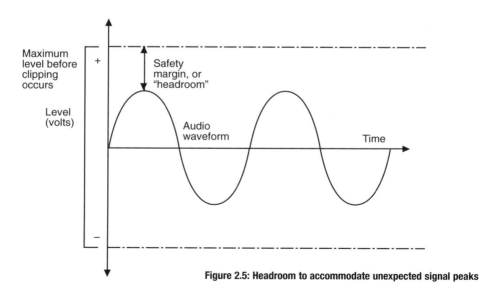

Maximum
level before
clipping
occurs

+

Safety
margin, or
"headroom"

Level
(volts)

Audio
waveform

Time

–

Figure 2.5: Headroom to accommodate unexpected signal peaks

0dB

Level

Time

Analogue tape saturates gradually, so
the amount of distortion increases
progressively as the level exceeds 0dB
on the record meter scale. This is
sometimes called *soft clipping*

**Figure 2.6: How analogue
tape and digital systems
overload**

0dB

Level

Digital systems can't accept any signal
above 0dB, so hard clipping occurs. This is
why digital level meters have no safety
margin shown beyond 0dB

nominal safe operating level for digital equipment is usually chosen to be
around 12dB or so below the 0VU clipping point. Figure 2.6 shows how both
analogue tape and digital systems respond to being overloaded.

If too small a signal is fed into a digital system, it's represented by fewer
bits, which again results in noise – just because something is digital, it
doesn't mean that the old analogue problems are left behind. With both
analogue and digital recording, it's vital to set the right recording level in
order to get the best possible sound with the least background noise. (The
basics of digital recording will be covered later in this book.)

setting gain structure

Put simply, to set up your gain structure means to ensure that every piece of
circuitry in your studio is running at its optimum signal level – not high enough
to cause distortion but also not low enough to allow excessive noise to intrude.

This means making sure not that only your recording levels are optimised but also those of any signals fed into your mixer, any signal-processing equipment plugged into your mixer and any tape machines fed from your mixer. This may sound complicated, but it isn't really. You just have to be methodical and pay attention to setting up your system properly before you start recording.

Good gain structure starts right back at the microphone pre-amplifier of your mixer, tape deck or cassette multitracker, so if you have a mixer or multitrack workstation equipped with PFL (Pre-Fade Listen) buttons, use these to monitor the individual inputs. By adjusting the input gain trim controls, you can get each signal reading an optimum level on the meters. This takes a few minutes but is absolutely vital to obtain a good recording. (If you're not already familiar with these terms, you should check out Chapter 3 on "Mixers".)

In digital systems, gain-structure management extends to ensuring that the maximum possible level of analogue signal is presented to the input converters of the computer soundcard or digital recorder. This may done by using either a mixer or a separate "voice-channel" device combining a mic pre-amp with compression and often some degree of equalisation. Compressing the input signal in the analogue domain offers some advantages over digital compression inasmuch as it increases the average signal level presented to the input converters, thus maximising the resolution of the signal once it is digitised. In digital signals, the maximum possible input level that can be used without clipping taking place is known as DFS (Digital Full Scale). Any signals exceeding this level will cause hard clipping, as all of the bits of the converter have already been "used up". Most digital recorders include a peak indicator of some kind to ensure that short-duration peaks don't cause clipping.

It's interesting to note that, in analogue systems, the signal distortion increases with rises in signal level, whereas in a digital system it's the loudest signals that are the least distorted. This is because, in digital systems, the louder a signal, the more bits of data are used to represent it, and so the more accurate the representation. With low-level signals, fewer bits are switched on, and so the representation of the signal is therefore less precise.

impedance

Electrical resistance is a familiar concept – the higher the resistance, the more voltage you need to force a current through it. It's measured in ohms, and most people will be familiar with Ohm's law, which states that $R = V/I$, where V is the voltage across the circuit and I is the current (in amps) flowing through it.

Impedance is essentially a circuit's resistance to an alternating current, such as an audio signal. In a purely resistive circuit, resistance and impedance are the same thing, but in a reactive circuit containing capacitors or inductors the impedance will vary depending on the frequency of the signal passing through it. Most audio equipment is designed to keep the impedance reasonably constant over the entire audio range, but this isn't always possible in components such as loudspeakers.

Input impedance is, in effect, the load that a circuit presents to the device trying to feed a signal into it. But how is output impedance defined? Input impedance is related to how much electrical current is absorbed by a circuit, whereas output impedance is related to how much current an output can supply. In order to get one piece of equipment to feed another without experiencing problems, we have to pay attention to impedance matching.

matching

In electrical terms, a matched connection is where a circuit with a given output impedance is feeding an input which has the same value input impedance. A 600 ohm output feeding a 600 ohm input would be a perfect match. This is an important concept in any system concerned with transferring the maximum amount of power from one circuit to another, the obvious example being an amplifier driving a loudspeaker. In mechanical terms, impedance matching can be thought of as the electrical equivalent of gear ratios in a car gearbox.

With low-level audio signals, we're no longer concerned about optimum power transfer – we simply want to get a signal from one place to another without doing it any damage. To achieve this, it's usual for the source impedance (the output impedance of the equipment providing the signal) to be made between five and ten times lower than the load impedance (that of the device accepting the signal). Not only does this prevent the signal from being unduly loaded but it also enables one source to drive two or three loads simultaneously.

To see how this works in practice, a mixing console has an input impedance of around one kilo-ohm, while a low-impedance dynamic microphone might have an impedance of 200 ohms or so. This satisfies the criteria for a good match, as the ratio is 5:1. Line inputs have a typical impedance of 50 kilo-ohms, while most equipment designed to drive such a load will usually have an output impedance measured in hundreds of ohms.

If the load impedance is considerably higher than the source impedance driving it, it should be possible to split the source signal to drive two or more loads. You can't, however, work the other way around and join two outputs together to mix them; the two output stages will try to dominate each other and the signal may be seriously distorted. In some cases, equipment damage may result.

Don't worry if this seems a bit academic, because modern-day equipment is invariably designed to interconnect without matching problems. If you have a cassette multitracker, you should read the handbook to see if you need to work with high- or low-impedance mics, but other than that everything should work together quite comfortably. The basic rules on impedance matching are:

• When transferring a signal from one device to another, the output impedance of the source device should be at least five times lower than the input impedance of the receiving device;

• A signal output may be split to feed two inputs, but you should never use a Y-lead to try to feed two outputs into one input. Two or more signals should only be mixed together using a mixer;

• When connecting loudspeakers to amplifiers, the loudspeaker impedance should be as near as possible to the output impedance quoted for the amplifier.

There are two "standard" operating levels in common usage: the -10dBV standard (for semi-pro and domestic recording equipment) and the +4dBu standard (for pro studio gear). These are close enough that, as long as you set your gain controls correctly, they will usually still work together, although the meter readings between the two types of equipment will not agree. In theory, mixing pro and semi-pro equipment will compromise your gain structure slightly, but in practice the deterioration in signal-to-noise ratio is insignificant.

decibels

Equipment specs quote them, meters read them and operating levels conform to them, but what is the decibel (dB) and where did it originate? Even though our VU meters are calibrated in decibels, the most experienced engineer can start to fumble when asked to explain exactly what they are and how they relate to terms like dBu, dBm, dBv and dBV. It's all a throwback to the pioneering days of telephones, but at least it's a standard – of sorts.

The term *decibel* means a tenth of a bel, the bel part being named after Alexander Graham Bell, hence the capital B in dB. The decibel doesn't necessarily relate to any fixed level of signal; it's most often used as a convenient way of expressing the ratio between two signal levels. The decibel scale is logarithmic, just like the human ear, so decibels on a VU meter correspond pretty closely to our subjective impression of loudness.

The method of calculating decibels for both voltage and power ratios is shown at the end of this chapter, and you might like to know that you can pick any power or voltage to be your 0dB reference level and then express all other values relative to that. For example, the record level meter on a tape machine is always set so that the optimum recording level is shown as 0dB, regardless of what that means in terms of magnetic flux at the record head. If a signal is lower than optimum, it's read as minus so many decibels, whereas if the signal is too high it's shown as plus so many decibels.

Because decibels are logarithmic, most calculations involve addition or subtraction rather than multiplication or division. For example, a doubling of voltage corresponds to a 6dB increase, so making the voltage four times as big would equate to a 12dB increase. Similarly, a voltage amplifier having a gain of 60dB amplifies the input signal 1,000 times. The same is true of specifications such as dynamic range – 100dB dynamic range means that the largest signal a circuit can handle is 100,000 times bigger than the smallest it can handle.

dBm

While decibels express only ratios, the dBm is a fixed value where 0dBm equates to 1mW of power dissipated into a 600 ohm load. This is of little direct relevance in the world of modern audio, but it was vitally important in the pioneering days of telephone, when small amounts of electrical power needed to be transmitted over long distances. Therefore, 0dBm refers to a signal of 0.775 volts applied to a load of 600 ohms, which dissipates a power of 1mW.

Today, the term dBm is often abused to signify a signal level of 0.775 volts, but unless the load impedance is exactly 600 ohms this is technically incorrect. Because exact load impedances are less of an issue in modern audio systems, the new term dBu (*u* meaning unloaded) was coined to signify a voltage level of 0.775 volts, regardless of load impedance. In other words, while dBm is a measure of power, dBu is a measure of only voltage. The term dBv (lower-case *v*) also means the same as dBu, although dBu is more commonly used.

A standard reference voltage level of 0.775 volts is pretty clumsy when one volt would be easier to manage. That's where the recently introduced dBV (note the upper case *V*) comes in; it signifies a signal level of one volt without regard to the load impedance.

standard levels

You may have heard it said that some recording equipment works at "plus four" or "minus ten", but what does that mean in practice? "Plus four" actually means +4dBu, an operating level adopted in pro audio due to historic rather than logical reasons and corresponding to an RMS signal level of 1.23 volts. This is a fairly convenient figure for use with modern op-amp circuitry, as it leaves a sensible amount of headroom before the circuitry runs into clipping.

The so-called "minus ten" level was introduced along with semi-pro recording gear, and is largely a Japanese concept. Correctly stated, this is -10dBV, which corresponds to 0.316 volts, or just under a third of a volt. Again, this is reasonable for use with op-amp circuitry, but many purists feel that the +4dBu system provides a better balance between noise and headroom.

Some musical instruments – such as electronic keyboards – have an even lower, -20dBV output level, allowing them to be used with domestic hi-fi equipment. Because of this, some effects units also have matching -20dBV low-level inputs corresponding to a signal level of only 0.1 volt RMS. Such equipment can cause problems, because a lot of mixer gain is required to bring the signal up to a manageable level, the unwanted side-effect being noise. For this reason, it may be wiser to use purpose-built keyboard pre-amps or DI boxes than to rely purely on the mixer line input to provide all of the gain.

digital levels

Once signals are in the digital domain, operating levels fail to have any meaning – all that matters is how many of the available bits are being "used". Nevertheless, problems can arise while matching analogue signal levels prior to conversion, and a number of users complain that their analogue equipment can't provide a high enough output signal to give a full-scale digital reading. There is a reason for this.

Analogue equipment can be driven beyond its nominal 0dB maximum level and still produce an OK-sounding signal. This is because the amount of distortion increases progressively until the equipment clips, which may be anywhere between 10dB and 20dB higher than the 0dB level. Because mild analogue distortion sounds benign, it's common practice to push the meters of analogue recorders and mixers a few decibels into the red, but you can't do this with digital equipment. In order to simplify the matching of analogue and digital equipment, the AES standards committee recommended that the input stages of analogue converters should be calibrated so as to allow a useful amount of headroom above the 0dB level. It seems, however, that different manufacturers have allowed different amounts of safety headroom, although a typical figure is around 15dB, which means that an audio input designed to accept +4dBu professional-level signals will actually read -15dB on the level meter when a +4dBu signal is present. To get a full-scale or 0dB reading, the input would need to be 4dBu + 15dBu, which is a rather hefty 19dBu. Pro analogue equipment has no problems with outputting peaks at

+19dBu, but some project-studio mixers and voice channels may start to struggle before this level is reached. One way around this is to use the -10dBv setting on the mixer's digital input stage, if it has one, but otherwise there's no alternative to using analogue equipment that can deliver these levels.

A similar problem arises when digital equipment is fed into analogue mixers, as the signal will peak again at around +19dB. Some mixers can't handle these high levels without distortion, so again it's necessary either to select the -10dBv output level, if there is one, or to upgrade to better analogue equipment. However, there is a third alternative, which is to fit resistive attenuator pads (10dB should do the trick) at the output of the digital recorder in order to reduce the level of the signal reaching the mixer.

calculating decibels

When comparing two power levels, the difference in decibels may be calculated by the equation

Number of decibels = 10 log (P1/P2) where P1 and P2 are the two powers being compared and where the log is to the base 10.

Don't worry if you don't understand how logarithms work, because few engineers actually get out their calculators when dealing with decibels. Instead, there are some useful figures that you should remember, the most common being that 3dB represents a doubling in power. It follows then that a ten-watt amplifier can produce 3dB more power than a five-watt amplifier. Similarly, a 20-watt amplifier can produce 3dB more power than a ten-watt amplifier. So, how much more powerful is a 20-watt amplifier than a five-watt amplifier? Simple – just add two lots of 3dB, which gives you 6dB.

Because of the mathematical relationship between power and voltage, the calculations are slightly different when it comes to working out voltage ratios in decibels. Here, the equation is as follows:

Number of decibels = 20 log (P1/P2) where P1 and P2 are the two powers being compared and where the log is to the base 10.

Note that we now have a 20 in the equation instead of a 10, which means that the answer is twice what it would be for a ratio of powers. In other words, double the voltage and the level goes up by 6dB; halve the voltage and the level goes down by 6dB.

mixers

Whether you use an all-in-one cassette multitracker or a separate multitrack recorder and mixer, the mixer is the hub of your studio. Not only does it allow you to change the level and EQ of signals, but it also provides a means of routing signals to and from tape or to external effects and processors. In principle, a mixing console is pretty straightforward, although I'd agree that large studio consoles can be intimidating at first sight. Even so, the principles are the same, and the concepts embodied in a cassette multitracker's mixing section also apply to studio consoles.

Mixers comprise several identical "building blocks" known as channels, and the purpose of a channel is to change the level of the signal fed being into it to enable the signal to be EQ'd and to provide routing. Routing includes sending the signal to what's known as a *mix buss* – an electrical circuit that allows the outputs from two or more channels to be added together to form a single, composite signal. In order to illustrate these concepts, I'll describe a simple, four-channel mixer that's designed to mix four signals into one. Because the mixer has only one output, in this case the output signal will be mono. For a stereo signal, we'd need two signal paths – one to carry the left speaker signal and one to carry the right speaker signal.

mic and line levels

Earlier, I emphasised that all electronic circuitry has an optimum operating range, and I introduced the idea of gain structure. Internally, mixers are designed to work within a particular range of signal levels, usually up to ten volts or so. Some signals – known as line-level signals – fall within this range, and these include the outputs from effects units, tape machines and many electronic instruments. However, the signal produced by a microphone is at a much lower level than this. To bring the mic level up to the internal line level used by the mixer, there's a low-noise microphone amplifier positioned right at the input of the channel, and this may also be fitted with phantom power circuitry, enabling it to be used with capacitor microphones.

Capacitor microphones require power to operate, and phantom power is simply a standard method of sending 48 volts along the mic cable from the mixing console. Phantom powering can only be used with balanced microphones. As a rule, if the body of the mic you're using is fitted with a three-pin XLR socket, it's balanced, but always check the data sheet that came with it to be sure. Use of unbalanced cables might cause damage to dynamic mics, as could plugging or unplugging them with the phantom power turned on. You can find out more about microphones in Chapter 4.

channel gain

Because not all microphones produce the same level of output, and because the output level depends on how close and how loud the sound being recorded is, the microphone amplifier is invariably equipped with a gain control, which determines the amount of amplification applied to the signal. In other words, the setting of the gain control relates to how much bigger the signal will be made. Line-level signals don't need to pass through the microphone amplifier, so mixer channels also have a line input. Normally, only the line or mic input may be used, not both at once.

The line input on a typical mixer will also be fitted with a gain control, and on most professional mixers the mic and line inputs will have separate gain controls, but on most home recording mixers and multitrackers, a common control is used for both mic and line gain adjustment.

mixer channels

Figure 3.1 shows a simplified schematic of a four-channel mono mixer with simple bass and treble equalisation. Separate mic and line gain controls have been shown to aid clarity, but in practice a single shared control is more likely on a mixer of this type. There are separate input sockets for both the microphone- and line-input signals, although on budget equipment it's possible that a single socket will be used for both. A switch is sometimes used to select between the microphone input and the line input, but not always.

After the input-gain stage comes the equalisation section, which can be as simple as the bass/treble (also known as hi/lo) arrangement shown here, or it can be a complex, multi-band affair, as is more common in serious semi-pro and professional mixers. (For more about EQ, see Chapter 5 on "Equalisation".) More sophisticated mixers have an additional switch which allows you to bypass the equalisation section when you're not using it.

Finally, the signal level is controlled by a knob or fader before it passes to the mix buss, sometimes via an On or Mute switch. (Note that here all four input

Figure 3.1: Simplified four-channel mono mixer

channels are identical, and a larger mixer would have more input channels.)

The combined signal on the mix buss passes through further amplification stages (known as the mix amplifier) controlled by the a master level fader or knob. This controls the output level of the mixer, allowing it to present the correct signal level to the amplifier or tape recorder connected to the mixer. The master fader may also be used to make controlled fades at the ends of songs.

stereo mixers

A stereo mixer is only slightly more complicated than a mono mixer, as can be seen from Figure 3.2. This is very similar to the mixer shown in Figure 3.1,

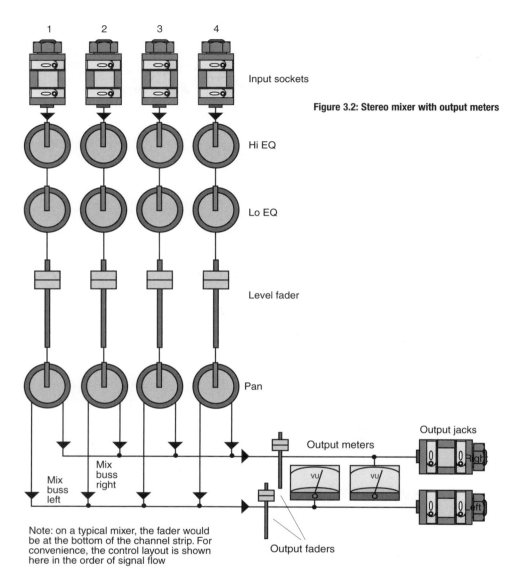

Input sockets

Figure 3.2: Stereo mixer with output meters

Hi EQ

Lo EQ

Level fader

Pan

Output jacks

Output meters

Mix buss right

Mix buss left

Note: on a typical mixer, the fader would be at the bottom of the channel strip. For convenience, the control layout is shown here in the order of signal flow

Output faders

except that the input channels have an extra control for panning the signal between the mixer's left and right outputs. When the pan control is turned completely anti-clockwise, the channel signal is routed exclusively to the left mix buss, while turning it clockwise routes the signal to the right buss and leaving it in the centre routes equal amounts of signal to the left and right busses, making the resulting sound (when reproduced over a stereo speaker system) appear to originate from midway between the speakers. These two busses are often referred to in the singular as a *stereo mix buss*, although in reality the busses are physically separate.

In a stereo mixer, there are two master faders, one for the left output and one for the right, although some mixers use a single stereo control in order to save on cost and space. Figure 3.2 also shows a stereo level meter, which allows the user to monitor the output level of the mixer. This will be familiar to anyone who has used a stereo cassette recorder, although the mechanism here could take the form of a moving-coil meter with a physical pointer or it could be a row of LEDs (Light-Emitting Diodes) arranged in the form of a ladder.

This type of simple mixer is much like those used in small PA applications, although the mixer section of a cassette multitracker isn't very different. A stereo mixer of this type is usually described in the form "something into two" – for example, a twelve into two (12:2) mixer has twelve input channels and two outputs (left and right).

auxiliaries

In the studio, we don't just want to mix and EQ signals; we also want to do things like add effects or send a mix to the performer's headphones. In a live situation, a cue mix is required to feed to the stage monitors, and there has to be some way of providing a different balance on the cue output to that on the main stereo mix outputs. For example, singers usually need to hear more of the vocals than of the instrumental backing.

pre-fade send

Both effects and cue (sometimes called foldback) monitoring can be handled using the auxiliary controls on a mixer, and Figure 3.3 shows how these fit into the picture. Here you can see two new controls: aux 1 and aux 2, where aux is short for auxiliary. Aux 1 is simply another level control feeding a mono mix buss which runs across the mixer to the aux 1 master level control and then to the aux 1 output socket, but the signal feeding the aux 1 control is taken before the channel fader and so is known as a *pre-fade send*. The implication of this is that the aux 1 signal level doesn't change if the channel fader is adjusted. In other words, any mix set up using the pre-fade aux send will be completely independent of the channel faders. This is just what we want for setting up a cue mix for the musician or singer doing an overdub. The overall aux 1 mix is controlled by the aux 1 master level control, and the aux 1 output would normally feed a headphone amplifier. Using a pre-fade send, the engineer can provide the musician with a monitor mix that's exactly to his or her liking.

post-fade send

The second aux control, aux 2, takes its feed from after the channel fader (post-fader), so its level is affected by any changes in the channel fader

1 2 3 4

Input sockets

Figure 3.3: Aux controls

Hi EQ

Lo EQ

Pre-fade aux out

Pre-fade aux send buss (foldback)

Level fader

Post-fade aux send (effects) Post-fade aux out

External (stereo out) effects unit

Pan

Effects return level

Output jacks

Right

VU   VU

Mix buss right

Mix buss left

Left

Note: on a typical mixer, the fader would be at the bottom of the channel strip. For convenience, the control layout is shown here in the order of signal flow

Output faders

setting. This is exactly what we need if aux 2 is being used to feed an external effect, such as reverb, because when the channel signal level is turned up or down we want the amount of effect to change by a corresponding amount.

By using different settings of the aux 2 control on each channel, it's possible to send different amounts of each channel's signal to the same effects unit. When the output from this effects unit is added to the main stereo mix, this has the advantage that different amounts of the same effect can be added to different sounds in a mix. A typical example might be where one reverberation unit is used to provide a rich reverb for the vocals, less reverb for the drums and little or none for the guitars and bass.

It's important to note that an effects unit used in conjunction with a channel aux send should be set up so that it produces only the effected sound and none of the original. This is usually accomplished by means of a mix control, either in the form of a knob or accessed via the effects unit's editing software. In either case, the mix should be set to 100% effect, 0% dry.

effects returns

The output of the effect unit may be fed back into the mixer via spare input channels or via dedicated effects-return inputs, also known as aux returns. Aux returns are electrically similar to input channels but usually sport fewer facilities. They'll have no mic inputs, and on a simple mixer they may have no EQ or aux sends of their own. Normally, they feed straight into the main stereo mix.

A spare input channel – or a pair of them panned hard left and right, for stereo – may be used as an effect return, and here you gain the benefit of EQ and access to the aux send busses – for example, you may want to add reverb to the cue mix. However, you must ensure that the corresponding aux send (in this case aux 2) is turned down on the return channel, or the effect signal will be fed back on itself, resulting in an unpleasant howl or scream. (The diagram in Figure 3.3 also shows how an external effects unit is connected. All of the controls shown in the figures are arranged in a logical order to illustrate the signal flow through the channel, although commercial mixers tend to have their pan and aux controls located above the channel fader for convenience.)

insert points

Another way to connect an effects unit or signal processor to a mixer is via an insert point. All serious stand-alone mixers have insert points on their input channels and also on the master stereo outputs, although self-

1   2   3   4

Input sockets

Hi EQ

Lo EQ

Note: the insert jacks are shown post-EQ. On some consoles, the insert points may be pre-EQ

External signal processor

Insert point

Pre-fade aux send

Insert point is a TRS jack so that the send and return signals can be carried by a single socket. To connect the external processor, a special twin-core screened cable must be used with a stereo jack at one end and two mono jacks at the other

Level fader

Pan control and busses omitted for clarity

Figure 3.4: Channel insert points

contained multitrackers don't always have them. An insert point is just a socket that allows the signal path of a normal channel or stereo master to be interrupted and re-routed through an external device. When no plug is inserted, spring contacts inside the socket complete the connection so that the signal flow isn't broken.

On most home recording mixers, the insert points are on stereo jack sockets, which means that you need a specially wired Y-lead or adaptor to be able to use them. The stereo socket is conventionally wired "tip send/ring return", with the cable screen being common to both send and return. Figure 3.4 shows the channel insert points in a typical mixer. Physically, they appear as stereo jacks, and are usually found near the mic- and line-input sockets.

effects and processors

This next paragraph is very important, and understanding its implications will save you a lot of trouble and frustration later on. While it's permissible to connect any type of effect or signal processor via an insert point, there are restrictions on what can be used via the aux send/return system. As a rule of thumb, only delay-based effects – such as reverb, echo, chorus, phasing, flanging and pitch shifting – should be connected via the aux system, and these are generally called *effects*. If the box uses delay to do its work, it's an effect, and if there's a dry/effect mix knob or parameter, the box is almost certain to be an effect. The unique thing about an effect is that it's added to the original signal. A *process*, such as EQ, doesn't add to the original signal, but instead changes it. Processors – such as compressors, gates and EQ – may only be connected via insert points, and under normal circumstances never via the aux sends and returns.

multitrack mixers

Cassette multitrackers have relatively simple mixer sections, and because everything is in one box you don't have any wiring to worry about, other than plugging in the mics. Things get slightly more complicated when you move up to a separate mixer and multitrack recorder, but most of what you've learned already still applies.

As touched upon earlier, a studio console doesn't just mix signals, it also acts as a central routing system, sending signals to the different tape-machine tracks, adding effects from external processors and mixing the outputs from the tape machine to produce a final stereo mix. At the same time, it has to function as a "mixer within a mixer" so that a separate control-room monitor mix can be set up while the performers are recording or overdubbing.

tracks or channels?

The terminology associated with mixers can be a little confusing, and a common mistake that even experienced users make is to refer to a mixer as having so many "tracks". In fact, mixers don't have tracks – they have channels (inputs) and groups (outputs). It's tape recorders that have tracks!

So far, we've described a simple input channel with input gain, EQ, aux sends, pan control and a fader, but on a multitrack mixer there are two different kinds of channel. The main input channel generally has the most comprehensive facilities, and is used to feed microphones and line-level sources (such as keyboards and samplers) into the mixer while recording.

When you're mixing your tape tracks, the input channels handle the output from the multitrack tape machine.

The other type of channel is the monitor channel, so called because it's used to set up a guide monitor mix based on the multitrack outputs while the performers are overdubbing new parts. Without some way of hearing a mix of the tracks that have already been recorded, there would be no way for the musician to keep in time or stay in tune with the music already recorded.

monitor channels

Monitor channels tend to have fewer facilities than the main input channels, because their main job is to provide a rough mix during the session. They may have little or no EQ and fewer aux sends than the main channel, although on an in-line mixer (so called because the main input and monitor controls are located in the same channel strip as the input channel controls) there's often a provision to switch all or part of the EQ between the main and monitor signal paths, and the same is often true of the aux sends. To make visualisation easier, I like to think of the monitor section as being like a separate mixer connected to the tape-machine outputs. The fact that this shares the same box as the main mixer (used for feeding stuff onto tape) is purely for convenience.

Because there's no need for a monitor mix when the recording is complete, most mixers allow the monitor channels to be used as extra line inputs at the mixing stage. These may be used as additional effects returns, or to add sequenced MIDI instruments, and they generally feed directly into the stereo mix.

groups

Until now, we've talked about mixers with simple stereo outputs, but for multitrack work we need some way of routing different signals to different multitrack inputs at the same time. That's where the mixer group comes in. Whereas a stereo mixer just has a left and a right output, a multitrack mixer has several additional outputs, each with its own fader. These separate outputs are known as *groups*, and an eight-group mixer is ideal for use with an eight-track tape recorder. The term "eight-group" simply means that the mixer has eight mix outputs in addition to the main stereo output. You may also see such a mixer described as an eight-buss console, because the eight groups are fed from eight mix busses.

Any of the input channels may be routed to any of the eight group outputs via routing switches linked to the eight group busses (as well as to the stereo output), and if two or more channels are routed to the same output they're automatically mixed together. As before, the channel faders set the relative levels of the various elements in the mix, but now the group fader controls the overall level feeding the tape machine or other multitrack device. During recording, the group outputs feed directly into the correspondingly numbered inputs of the multitrack tape machine, enabling any mixer input to be routed to any tape track without the need to replug any cables.

routing

On a cassette multitracker, routing the desired input signals to tape is relatively straightforward, as you usually have only four tracks to play with. On a multitrack mixing console, however, you'll find a set of routing buttons next to the channel faders, which are used to send the channel signals either to the various group outputs (which are connected to the multitrack inputs) or to the stereo mix. At mixdown, the stereo mix is used to feed the stereo-mastering recorder, but the stereo output also feeds the control monitor during recording, overdubbing and mixing so that you can hear what you're working on.

pan and routing

Within each input channel, a single routing button handles the routing for a pair of groups, with the pan control being used to change the balance of what's sent to the odd- and even-numbered groups. If you wanted to route a channel only to output group 2, for example, you'd press the routing button marked "1/2" and turn the pan control fully clockwise so that all of the signal went to group 2 and none to group 1. Leaving the pan in its centre position would send equal amounts of signal to groups 1 and 2. To record something in stereo (for example, the different drum mics over a drum kit), the relevant channels would be routed to a pair of groups and the pan control used to position the various sounds between them. The outputs from these two groups would then be recorded to two tracks of tape. When mixing, these two tape tracks would be panned hard left and right to maintain the stereo image that was created during recording.

routing buttons

On an eight-group mixer (the most popular format for project-studio use), the routing buttons would be marked 1/2, 3/4, 5/6 and 7/8, with a further L/R button for routing the channel directly to the stereo mix. Figure 3.5 shows the signal flow through the routing buttons of a typical console, including the signal path to the group fader and group output socket. Note that you don't have to use an eight-group mixer to work with an eight-track tape machine; you could use a four-group mixer, as long as you don't need to record more than four groups at a time. You can still record more than four tape tracks at

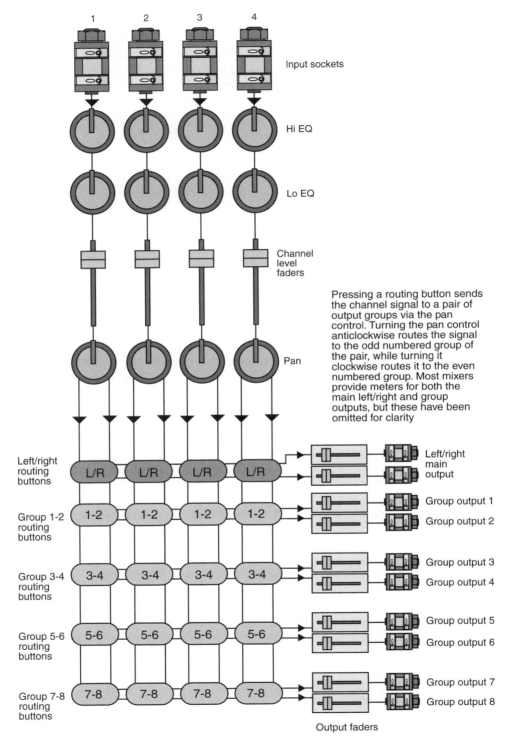

1 2 3 4

Input sockets

Hi EQ

Lo EQ

Channel level faders

Pressing a routing button sends the channel signal to a pair of output groups via the pan control. Turning the pan control anticlockwise routes the signal to the odd numbered group of the pair, while turning it clockwise routes it to the even numbered group. Most mixers provide meters for both the main left/right and group outputs, but these have been omitted for clarity

Pan

Left/right routing buttons   L/R   L/R   L/R   L/R

Left/right main output

Group 1-2 routing buttons   1-2   1-2   1-2   1-2

Group output 1
Group output 2

Group 3-4 routing buttons   3-4   3-4   3-4   3-4

Group output 3
Group output 4

Group 5-6 routing buttons   5-6   5-6   5-6   5-6

Group output 5
Group output 6

Group 7-8 routing buttons   7-8   7-8   7-8   7-8

Group output 7
Group output 8

Output faders

Input channels   L/R meters   Group output meters

In a typical split-console mixer, the tape monitor section is separate and located to the right of the master section

Group output faders

Master section, including L/R master faders

Figure 3.6: Split console arrangement

a time by using channel direct outputs, insert sends or even spare aux sends to feed additional tape tracks.

By connecting group output 1 to tape inputs 1 and 5, and group output 2 to tape inputs 2 and 6 and so on, you can still record on all eight tracks without having to replug any cables. The tape machine's Record Status buttons determine which of the two possible tracks each group will record onto.

split and in-line monitoring

On a conventional "split" mixing console, the group faders and the monitor channel controls are situated on the right-hand side of the mixer. Between the main input channels and the monitor section is the master section, which includes functions such as the master stereo faders, the aux send and aux return master controls. On a more advanced mixer, you'll also find things like the test oscillator, the talkback mic, mix/two-track monitoring, headphone-level control and so on. An eight-group console needs a minimum of eight monitor channels in order to provide an off-tape monitor mix, but many models have 16, allowing the mixer to be used with a 16-track recorder using the split wiring arrangement described in Figure 3.6. The basic requirements for a monitor channel are level and pan controls, so that a stereo cue mix can be provided from the outputs of the multitrack recorder. In practice, though, most monitor channels have some form of basic EQ and also have aux controls

are fed via the input
channels

Figure 3.7: Signal flow during recording

Monitor section shown
below recorder to clarify
signal flow

Track recording levels set
via group faders

Split-format recording console

Multitrack recorder

Track 8

Recorder inputs   Track 1

During recording, the input
channels are routed to the
appropriate tape tracks and
the recording levels set using
the group faders. The control
room monitor mix is based on
the outputs from the multitrack
recorder, mixed though the
monitor section of the console

Monitor speakers

Left/right
faders

Monitor section of mixer

Monitor amplifier

Monitor amplifier fed
from control room
monitor output

54

that feed the same aux busses as the main mixer input channels. Figure 3.7 shows a multitrack mixer with the monitor section shown separately. In reality, the monitor section is housed in the same box as the rest of the mixer, but it can help to visualise it as a separate mixer within a mixer. The diagram shows the direction of signal flow during recording.

tape monitoring

Why is it that the monitor section always monitors the tape-machine outputs? What happens if you want to hear what you're playing at the same time as you're recording? Fortunately, modern multitrack tape machines are far simpler than they used to be when there was a time delay between the record and playback heads and when there were separate switches on the tape machine to switch each tape track between Input, Sync and Playback Monitor mode.

Modern tape machines take care of monitor switching without you even having to think about it, and the relevant signal is always present at the tape-output socket. If a track is being recorded, you hear the tape input, but if the track is in Playback mode then you hear what's on tape. However, older tape machines usually have a switch which allows each monitor channel to be fed from either the multitrack output or the group output (which is the same thing as the multitrack input).

console formats

Currently, virtually all budget recording consoles adopt the in-line format, which differs from the split concept in that the monitor controls reside in the same channel strip as the main input channel controls. In a split console, the monitor section is usually in the master section or to the right of it, giving it more of a separate feel. In-line consoles may seem confusing at first, but the advantage with them is that, instead of being limited to just eight or 16 monitor channels, there's one monitor channel for every input channel. This layout usually results in a mixer that's deeper, front to back, than one which follows an equivalent split design, but it also means that the mixer can be made narrower and yet still have the same number of channels – an important consideration in a studio where space is limited.

split EQ and aux sends

Most monitor channels have at least one aux send control, so that effects may be added to the foldback or cue mix, but there may be little or no room for EQ controls. Depending on the model and make of in-line mixer, you may get just a simple bass and treble EQ, or no EQ at all. To help compensate, there's often a switching arrangement that allows the monitor channel to share part of the main input channel's EQ. For example, if the main EQ is a four-band affair with two sweep mids, the monitor channel may be able to make use of the hi and lo EQ, leaving the main input channel with two sweeps. In such cases, the sweep range is usually wide enough to allow the two mids to cover the entire audio spectrum. Another common arrangement is for a couple of the aux sends to be switchable between either the input or the monitor channel.

mixing down

When mixing down with a split console, you have to route all of the tape tracks to the main input channels and then set up the mix from scratch. With an in-line console, however, as each track is recorded, you can operate a "flip" switch in the channel strip which routes the tape signal through the main input channel path, leaving the monitor input free for later use. The benefit of working in this way is that you can be working on your mix and fine-tuning the balance and EQ as you go along. By the time you've finished recording, you should already have the basis of a good mix set up.

monitors as line-ins

Once the flip switch has been operated, the monitor channels are connected to the console line inputs allowing many line-level sources to be fed into the mix. In these days of large MIDI systems, many of which are used synced to tape, these additional inputs are a necessity, not a luxury. Furthermore, these spare monitor channels may be used to handle extra effects returns if you run out of conventional effects return inputs. (At this point, it's worth reiterating that an effects return is just another kind of input channel.)

all-input mixing

Although both in-line and split consoles have separate monitor channels to provide an off-tape control-room mix while recording, it seems that a great many people don't use them for that purpose at all. Instead, they operate their mixers in so-called "all-input" mode.

If you have an eight-track tape machine, and if you have enough mixer input channels, you can leave the outputs of your tape machine permanently connected to the first eight channels of the mixer, routing these directly to the stereo L/R mix. The remaining channels may then be used to handle the signals being recorded. This does away with the need to switch the off-tape signals between the monitor and input channels, and it also means that you can build up your mix, complete with added effects, as you record. In effect, your control-room mix also becomes your final mix.

The permanently redundant monitor channels may then be used as inputs for MIDI instruments being sequenced in sync with the multitrack recorder, or as effects returns. The only limitation of working in this way – other than having to ensure that you have a mixer with enough input channels – is that the monitor channels can't be routed via the groups to create subgroups – they always feed directly into the stereo L/R mix. There's no right or wrong way to use your console; it's just a matter of finding a system that works for you.

subgrouping

Just as the monitor channels change roles when switching from recording to mixing, so does the group routing system. During recording, the groups are used to route signals to tape, but when you mix they can be routed back into the stereo mix. As always, there's a very good reason for this.

Imagine that you have backing vocals recorded over four or five tracks of your multitrack tape. To change the overall level of the backing vocals, you'd have to change the level by moving several faders at once, which is both cumbersome and inaccurate. A more effective approach is to create a *subgroup* of the backing vocals by routing the vocal channels to a pair of groups rather than directly to the left/right mix. In this way, the whole stereo backing-vocal mix can be controlled by just two group faders. Some consoles have the groups permanently routed to the stereo mix, while others provide "groups-to-stereo" buttons for each group fader, and these generally route all odd-numbered group faders to the left and all even-numbered ones to the right.

A better system – which is usually missing from budget consoles for reasons of cost – is to provide group pan controls. If you have group pan controls, you can then create mono subgroups and still pan them anywhere in the stereo mix. If you don't have group pan controls, you always have to use up two group faders for every subgrouping operation, apart from those where the end result will be panned either hard left or hard right.

In a typical mix, you might create subgroups from things like drums, backing vocals and keyboards, which would reduce the number of faders which would need to be moved during the mix. Note that any effects that are to be added to these subgroups using the aux sends should be returned to the same subgroup (using the channel or effect-return routing buttons), or the effect level won't change when the group fader is moved.

Figure 3.8 shows the signal flow at mixdown. In this example, the monitor channels are being used as extra line inputs, and the line depicting signal flow shows how subgroups actually work.

Effects unit (mono in, stereo out) connected to aux send and return points on the console

Sequenced MIDI modules (stereo) fed to spare tape-monitor inputs

Multitrack recorder

Master stereo recorder fed from main mix output

Monitor system fed from control room monitor output

Figure 3.8: Signal flow when mixing

choosing a mixer

When choosing a mixer as part of your system, don't look at your system as it is now but as it might be in a year or two's time. If you don't, you're bound to run out of channels as your MIDI system expands or as you add more tape tracks. If you have a very large MIDI set-up, consider whether buying a separate rack submixer would make more sense than buying one big multitrack console, and find out if expander modules are available for the mixers on your shortlist. If you've moved into digital multitrack, you have the option of using multiple machines to provide more tracks, but will your choice of mixer allow for this? You may even be considering mix automation, in which case you should find out if there's a system that can be added to your mixer at a later date.

You can never predict every future requirement, and even if you could you probably couldn't afford to buy a mixer that would cover every eventuality, but a little forethought will help you choose something that you aren't likely to have to sell at a loss in six months' time, when you've outgrown it.

digital mixers

Digital mixers do essentially the same job as their analogue counterparts, the main practical difference being the user interface. There may also be a digital link between the mixer and compatible digital multitrack machines, which preserves signal integrity and simplifies wiring.

Because digital mixers can incorporate more features than can be squeezed onto the average analogue console, it would be impractical to provide a physical control for each function. Instead, there tends to be a physical fader provided for each channel (often motorised, in the case of an automated mixer) but only one set of EQ and aux send controls. A selector button located by each fader allows the control section to become active for that particular channel, and a display screen usually provides further information, as well as a physical representation of some of the virtual controls.

Most modern digital consoles include effects, dynamic processing and the ability to automate complete mixes, right down to controlling EQ and aux settings, making it possible to recall an old mix many months after it was first created and get it back exactly how it was originally. Only a couple of years ago, I would have thought digital mixers to be beyond the scope of this book, but now they're already starting to appear in digital multitracker-type products.

digital advantages

It's arguable whether digital mixers have any sonic advantage over analogue consoles, and they're certainly less straightforward to use, but they do make it possible to access and automate a great number of functions at a relatively low cost and in a very compact form. Already we've almost reached the stage where it's cheaper for a manufacturer to build a completely automated digital mixer than an equivalent manually operated analogue mixer.

One very real advantage of using a digital mixer with a digital multitrack recorder is that the signal is kept in the digital domain for as long as possible. Indeed, by using a digital master recorder (such as a DAT machine), once the mic signal has been recorded to digital it need never leave the digital domain until it reaches the end user's hi-fi system. As a rule, signal deterioration occurs whenever analogue signals are converted to digital signals or vice versa, so once a signal is in the digital domain it makes sense to keep it there.

chapter 4

microphone types

E very microphone performs the same basic task of converting sound energy into electrical energy, but there are many different types of microphone and one of the recording engineer's many skills lies in knowing how to pick the best type for a particular job. If the right choice is to be made, it helps to have a basic knowledge of how microphones work and in what areas the various types differ.

In music recording, we encounter mainly dynamic or capacitor microphones, with dynamic mics being the most common because of their suitability for stage work. In professional applications, you may also come across ribbon microphones, which are favoured for classical music applications, but ribbon mics are very rarely seen outside professional studios or broadcast companies.

One factor that all microphones have in common is that the air vibrations that constitute sound are used to move a lightweight diaphragm, the movement of which is then used to generate an equivalent electrical signal. To put it more directly, the rapid positive and negative changes in air pressure which we perceive as sound are converted by the microphone into analogous positive and negative fluctuations in an electrical current.

dynamic mics

A dynamic mic comprises a lightweight, rigid diaphragm attached to a coil of wire suspended in a magnetic field created by a permanent magnet and an air gap. As the diaphragm moves in response to sound, so does the coil, and a tiny electrical current is generated in exactly the same way as a spinning dynamo produces electricity. Faraday's laws dictate that moving an electrical conductor in a magnetic field will cause an electrical current to flow in that conductor, which is exactly what happens when the diaphragm (and hence the coil) is set in motion by a sound. Dynamic mics are relatively inexpensive and mechanically robust, and they require no electrical power to operate, which makes them attractive choices for many home recording applications.

Lead-out wires

Magnet

N

Coil

Diaphragm

Figure 4.1: Dynamic mic schematic

On the other hand, the sound energy has to move both the microphone's diaphragm and the coil attached to it, the outcome of which is that high-frequency vibrations are opposed by the combined inertia of the coil and diaphragm. Inertia resists acceleration, and a vibrating microphone diaphragm has to accelerate and decelerate many times each second as the diaphragm moves first one way and then the other. In practical terms, this means that dynamic models are struggling pretty hard by the time you get to the upper frequencies of the human hearing range, and few models produce a meaningful output far beyond 16kHz. Figure 4.1 shows a typical dynamic mic schematic.

Another side-effect of the finite mass of the diaphragm/coil assembly is that the dynamic microphone isn't particularly efficient – the signal needs to be amplified many times before it's large enough to be usable. Unfortunately, the more you have to amplify a signal, the more electrical background noise is added. With loud or nearby sounds, this presents no problem, but the dynamic microphone copes less well when you're working with quiet or distant sound sources.

The ribbon mic is a form of dynamic microphone, except that the diaphragm and voice coil are replaced by a thin metal ribbon suspended in a magnetic field. In this type of microphone, the ribbon moves in response to sound energy, and the resulting electrical signal is induced in the ribbon itself. The ribbon is lighter than the combined voice-coil and diaphragm assembly of a conventional dynamic microphone, which makes it slightly better able to cope with high frequencies, although the main advantage of ribbon microphones is their smooth, detailed sound.

capacitor mics

Capacitor microphones – sometimes also known as condenser mics – have been around for decades, but they still represent the state of the art in microphone technology. Capacitor mics don't need voice coils, because they work on an entirely different principle. This means that the diaphragm can be made much thinner and more flexible, and because of its lower inertia it can follow high frequencies with ease.

In practice, the diaphragm is just a few microns thick, and this is given a metal coating only a few atoms thick in order to make it electrically conductive. Holes are drilled in the fixed back-plate to prevent air from being trapped between the plate and the diaphragm, which would act as a cushion pushing against the moving diaphragm and would adversely affect the microphone's performance. The result is a very sensitive microphone that's capable of resolving high-frequency detail right up to the limits of human hearing and beyond.

As the diaphragm vibrates, its distance from the stationary metal plate varies, and if a fixed electrical charge is applied between the diaphragm and the plate, a corresponding change in electrical voltage is produced. This change in voltage is amplified by circuitry within the microphone, which is why capacitor microphones need electrical power to operate. Power is also needed to provide the electrical charge on the diaphragm. Figure 4.2 shows how a capacitor mic works.

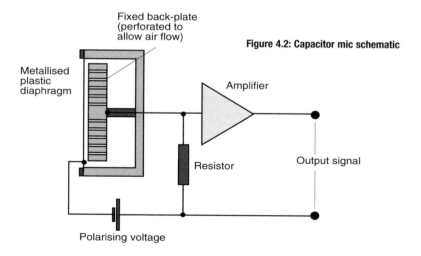

Fixed back-plate (perforated to allow air flow)

Figure 4.2: Capacitor mic schematic

Metallised plastic diaphragm

Amplifier

Resistor

Output signal

Polarising voltage

While the operating principle of all capacitor mics is the same, they can be built with diaphragms of different sizes and thicknesses and of different materials. Small-diaphragm models tend to sound extremely accurate, while large-diaphragm models often have a warm, flattering sound, making them popular for studio vocals.

capacitor pros and cons

Capacitor mics exhibit a significant increase in sensitivity compared with dynamic models, making them more suitable for recording both quiet and distant sources. They can also resolve high-frequency detail up to and beyond the limit of human hearing. So, if they're so good, why use anything else?

Capacitor microphones need an internal pre-amplifier in order to amplify the signal from the capsule and to provide impedance matching. This adds to the manufacturing cost, and a source of power is also needed, not only to run the pre-amp but also to provide the electrical charge on the diaphragm. The most common source of microphone power is the 48V phantom power source built into most mixing consoles, although tube-based capacitor mics tend to have their own dedicated power supplies.

Because of their complexity, good capacitor microphones are significantly more expensive than their dynamic counterparts and tend to be less robust. However, they're much more sensitive, making them suitable for recording both quiet and distant sources, and they can resolve high-frequency detail much better than a dynamic microphone can.

The broader market created by the project studio has meant that lower-cost capacitor models are now available, some of which rival the professional models in terms of performance.

electret mics

A variation on the capacitor mic is the electret mic. On these models, instead of the capsule being charged from an external voltage supply, the diaphragm contains a permanent electrical charge sealed in an insulating material. A pre-amplifier is still required to amplify the signal from the capsule, but this may be battery operated in some models.

The original electret mics performed quite poorly, for the simple reason that building a diaphragm that could hold a magnetic charge meant making it thicker and heavier than that found on a true capacitor model. Greater thickness means greater mass, and this leads to poor sensitivity and a poor high-frequency response, just as with the dynamic mic.

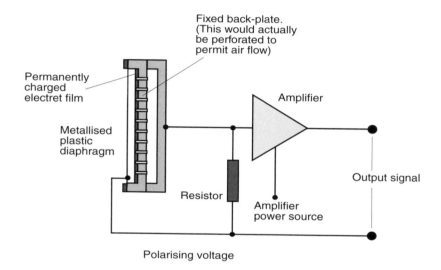

Fixed back-plate.
(This would actually
be perforated to
permit air flow)

Permanently
charged
electret film

Amplifier

Metallised
plastic
diaphragm

Output signal

Resistor

Amplifier
power source

Polarising voltage

back-electret mics

The performance of the electret mic improved dramatically when manufacturers decided to try out a design where the permanently charged material was fixed to the capsule's stationary back-plate, thus allowing the same metallised plastic diaphragm to be used as on true capacitor models. The result was the back-electret microphone, and the best examples of these can rival a conventional capacitor microphone in all aspects of performance. In theory, the electrical charge on the capsule of an electret mic will leak away, but modern models are expected to remain stable for several decades. Figure 4.3 shows the construction of a back-electret microphone.

It's possible to buy a good back-electret mic for little more than a dynamic mic would cost, yet they out-perform their dynamic counterparts by a significant margin in applications where sensitivity and high-frequency response are important. Lower-cost back-electret microphones often offer a choice of battery or phantom power operation, whereas better models operate from phantom power only, as the increased voltage provides them with more headroom.

Omnidirectional
This pattern picks up
sound equally in all
directions

Cardioid
Picks up sound
mainly from the front
and is least sensitive
at the rear

Omnidirectional
This pattern picks up
sound equally in all
directions

Cardioid
Picks up sound
mainly from the front
and is least sensitive
at the rear

Figure 4.4: Common microphone patterns

cardioid mics

In the project or home studio, where serious acoustic treatment isn't usually an option, most recording is done using unidirectional-pattern mics, so called because they pick up sound from mainly one direction. The common name for this type of microphone is *cardioid*, which means literally "heart shaped". While the microphone may not be heart shaped, the pick-up pattern, if plotted on a circular graph, does roughly resemble a heart. This shows that the microphone is most effective when picking up sounds from in front, which helps to keep individual sounds separate and minimises the effects of room reflections.

proximity effect

The so-called proximity effect, which applies to cardioid-pattern microphones and figure-of-eight models, results in a significant bass boost when the microphone is used with sound sources closer than a couple of centimetres. Used creatively, the proximity effect can give the experienced vocalist a means of adding tone and expression to a performance, but in the studio it's an unwelcome source of inconsistency.

omni mics

Omni mics – ie those that pick up sound equally well in all directions – are generally technically superior, but if you use them you run the risk of picking up unwanted sounds as well as the sounds you want. For example, where several instruments are playing in close proximity, each with its own microphone, using omni microphones may allow too much unwanted sound leakage from one instrument into a mic intended for another instrument.

Some of the better capacitor mics have switchable polar patterns, enabling them to work as omni mics, cardioid mics or even figure-of-eight mics. The figure-of-eight-pattern mic is equally sensitive both at the front and at the back, but the sides are completely dead, whereas the figure-of-eight microphone is particularly useful in certain stereo-recording applications. Figure 4.4 shows the three main polar patterns.

PZM mics

The PZM (Pressure Zone Microphone) – also known as a boundary microphone – is a special type of microphone which uses an omnidirectional capsule suspended in close proximity to a reflective back-plate, or boundary. When a conventional microphone is placed within a room, it receives both direct and reflected sound, and cancellation effects occur because of phase differences caused by the longer path of the reflected sound. The result is a so-called comb-filtering effect, where the frequency response of the combined direct and reflected sound shows a series of closely spaced peaks and troughs, rather like the teeth of a comb.

By placing the mic capsule very close to the boundary, the direct sound and any sound reflected from the boundary will arrive at the capsule at virtually the same instant, thus avoiding the comb-filtering effect. Furthermore, because the reflected sound is essentially the same intensity as the direct sound, a doubling of output level occurs.

Because sound can't be received from the other side of the boundary (because the boundary itself is in the way), the polar pattern is confined to a hemispherical pattern rather than the usual spherical pattern of the

Boundary layer, where sound exists only as a variation in pressure. Here the direct and reflected sounds combine in phase

PZM
Has a hemispherical polar pattern above the cutoff frequency of the boundary plate. For full-range applications, a boundary of around 1m^2 or greater is recommended

Boundary plate

Mic capsule facing plate

Cable

Figure 4.5: PZM mic

conventional omni microphone. However, for the boundary to reflect low frequencies effectively (and to enable it to reject low frequencies from the rear), the boundary size must be at least a quarter of the wavelength of the lowest frequency along each side. The boundary plate on which the capsule is mounted is far too small to be effective at low audio frequencies, so it's common practice to mount the microphone on either a rigid board, measuring one metre square or more, or to place the microphone on a wall, floor or tabletop. If mounted on a tabletop, the microphone will pick up sound from all directions, except down, and effective stereo recordings may be made by placing two PZM mics a metre or two apart. The main benefit of this type of microphone is the uncoloured sound that it produces, due to the lack of undesirable comb-filtering effects.

For an inexpensive introduction to this fascinating method of miking, try the Radio Shack/Tandy low-cost PZM. This is an electret model that runs from batteries, so phantom power isn't required, and PZM mics are suitable for recording both vocals and instruments. For budget vocal recording, try a low-cost PZM mic taped to a mirror with a pop shield placed directly in front of it. A pop shield is simply a piece of fine gauze or mesh (nylon stocking material is best) designed to break up blasts of air from the singer's mouth.

mic characteristics

A theoretically perfect mic would have a flat frequency response over the whole audio range, but this isn't always what we need. For example, some mics are designed with a deliberate degree of treble boost or presence to help vocals cut through a mix. Different models apply the treble boost in different parts of the spectrum, so it's important to choose a mic with characteristics that complement the singer's voice.

Dynamic microphones don't have as good a frequency response as capacitor models, but they may still be used in the studio because they deliver a more solid, hard-hitting vocal sound. They're also often used for miking drums, electric guitars, bass guitars and some brass instruments. Dynamic mics with extended low-frequency responses or pronounced bass-boost characteristics are also built especially for miking kick drums.

Capacitor mics are the mics of choice for most vocal work and for most acoustic instruments. They're also used for stereo drum overheads, as their good high-frequency response lets them capture cymbal sounds with great accuracy. Good back-electret models may be used in the same way as capacitor models – the only practical difference is that back-electrets aren't built with switchable pick-up patterns.

choosing a microphone

When choosing a microphone for a particular task, first determine whether the sound source is loud and close or quiet and distant. If loud, you can choose either a dynamic microphone to give a solid, punchy sound, or a capacitor microphone, which will produce a more transparent, detailed sound.

If the sound source is quiet or distant, a capacitor or a back-electret microphone are the preferred choices, because of their greater sensitivity. The directional characteristics of the microphone will depend on how close you can get to the sound source, how far away other sound sources are and the effect that the room has on your sound. If several loud sources are close together, a cardioid-pattern microphone will help to reduce the spill, but in less difficult circumstances an omni-pattern microphone may produce a more natural sound.

Finally, should you choose a mic with a relatively flat frequency response or one with a presence peak? This is purely subjective, and when working with vocalists, particularly, it's often best to try two or three different types of microphone to see which one suits the voice best. If the singer has a bright, sibilant voice, a model with a strong presence peak might make this worse; on the other hand, however, a voice lacking in definition will benefit from the extra brightness of a model with a presence peak. Making the best choice is all part of the engineer's skill, and this only comes with experience. Nevertheless, knowing what the important differences are between various types of microphone makes the choice much easier.

direct injection

Whenever you use a microphone, the resulting sound depends on both the quality of the microphone and on the acoustic character of the recording environment. All recording of actual sound must be done using a microphone, but many electronic musical instruments can be recorded using a method known as DI (Direct Injection). Direct injection involves plugging a signal from an electronic or electric musical instrument into a recording system – often using some form of pre-amplifier or matching transformer – rather than using a traditional mic. DI recording techniques are suitable for bass and lead guitars (with suitable pre-amps), synths, samplers, drum machines and so on.

guitar DI

Synths, samplers and drum machines can usually be connected directly to the line input of a mixer or multitracker, but because of their relatively high source impedance guitars and basses have to be DI'd via a matching circuit of some kind. One solution is to use an active DI box, which matches the impedance of the guitar to that of the multitracker. These may be powered from batteries or from their mixer's own phantom power supply.

While guitars and basses may be successfully DI'd using an active DI box, only clean sounds can be recorded in this way, because a guitar played through a guitar amplifier or combo is tonally coloured by the amplifier's circuitry and by the characteristics of the loudspeaker and its cabinet. To successfully record a convincing rock guitar sound, for example, it's best either to use a dedicated guitar recording pre-amp or to go back to miking up your amp. Very often, miking a small practice amp will produce just as large a sound as miking a big stack. (See Chapter 7 on "Miking Techniques" for more information on how to record various instruments.)

speaker simulators

Any attempt to DI a guitar overdrive pedal will result in a rather thin and buzzy tone, because you no longer have the guitar amp's circuitry or speaker to shape the sound. Most of the unwanted upper harmonics are filtered out by the restricted frequency response of a typical guitar loudspeaker, and for this reason recording guitar pre-amps include a piece of circuitry that functions as "speaker emulator" by mimicking the frequency response of a guitar speaker. Separate speaker-simulator boxes – both active and passive – are also available that can be used with pedals, the pre-amp output from a regular guitar amp or even the speaker output from a guitar amp.

chapter 5

equalisation

qualisation can come in many forms, from the simple treble/bass
control to the multi-band parametric equaliser; but however you dress
it up, equaliser is just another word for tone control. The term
equalisation came about because the very first equalisers were developed to
help counteract or equalise other shortcomings in the system, but today
equalisation is often used creatively, and not just to fix problems. To
understand EQ, it's first necessary to understand a little about the audio
spectrum as it relates to human hearing.

hearing range

Check out any textbook on audio and you'll see the limits of human hearing
quoted as being around 50-20kHz, although those very same books will also
point out that very few individuals – other than young children – can hear
pitches anything like as high as 20kHz. A more realistic figure might be around
15kHz for an adult, decreasing further as the years pass. What's really puzzling,
though – and this is scope enough for a book in its own right – is that, even
when your measured hearing response starts to fall off at way below 20kHz,
it's still very easy to hear the effect of equalisation applied at the top end of the
spectrum, where you wouldn't expect to be able to hear the change. The plot
thickens further when reputable studio engineers claim to be able to
differentiate between two otherwise identical circuits, where one has been
modified to handle frequencies up to 50kHz and one handles frequencies up
to 30kHz. In theory, both limits are well above the limit of human perception,
so it seems that what goes on outside the audible spectrum has a way of
influencing what we perceive within the range of our own hearing systems.

You can try this for yourself by comparing a good capacitor mic (ie one with an
audio bandwidth in excess of 20kHz) with a dynamic microphone chosen to be
nominally flat up to 15kHz or so, after which its response rolls off. Provided that
both have reasonably flat responses below their cut-off points, they should
sound much the same to someone who is, in effect, deaf to all frequencies
above 15kHz. In practice, however, the high-frequency detail captured by the
capacitor mic lends it an entirely different character to the dynamic mic.

Figure 5.1: Shelving filter response

types of equaliser

Although all equalisers do essentially the same job, there's a great deal of difference between a simple two-band treble/bass tone control and a multiband studio equaliser. The simplest equaliser is the shelving equaliser, a device that applies cut or boost, rather like a volume control, but only to the frequencies above or below the cut-off point of the equaliser, depending on whether the equaliser is based around a high-pass or a low-pass filter.

shelving filters

A low-pass shelving filter, as its name suggests, passes all frequencies below its cut-off frequency but affects all frequencies above it. Similarly, a high-pass filter passes all frequencies above its cut-off frequency but affects all frequencies below it. Figure 5.1 shows the frequency-response graphs of a typical treble/bass EQ using high- and low-pass filters. Note that the filter graph shows up as a slope at the cut-off point – it's neither possible nor desirable to have a filter that does nothing at one frequency and then, when moved up by just 1Hz, comes in with full effect. Simple shelving filters typically have a 6dB per octave slope so that their influence is felt more progressively.

bandpass filters

A filter that passes frequencies between two limits is known as a *bandpass filter*. If you have a mixer with a mid-range control, it's a bandpass filter. On a typical mixer, the bandpass filter will have variable cut and boost, and it will be tunable, so that its centre frequency can be varied. This is known as a *sweep*

Figure 5.2: Bandpass filter response

equaliser because, although the filter frequency can be changed, the width of the filter can't. Figure 5.2 shows a typical bandpass filter response.

parametric EQ

A parametric EQ is very similar to a sweep bandpass EQ, except that a third control is added to allow the width of the filter to be adjusted. The width of a filter is sometimes described as its Q value, where Q is the filter frequency divided by the number of hertz that the filter affects. Because the filter response is curved, the actual frequency width is measured between the points on the graph where the signal level has fallen by 3dB. A high value for Q corresponds to a very narrow filter, whereas a low value of Q corresponds to a wide filter. High Q values are useful for picking out sounds that occupy a very narrow part of the audio spectrum, whereas lower Qs produce a smoother, more musical sound.

A studio parametric EQ may have several filter sections so that three or four parts of the frequency spectrum can be treated simultaneously. Parametric EQs can be time consuming to set up properly, but they are the most powerful and most flexible of all types of EQ. Figure 5.3 shows a typical parametric equaliser response.

graphic equaliser

A graphic equaliser can be recognised by a row of faders across its front panel, each of which controls a narrow section of the audio spectrum. For

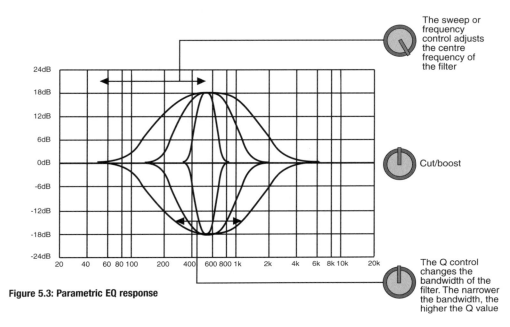

The sweep or frequency control adjusts the centre frequency of the filter

Cut/boost

The Q control changes the bandwidth of the filter. The narrower the bandwidth, the higher the Q value

Figure 5.3: Parametric EQ response

example, a 30-band graphic equaliser provides independent control over 30 different bands spaced a third of an octave apart.

Other than the highest and lowest faders, which control shelving filters, each of the filters in a graphic equaliser is a fixed-frequency bandpass filter, applying boost when the fader is moved up from its centre position and applying cut when the fader is moved down. Graphic equalisers have the advantage of being very easy to set up, but unless they're very well designed, or used sparingly, they can have an adverse effect on the sound. They're also less flexible than the parametric EQ, which can be exactly tuned to specific frequencies. With the graphic equaliser, the range covered by each fader is fixed, and the width of each individual band of a third-octave equaliser is actually rather wider than a third of an octave, thus allowing a smooth overlap between bands. Figure 5.4 shows the response of a typical graphic equaliser.

the psychoacoustics of EQ

Over the past couple of decades, EQ has moved further away from the corrective domain and has joined the more obvious effects boxes as a creative effect in its own right. Instead of simple bass and treble "tone" controls, most recording mixers now offer additional mid-band control, often with a variable frequency or sweep function, and in more sophisticated systems there's parametric EQ, which provides several bands of control where frequency, bandwidth and degree of cut and boost are all adjustable.

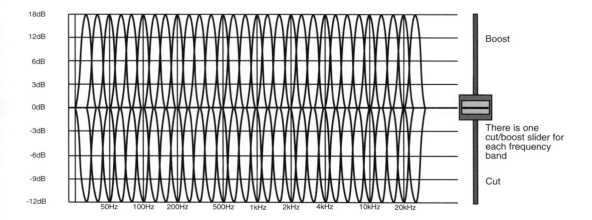

Figure 5.4: Graphic equaliser response

EQ and its perceived effect has much to do with psychoacoustics (the way in which various nuances of sound affect our perception of the world around us) and, like so many areas of psychology, the roots of psychoacoustics undoubtedly date back to the days when survival was more important than setting up a really hot mix.

the effect of air

Nature has its own built-in EQ system in the form of distance. Low frequencies propagate slightly faster than high frequencies, so the further away the sound source, the greater the time lag between the fundamental pitch of a sound and its higher harmonics. Although this in itself doesn't change the spectral content of the sound, the change in the phase relationships of the various harmonics does cause us to perceive the sound as being more distant and, in terms of survival, less demanding of our immediate attention.

The other thing that happens when a sound has to travel a long way is that the high frequencies are absorbed by frictional losses within the air itself, and the higher the frequency, the greater the absorption. This does affect the spectral content of the sound, and the further away a sound source is, the less bright it sounds. Again, less bright equates to more distant and less deserving of immediate attention, especially when closer sounds are being registered at the same time. In a real-life setting, this might go along the lines of the howling wolves in the distant forest being less of a threat than the sabre-toothed tiger dribbling and spitting six feet in front of you! In other words, nature's EQ is a means of making us pay attention.

Sabre-toothed tigers and wolves aren't generally a problem in today's urban environment, but we still exhibit essentially the same instinctive reaction to sounds. It therefore follows that, to get somebody's attention, you have to place a sound very close to them, and as recorded music is simply an illusion – stereo doubly so – you have to use the tools at your disposal to create the illusion of closeness. And that's what we're doing, often unconsciously, when we use EQ.

what does EQ do?

Equaliser circuits are simply designed to lift or cut parts of the audio spectrum relative to other parts. Think of EQ as a frequency-selective volume control. However, one of the side-effects of EQ is that the circuitry also introduces phase differences between the high- and low-frequency components of a signal. A touch of high-frequency EQ and an increase in gain can make a distant sound appear closer by compensating for the high-frequency loss due to air absorption, and at the same time the phase changes introduced by the equaliser can help offset the fact that the higher harmonics have been delayed due to their passage through air. If adding high-frequency EQ can make distant sounds appear to be closer, it stands to reason that close-miked sounds can be made to appear even closer still by the addition of top end.

subjectivity

Why do different models of equaliser sound different even though they claim to be working at the same frequency? While the effect of an equaliser's performance on the spectrum of the signal being processed is well documented, there's usually far less said about the way in which the equaliser affects the phase of the signal, and there's now a widely held belief that what an equaliser does to phase is just as important as what it does to frequency response. Indeed, some engineers believe that you can build an EQ that affects only phase and not the frequency spectrum, and in some respects these opinions are given credence by the success of various enhancer circuits which have a minimal effect on the frequency spectrum of the sound being processed and yet create a significant impression of closeness and clarity. It's also true that a very small adjustment on a good equaliser will bring a sound out of a mix, while if you use a less sophisticated equaliser you might have to crank up the treble to a point at which the signal sounds harsh and nasty before it achieves the required degree of "up-frontness".

audio cues

Audio is a complex subject, and there are non-EQ-related audio cues to distance which also need to be simulated in order to create a convincing sense of distance or proximity. For example, if someone suddenly whispers in your ear, you hear far more direct sound than reverberant sound, whereas a distant sound may have a wide stereo spread and (depending on the environment) may contain a high proportion of reverberant information, especially in rocky or wooded areas.

the deep end

If high-frequency EQ affects the apparent proximity of a sound by grabbing our attention, low-frequency sounds seem to have a more subliminal effect, which is why repetitive, rhythmic sounds usually include a lot of low-frequency information. You can have a really deep bass sound going on, which can add to the excitement of a track but without ever drawing your attention away from whichever sounds have been placed "up front" in the mix. However, even the deepest sounds usually contain some high-frequency harmonics, so you can still use high-frequency EQ to move these sounds forward in the mix if you want to make them demand attention.

perspective

If everything in a mix is close miked and given roughly the same EQ, it's all going to try to push to the front, where it will compete for our attention, and the human brain is noted for its intolerance of being asked to concentrate on too many different things at the same time. In a musical context, this leads to fatigue and a general sense of not wanting to listen any more. To check out what I mean, listen to a CD that's been recorded with everything too bright and you'll soon want it to get out of your face. If used intelligently, EQ can place sounds in perspective, with lead vocals and solos at the front, supporting instruments slightly behind and sound effects at a distance. A mix is like a painting, and if all of the colours are too bright there'll be no way of differentiating between the foreground and the background.

spectral mixing

Most of the techniques discussed so far can be tried with a simple bass/treble EQ, but if that's the case then why do we need mid-range controls or parametric equalisers? One obvious application of a bandpass filter – which is what mid-range and parametric equalisers are – is that you can "tune" the equaliser to the fundamental pitch of an instrument and then add boost to increase the instrument's apparent level without having too much effect on the sound on either side. If the level of the instrument is then reduced by turning down the gain, so as to restore the original subjective balance, frequencies produced by that instrument that are well away from the fundamental frequency will also be reduced in volume, which helps to reduce spectral overlap between sounds that might otherwise be too similar. To my mind, this is a corrective process rather than a creative one, and if you can choose more appropriate sounds at source you'll probably find that the end result is better than using EQ to "bend" the sounds to fit. However, spectral mixing does work, and it's worth exploring it so that you'll know its benefits and limitations.

loudness curve

One aspect of natural sound relates not to the sound itself but to the way in which the human hearing system works. While a good hi-fi amp has a perfectly flat frequency response, the human hearing system comes nowhere near being flat. What's more, the frequency response changes depending on the level of the sound being heard. As a sound gets louder, we perceive more low end and top end, but the mid range becomes progressively more recessed. Looking at a frequency-response graph, you'd see a curve with a dip in the centre, often known as a smile curve, because of its obvious shape. The louder the sound, the deeper the smile. The loudness button on a stereo system emulates this smile curve so that you can play back material at a low volume level and yet still get some impression of loudness.

In the studio, you can create a similar loudness effect by pulling down the mid EQ. Even physically quiet and distant sounds will appear louder, but they'll still seem far away. Pulling down the mid range can also make a mix appear to be less cluttered, because a lot of the information that's clamouring for our attention resides in the upper mid range. Using this knowledge, you could, for example, EQ an entire rhythm section to make it sound louder and then overlay it with conventionally EQ'd vocals and solo instruments. It's easy to make a mix sound loud by cranking up the monitors, but there's more skill in making a mix sound loud and powerful regardless of the playback level.

EQ for positioning

I believe that there's value in listening to the various elements in a mix and then deciding on a pecking order in terms of which sounds deserve the most attention and which ones play more of a supportive role. Then you can set up your EQ to help reinforce the natural sense of perspective. Most people try to achieve perspective by using the level control – everyone knows that the further away a sound is, the quieter it is – but now you know that you can also roll off a little top just to consolidate the illusion.

EQ cut

In most instances, the less EQ boost you use, the more natural the final sound will be. For this reason, rather than adding lots of top to vulnerable sounds such as vocals in order to get them to sit at the front of the mix, try being more restrained in your use of EQ and instead use high-end cut on things like low-level pad sounds, backing vocals and whatever else is playing a subordinate role. This is particularly relevant to those who don't have access to really sweet-sounding, up-market EQs; most console EQs are a little unsubtle when used in anything but moderation.

No one approach will solve all of your EQ problems – some difficult mixes are simply down to an unfortunate combination of instruments or sounds, or even plain bad arrangement. On the other hand, if you can get closer to the results you're after by using less EQ, you might just break the unfortunate trend of mixing fatiguing, over-bright records.

music and the audio spectrum

Having put forward an explanation for why I think equalisation works, it's time to look at the more common instruments used in pop music to see how EQ can be used to shape them. The first thing we need to know about an instrument is the range of frequencies it can produce, although if you don't have the figures written down then a little experimenting with EQ will soon tell you where the key elements of the sound reside.

The low-frequency limit of an instrument is usually defined as the fundamental frequency of its lowest note, but the high-frequency end is less easy to quantify. This is because nearly all musical sounds include harmonics that extend right to the top end of the audio spectrum and beyond, even though the level of these harmonics is probably very low.

bass instruments

Starting right at the bottom of the spectrum, with bass sounds, the bass drum puts out most of its energy in a narrow band between 40Hz and 150Hz, depending on how it's tuned, but the attack transients reach right up into the upper mid range. This can be confirmed by applying some EQ boost at around 4-6kHz, where the difference in the attack characteristic is very noticeable.

The lowest note on the amplified electric bass guitar is 41Hz, but the higher notes contain significant energy right up to 2kHz or 3kHz. Likewise, the traditional pipe organ goes an octave lower, down to 20Hz, where sounds are felt rather than heard. The organ's high notes may generate significant energy up at 8kHz and beyond.

The electric guitar has a starting point one octave higher than the bass guitar, at 82Hz, and there's little energy above 4kHz, because of the restricted range of electric guitar speakers. Even so, it would be a mistake to draw too many conclusions from the upper limit of any sound, because EQ applied above this arbitrary limit will almost certainly have some audible effect.

Moving a little higher up the spectrum, vocals can range from around 80Hz-1kHz, depending on the style and sex of the performer. Again, there's a significant amount of energy above that range, which is why live-mic manufacturers often build in a presence peak at 3kHz or 4kHz.

Brass instruments also tend to occupy the mid range of the spectrum, typically at 80Hz-1kHz, unless you count the tuba, in which case you can add almost an octave to the bottom of that figure. Few instruments produce the majority of energy at the high end of the spectrum, the piccolo and xylophone coming closest in the 600Hz-5kHz range. The upper harmonics of cymbals, bell trees, triangles and suchlike also extend well beyond the limits of human hearing. Sampled and synthesised sounds haven't been included, because they can cover whatever range the electrical circuitry is capable of supporting, which in theory can be the entire audio spectrum.

reasons to EQ

Some classical purists might say that you don't need EQ at all, but in the real world of pop recording, where the emphasis is on appropriate rather than accurate sounds, equalisation has become a way of life. After all, when was the last time you heard a pop record with a drum sound that bore any resemblance to an acoustic drum kit? Also, as explained earlier, EQ can be used to create or emphasise perspective within a mix.

The close miking of drums was originally devised to cut down on spill from other instruments, but the sound it produced (with some contribution from EQ) was so distinctive that it rapidly became the norm for pop records and the actual acoustic sound of the kit was largely forgotten.

In the case of the electric guitar, circumstance also dictated sound. During the pioneering days of electronics, amplifiers were pretty crude and tended to distort drastically at high volume levels. Likewise, speaker design wasn't really up to handling much power, and the brute-force twelve-inch guitar speakers that became so popular couldn't reproduce any of the higher harmonics produced by guitar pick-ups. If modern technology had been available from the outset, electric guitars might have sounded as clean and bright as the acoustic guitar, but as it turned out the combination of limited-bandwidth speakers and excessive amounts of distortion led to the rock sound that we now take for granted.

Now that low-distortion, high-bandwidth digital sound processors are available, it's ironic that designers are all trying to write algorithms that successfully duplicate the sound of vintage guitar amplifiers. The reason why I cite these examples is to show that equalisation can be used to shape familiar sounds in different ways – it isn't there just to fix problems caused by inappropriate recording techniques or equipment deficiencies.

separating sounds

EQ can be used creatively in many ways, but one of the most popular applications is to separate two similar sounds within a mix where the degree of overlap might cause the sound to become confused or muddled. Some overlap is inevitable, but if, say, two electric guitars or a brass sample and string sample are fighting for the same space in a mix, EQ can often be used to reshape the sounds, forcing them into slightly narrower areas of the spectrum. For example, a peaking equaliser can be used to add a degree of bite to one sound at one frequency while the other sound can be peaked up at a different frequency. Similarly, the top or bottom end of a sound can be "trimmed" to avoid conflict, a typical example being the acoustic rhythm guitar in a pop mix, where it's common practice to filter out the bottom end quite drastically. This leaves a bright guitar sound that sits well in the mix but without the bassy, boxy element that might overlap with the other mid-range instruments or the vocals.

At this point, it's valuable to examine a few common instruments to see how EQ can be used most effectively.

bass guitar

During the '60s, the bass guitar was used to provide little more than a low-frequency pulse; its sound was invariably dull in comparison with today's bass sounds. In contrast, the contemporary bass guitar sound is partly a result of changing from tape-wound to wire-wound strings, of new playing styles and of the degree of equalisation that can now be applied by using a modern bass guitar amplification system.

Boosting at around 80Hz can pull out the low bass, while boosting between 500Hz and 800Hz adds a nicely aggressive bite. Boosting higher up the spectrum tends to bring out the finger noise and little else, so if a bright sound is what you're after then try getting it as close as you can to what you want before you add EQ. Playing technique has a lot to do with the tone of a bass guitar, and no amount of EQ will compensate for a feeble finger-style of playing.

A touch of low-mid cut at around 200-250Hz can sometimes be effective in combination with a little low-end boost. This warms up the low bass end without allowing the low-mid area to get uncontrollably boomy.

bass synths

Bass synths can be treated in much the same way, although their ability to produce higher harmonics means that EQ at higher frequencies will also be effective. However, be cautious when using very bright bass synth sounds, as they can so easily fill up all of the space in a mix, leaving the whole thing sounding congested.

guitars

The electric guitar isn't a natural instrument, so anything you want to do to it using EQ is OK if it works on an artistic level. If you need to add warmth to the sound of an electric guitar, concentrate on the area between 125Hz and 200Hz. (There's no point in adding boost much below this region, as the lowest note's fundamental frequency is 82Hz.) Bass boost will only bring up the cabinet boom and make the overall sound muddy, and it could also conflict with the bass guitar. Equally importantly, boosting the bass end will accentuate any mains hum in the signal. Most guitar pick-ups capture a surprising amount of hum, especially single-coil models.

To add attack to the sound, go for the 2-4kHz region of the spectrum, but don't add any really high-end boost unless the guitar is DI'd, as there's not much coming out of a guitar speaker above 3kHz or 4kHz – all you'll do is bring up the background noise. If the guitar is being used with an overdrive sound, this will tend to go buzzy or fizzy.

In a congested mix, two similar-sounding electric guitars can be separated by adding bite at different frequencies, say one guitar at 3kHz and one at 4kHz. However, this is rarely as successful as getting a different sound at source, and using two different amplifiers or pre-amp settings while recording the two parts will help in this. It also makes sense to use different types of guitar – perhaps one with single-coil pick-ups and one with humbuckers. If you're miking the guitar amp, try using different mics for the different parts – using a dynamic for one take and a capacitor for the other will make a noticeable difference, even if the guitar, amp and player remain the same.

I try to record acoustic guitars with as little EQ as possible, preferring to move the mics in order to get the right basic tone, but players and producers always seem to want to add more top end, so some EQ is inevitable. More severe EQ may be called for if the acoustic guitar is playing rhythm in a pop mix, because the body resonance can clash with the other instruments in the arrangement. To thin out the sound a little, try cutting below 200Hz. Boosting in the region of 4-6kHz adds a nice American jangle, but you need a good guitar with fresh strings to really make this work. You also need to use a good-quality capacitor microphone, as dynamic mics are insufficiently sensitive and fail to reproduce the high-frequency detail which characterises a good acoustic guitar sound.

vocals

When recording vocals, always use a pop shield, as no amount of EQ will fix popping once it's on tape. General brightening can be achieved by using the shelving high EQ control on the mixer, but keep a wary ear open for sibilance. Boosting lower down, at 1-2kHz, gives a rather honky, cheap sound to the vocals and so isn't recommended, other than as a special effect. Presence can be added by boosting gently at 3-4kHz by using the upper-mid sweep equaliser, but be sparing with this as the natural character of the voice can easily be lost. In a mix of backing vocals, rolling off a touch of bass often helps the sound fit in better with the mix.

drums

Drums are a special case when it comes to equalisation, because the accepted pop and rock drum sound is not that of a natural kit. The trick is to make the drums sound both bright and solid but not too thick.

kick drums

A close-miked bass drum or kick drum without EQ will often sound less than ideal, although you may strike it lucky. Most often there is a need to add definition to the hit, plus a degree of low-frequency weight. For a straightforward, punchy sound, a little boost at 80Hz will almost always improve matters, but to get a deeper sound, without the end result being either boomy or too stodgy, try adding 10dB or so of boost with your shelving bass control (most consoles have their bass controls at 50Hz or 60Hz) and then wind in 10dB or so of cut at around 220Hz using the lower-mid control. The two controls work together to produce a narrow area of low-frequency boost rather than the rather wide, uncontrollable boost obtained by using the low EQ on its own.

To add definition to the beater impact, boost the upper-mid range between 3kHz and 6kHz, and choose the final setting by ear. A wooden beater is far better than a felt one for producing a modern kick-drum sound, and the slap can be further enhanced by taping a piece of thin plastic – a credit card, for example – on the drum head at exactly the spot where the beater impacts.

toms

Toms may be handled in much the same way as bass drums, with boost in the 80-120Hz region adding punch and depth. Careful adjustment of the upper-mid control can help pick out the stick impact, and if the tom rings on too much, or if it rings in sympathy with other drums, you can usually afford to roll off quite a lot of low bass without the result sounding thin in the context of a mix.

snares

Snare drums are quite unpredictable, and you never quite know how they're going to sound until you've put up a mic and listened to the result over the monitors. The sound can be fattened by boosting the 90-140Hz band, while the bite can usually be located in the 3-7kHz region. When searching for the right area, it's easiest to apply full boost and then tune for the appropriate pitch. Once you've found it, you can back off the degree of boost until you have a sound that you can live with. If the drum still doesn't sound crisp enough, consider switching to a capacitor mic.

cymbals

Always record cymbals at a low level to prevent tape overload and keep in mind that they always cut through more loudly than you expect. Brightness can be added by using the shelving high EQ control, or you can tune the upper-mid control until you find a "sweet spot". In general, cymbals are recorded as part of the overhead mic mix, and in some cases it can help to roll off the bass end quite significantly in order to prevent the drum sounds picked up by the overheads from obstructing the drum sounds from the close mics.

strings and brass

Relatively few home-studio owners get a chance to work with live brass or string players, but the high-quality sound that comes from a modern sample library patch can be EQ'd in much the same way as the real thing. Brass and stringed instruments work on entirely different principles, but they do respond to equalisation in similar ways. The sound can become nasal or honky between 1kHz and 3.5kHz, which means that a little subtle cutting in this region can sweeten things up. To add high-end sizzle, move up to the 6-10kHz band and try a little boost there, but don't overdo it or the sound will become "spitty". For a warm pad sound from string or brass samples and synth patches, roll off a little top and add a hint of boost between 300Hz and 400Hz.

piano

You'll need a pair of good mics to record a real piano, but again you can apply the following suggestions to piano samples if they're not already to your liking. The bass end can be warmed up by gently boosting at 90-150Hz, while the attack detail can be brought out by bringing up the 4-6kHz section of the spectrum. If the sound is boomy, look for the offending area between 250kHz and 350Hz and apply just enough cut to keep it under control.

Because the piano is such a natural and familiar instrument, it pays to use less EQ and concentrate instead on putting suitable mics in the right place. Electronic pianos can be equalised in the same way, although many models offer such a range of piano sounds that equalisation may be quite unnecessary.

overview

Equalisation should always be brought into play after you've done your best to get the right sound at source, and there's a huge subjective difference in sound between a budget and a top-quality studio equaliser. Although difficult to quantify, really good equalisers allow you to make more drastic changes without the sound appearing unnatural.

It's also important to understand that the human ear is far less critical of EQ cut than it is of boost, and so, if you can solve the problem by cutting the area of the spectrum that seems to be too loud, the result will be more natural. Often a combination of cut and boost is required, but always use the bypass switch to flip back and forth between the equalised and unequalised sounds in order to make sure that you really have improved matters. Equally, when you've EQ'd an instrument in isolation, make sure that the setting you've chosen works in context with the rest of the mix, as parts invariably sound quite different once everything else is playing.

If you strive to get your sounds right at the outset, EQ is an invaluable ally in shaping those sounds to your liking, but don't make the mistake of thinking that it can be used to salvage poor work.

chapter 6

setting up a home studio

To the uninitiated, a home studio is a bewildering jumble of speakers, cables, boxes and winking LEDs, but no matter how complicated the system, the essential components are roughly the same. You have to have a source of sound to record, such as the output from a microphone; you have to have a machine on which to record material; and you need some form of loudspeaker and amplifier system in order to play back your work. At its simplest, you could make recordings with just a stereo cassette deck, a pair of headphones and a couple of electret microphones, but I'm assuming that most people reading this book will either have (or aspire to own) a four-track, cassette-based system or a separate multitrack tape recorder and mixer. It's also possible to set up a combined MIDI and audio studio using a simple mixer, a PC and a suitable soundcard, but that particular avenue will be explored in a separate chapter.

the components

The nerve centre of a commercial recording studio is the mixing console; however, if you have a cassette Multitracker, Portastudio or one of the MiniDisc- or hard-disk-based integrated multitrackers, the mixer and multitrack recorder are combined in a single piece of hardware. This not only saves space but it also cuts down on the amount of wiring required. It also sidesteps any potential matching problems between the recorder and mixer. (The terms Multitracker and Portastudio are registered trademarks of Fostex and Tascam respectively, so I'll use the term multitracker with a lower-case M to describe a generic combined multitrack recorder and mixer.)

what else do you need?

You could just plug a microphone or two into your multitracker, put on a pair of headphones and start recording, but unless you're going to work at a very basic level you're going to need some other hardware to go with it.

The first extra you're definitely going to need is a stereo tape machine on which to mix your finished recordings, and the better the machine, the better the quality of your final recording. A good cassette deck will give acceptable results for demo work, but if you want to try for more professional-quality results then choose a DAT (Digital Audio Tape) recorder. These are rather more expensive than hi-fi cassette decks, but they can record at true CD (16-bit) quality.

Almost as good as DAT, but rather cheaper, are the new DCC machines, which were originally intended for the consumer marketplace. Technically, the sound quality with these isn't as good as DAT, because data compression is used to squeeze a lot of information onto a relatively small amount of tape, but in practice few people can tell the difference, especially with pop music. Certainly, the side-effects of data compression are insignificant when compared to the side-effects of the analogue tape noise-reduction systems used on semi-pro multitrack and domestic stereo tape machines. Sony's MiniDisc system is also a possibility for home mastering, although it tends to cost rather more than DCC. On the plus side, MiniDisc offers instant access to recorded material, much like a conventional CD player.

Other stereo-mastering options are to use the audio tracks of a hi-fi video recorder or to buy an open-reel stereo recorder, such as a used Revox or Tascam 32. Open-reel mastering machines have the advantage that you can edit your recordings using a razor blade and splicing tape. They also produce much better recordings than analogue cassette machines.

Whatever mastering format you choose to mix down to, the machine is known as a *master recorder*, and the stereo mixes you produce are called *master tapes*. It's from these master tapes that any subsequent copies (or records and CDs) are made.

the monitoring system

It's never a great idea to do all of your recording and mixing over headphones, as they often give quite a different impression to loudspeakers, especially when you're trying to evaluate bass sounds. Ideally, you should check your work on both headphones and speakers. For home use, a stereo hi-fi amp of at least 30 watts per channel is recommended, along with a pair of accurate loudspeakers. Ensure that your hi-fi amplifier has either aux, CD or tuner inputs – you can plug your multitracker's stereo monitor output into any of these. However, you can't use the phono record-deck inputs, as these have built-in tonal correction.

loudspeakers

No matter how sophisticated your studio, everything you do will eventually be judged by what comes out of your monitor loudspeakers. Choose the most honest-sounding speakers you can find, even if they don't sound the most impressive. Medium-sized two-way hi-fi speaker systems are usually fine for home recording, although dedicated near-field monitors tend to be more resistant to abuse. Whatever speakers you choose, try to listen to a selection of well-recorded CDs over them so that you get familiar with the sound. In this way, your mixes are likely to be more accurate, making it more likely that they'll also sound good on other hi-fi systems. It also pays to double-check your mixes on a cheap system, such as a ghetto blaster or a car stereo system.

microphones

You're going to need at least one microphone to record vocals and acoustic instruments, and most studio set-ups will need more than one, especially if two or more performers want to record at the same time. Choosing the right microphone can be confusing, so refer back to Chapter 4 on "Microphone Types" to make sure that you know how the various types differ. If you already have a decent dynamic live vocal mic, it should handle most jobs adequately, although a capacitor microphone is better for recording quieter acoustic instruments.

You should also read your multitrack workstation's manual before buying a mic to see whether you need to use high- or low-impedance models. All professional mics have low impedance and are balanced, although they can be used unbalanced with a suitable lead. If the mic has an XLR connector built into the handle and comes with a separate lead, it's almost certainly a low-impedance model and balanced.

Capacitor mics require 48V phantom power, and few multitrack workstations provide this. If you want to use one of these mics, you'll need an external mic pre-amp with its own phantom power source. A more cost-effective solution is to choose a good back-electret mic that can run on an internal battery.

effects

Modern recordings make extensive use of electronic effects, even though this may not be obvious from listening to the record. The most useful effect is without doubt the reverb processor, but most of today's effects units provide a whole range of different effects for you to use. These are

Monitor
loudspeakers

Power amplifier

Stereo master recorder

Mics

Left/right main outputs

Control room
monitor outputs

Stereo tape
returns

Effects
send

Reverb unit

Effects
returns

Cassette multitracker

Phones
output

Headphones

Figure 6.1: Recording system connections

commonly known as *multi-effects units*, and there's a full chapter on effects later in the book. As a minimum, you'll need one stereo reverb unit, but the ideal situation is to have at least one good reverb unit and one multi-effects unit. (Refer to the chapter on effects for more details of what the various effects do and how they should be connected.)

the system

Figure 6.1 shows how the various parts of a home recording system based around an integrated multitracker are connected. If you're using a hi-fi system to provide monitoring, the amplifier should be switched to Aux when recording and overdubbing and to Tape when you want to hear your stereo mixes played back from the mastering machine. All cables should be kept as short as possible.

When setting up your studio, everything should be within reach and the speakers should be positioned symmetrically about the listening position. However, don't place speakers too close to corners or the bass response will change unpredictably.

facilities

Studio effects can be very flexible, but you'll need a multitrack workstation equipped with effects send and return facilities to make full use of them. Fortunately, all but the very cheapest "musical-notepad"-type multitrackers have aux sends and returns. (If the term "aux" is unfamiliar to you, refer back to the chapter on "Mixers".) Modern digital effects units have stereo outputs, so a multitrack workstation with at least one stereo aux return or two spare input channels is required.

The other important signal processor that it's hard to live without is the compressor. A compressor is basically a type of automatic level control that tries to smoothe out the differences between loud and quiet sounds, and most vocal tracks benefit from compression to keep them sounding even. If you intend to use a compressor, you'll need a multitracker with insert points on at least some of the channels. An insert point is a socket that lets you patch an external processor "in line" with the signal passing through the mixer channel.

You can't plug a mic directly into a typical compressor (or any other signal processor, for that matter), as they are normally designed for line-level operation only. However, so-called voice channels are available, which combine a mic amp with a compressor and sometimes an equaliser. These may be used to treat a mic signal directly, and purists often prefer to plug these directly into their multitrack recorders, thus bypassing their mixers altogether. This may or may not be possible on a multitracker, depending on the facilities available, but where it is possible it usually results in a noticeable improvement in sound quality.

headphones

Although I've already pointed out that headphones aren't great for critical mixing without at least double-checking your mixes on loudspeakers, they're useful for working at times when making excessive noise would be antisocial, and they're absolutely essential for performers who want to monitor while overdubbing. Don't skimp on headphones – even a really good pair will cost significantly less than a decent pair of near-field monitor speakers.

open phones

Open or semi-enclosed hi-fi headphones usually sound most natural, but they tend to be bass-light when compared to fully enclosed phones. High-quality headphones are particularly useful for checking stereo positioning and for showing up noises or distortion that you might miss when listening over loudspeakers. Provided that you check your mix over loudspeakers at critical points, headphones can allow you to work at night, when you might otherwise have to stop because of noise constraints. Open phones are probably the nicest to work with, although you'll need to ask your speakers for a second opinion concerning the bass end of your mix.

enclosed phones

For monitoring while overdubbing, enclosed headphones are preferred, because they don't allow much sound to leak in or out. Some of the better enclosed headphones are accurate enough for checking mixes, so if your budget only stretches to one pair of phones then a good enclosed pair might be the best option. However, try out as many pairs as you can and find out how the sound compares with what you hear over loudspeakers. Check your multitrack workstation's manual to see what impedance of headphone it can drive.

system connections

Most of the signal connections in a typical home studio are made using regular instrument jack leads or RCA phono hi-fi cables. Only microphones require special cables, although the type that you need to use will depend on the input connectors of your mixer or multitracker. Very basic models may have inputs on jacks, whereas more serious models will have balanced

XLR inputs. Multitrack workstations and cassette decks usually connect to hi-fi power amplifiers by means of standard RCA phono leads, although most professional amplifiers have balanced inputs on XLR connectors or balanced jacks.

Speakers should be connected by using heavy, twin-cable, non-instrument co-ax leads. Keep the speaker cables as short as possible and make them the same length. There's no need to buy expensive speaker cables – what matters most is that they're thick enough to have a very low electrical resistance. Not only will inadequate speakers cable cause a loss of volume, but the sound will also be compromised.

Setting up a system using a separate mixer and multitrack recorder isn't much more complicated, but you will need a bunch of cables to carry the mixer's group outputs to the multitrack machine's inputs and another bunch of cables to link the multitrack's output to the mixer's tape inputs. All signal cables between the mixer and multitrack recorder must be screened.

mains wiring

In a typical studio, there are lots of mains-powered boxes, but mains wiring should be kept as far away from the signal wiring as is practical and, if possible, mains and signal leads should cross at right angles in order to reduce the amount of interference picked up from the 50Hz or 60Hz mains. The worst situation for interference is where mains and signal cables run close alongside each other for any distance, as the signal cable tends to act as an aerial and picks up the hum radiated by the mains cable.

Don't remove the earth leads from any equipment that's supposed to be earthed, and check your mains plugs regularly; loose wires are not only dangerous but will also cause intermittent crackles and buzzes. The use of multiway connector blocks is inevitable in the small studio – mine contains dozens of the things – but avoid plugging leads into them and pulling them out too often, as the socket spring tends to go slack eventually, and this can result in bad contacts.

studio layout

As touched upon very briefly earlier, you should set up your equipment so that it's easy to reach when in use. In the larger studio, it may not be possible to reach everything, but you should at least be able to get your hands on the controls you use most often. If you play keyboards or have a MIDI sequencer, you'll also need to think about where these go.

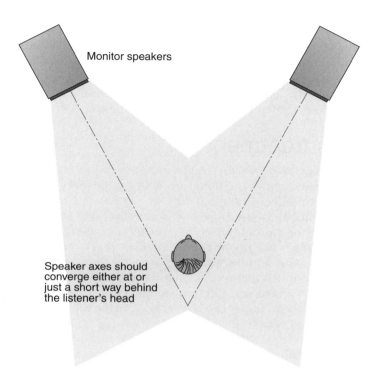

Monitor speakers

Speaker axes should
converge either at or
just a short way behind
the listener's head

Figure 6.2: Monitor positioning

speaker placement

It's important to have the speakers set up symmetrically and in front of you, as otherwise your stereo image will be affected. When using small speakers in a home studio, it's usually best to have them around one metre away and about the same distance apart, as shown in Figure 6.2. It's also advisable to keep the speakers at least half a metre away from corners, as putting speakers close to corners causes an artificial increase in bass, which may affect the way that you mix. Backing speakers right up against a wall may also cause an artificial increase in bass response. In a rectangular room, it's usually best to position the speakers along the longest wall.

While it's quite common to see speakers standing on a shelf, on a table or on top of a mixing console, acoustically it's better if the speakers are on stands behind your equipment desk or mixer, as this cuts down on unwanted reflected sound. It's also better to mount the speakers upright rather than to lay them on their sides, as this will produce a wider listening area within which the mix sounds accurate. The optimum listening position is exactly between the speakers, and this is sometimes called the "sweet spot". To ensure that the sweet spot is as wide as possible, the speakers should be angled so that the tweeters point either at or just behind the listener's head. The tweeters should be at head height or the speakers should be angled to point at the engineer's head.

acoustic treatment

Professional recording studios are designed to include elaborate acoustic treatment, but in the home studio there's usually insufficient budget and space to add anything but very simple acoustic treatment. When mixing, most problems are caused by loud reflections from the walls, floors and ceilings of a room, which all confuse the direct sound of the speakers. From this, you might rightly deduce that cutting down on excessive reflections is an obvious move, although you don't want to deaden your room so much that it sounds as though you're in a padded cell. Ordinary carpets, curtains and soft furnishings help enormously, and if you can hang heavy rugs or drapes on the rear wall, facing the speakers, this will deaden the sound even more.

It's important not to try too hard and absorb too much reflected sound, because bass frequencies tend not to be absorbed as much as high frequencies. If you do add too much absorbent material, the room is likely to sound dull and bassy, so aim for something like the acoustics of a domestic living room rather than something that sounds completely dead. In a typical carpeted room, little extra treatment should be necessary. One of the benefits of near-field monitoring is that, because the speakers are physically close, you hear more of the direct sound from the speakers and less of the reflected sound from the room, making room acoustics less of an issue. Also relevant is the fact that the near-field monitors don't produce a lot of deep bass, and although heavy bass might sound impressive, unless the control room is acoustically treated, the bass that you hear is likely to be very misleading. It's much better to have an accurate sound with less bass.

If the room is excessively reverberant, try hanging a rug or a thick drape on the rear wall and two smaller ones on the side walls on either side of your normal listening position. If you can hang the rugs at around 30mm from the walls, they'll be more effective than they would be if they were fixed directly onto the walls. Foam acoustic tiles or slabs of two-inch fireproof furniture foam are also very effective at mid and high frequencies. Bedroom studios often work well with little or no extra treatment, because the carpets, curtains and bed are very effective at absorbing sound.

Monitor speakers

Cassette multitracker

Power amplifier, stereo mastering deck and effects units

Sequencer and MIDI sound modules

If space is tight, a tiered keyboard stand may be used to place the multitracker above the keyboard, as shown here. Ensure that everything that's needed on a regular basis is within easy reach so that you can work in the correct position relative to the speakers

Power amplifier, stereo mastering deck and effects units

Monitor speakers

Sequencer and MIDI sound modules

Keyboard

Multitrack Recorder

In a more sophisticated set-up, it may not be possible to have everything in front of you, in which case priority should be given to positioning those pieces of equipment required during mixing. The keyboard and MIDI system may be set up to one side, as accurate monitoring isn't as essential when playing as it is when mixing. A swivel chair will make it easier to change from the mixing position to the playing position

Drum machine

Figure 6.3: Examples of typical system layouts

It should be noted that acoustic treatment isn't the same thing as soundproofing. Hanging acoustic tiles around the walls or sticking egg boxes everywhere may change the acoustics of the room, but it will do little to prevent unwanted sound from leaking in or out.

Figure 6.3 shows a possible studio layout, incorporating a MIDI keyboard and sequencer, and the positioning of additional absorbent material is indicated. The layout is similar where a separate mixer and multitrack recorder are used, with the mixer being at the centre of the action, although it may be more convenient to move the recorder to one side or the other.

patchbays

Patchbays often look daunting, but their sole purpose is to bring some degree of order to the potential wiring chaos of the recording studio. While many of the connections in a typical studio can be left alone, many more need to be changed on a daily basis. For example, you may have a compressor that needs to be patched into different mixer insert points as required, or you may want to move an effects unit from one send to another. Then there are those occasions when you need to copy a DAT tape, perhaps via an equaliser and enhancer onto cassette, but later in the day you might need the enhancer to process a stereo subgroup on your mixer or the equaliser to process a couple of input channels. No matter how you try to rationalise your system, you never seem to get by without having to repatch things.

Rewiring in a system without patchbays is awkward, mainly because most bits of studio gear have their connections at the back, where you can't get at them easily. Similarly, mixer insert points may or may not be easily accessible, depending on the make and model, but most use stereo jacks, and so, unless you have an endless supply of Y-leads or adaptors, they're not easy to use, even if you can get to them.

A properly-thought-out patchbay will bring out all of your regularly-used audio connections to a single patch panel, enabling you to make any necessary connections by plugging in short patch cables. However, it rarely makes sense to bring absolutely everything out to a patchbay, because there are some things that you may never need to change. For example, if you have more effects sends and returns than you have effects units, you could leave your effects permanently wired to the console rather than use a patchbay. If you have any spare console sends and returns, you could then bring these out to the patchbay in order to enable you to patch in effects brought around by clients or friends.

jack bays

At its simplest, a patchbay can be thought of as a system of extension cables that brings the necessary input and output points to an easily accessible panel. Most semi-pro studios use standard jack patchbays, because these are relatively inexpensive and they interface easily with most musical and hi-fi equipment, such as synths, effects, pedals, guitar pre-amps, cassette decks and so on.

The most common form of jack patchbay uses standard jacks both for patching and for rear panel connections, which means that you can wire up all of your system using conventional jack leads, making it easy to reconfigure your patchbay when you want to integrate a new piece of equipment. So-called "hard-wired" patchbays – where the rear connections are soldered directly to the cable harness – are cheaper and arguably more reliable, but changing things later is less straightforward. Currently, the most popular type of jack patchbay fits a 1U panel and has two rows of 24 sockets. Convention dictates that the lower sockets are inputs and the top row are outputs.

Where a patchbay is used to provide access to the ins and outs of effects processors, to the input channels of a mixer and so on, a basic non-normalised patchbay is required. In other words, the socket at the back of the patchbay connects directly to the socket on the front and nowhere else. This kind of connection system is known as *non-normalised* – the sockets are purely extensions of whatever the patchbay is connected to.

normalising

In the case of insert points, another type of patchbay is needed on which the upper and lower sockets are connected by means of so-called *normalising contacts* when no patch plugs are inserted. The reason for this is related to the way in which console insert points are wired. Usually, there's a stereo TRS insert jack socket on the console which includes a pair of switch contacts so that the insert send is connected directly to the insert return if no jack is inserted. If this weren't the case, there would be no continuous signal path through the mixer channel, unless a processor of some type was plugged into the insert point. (Chapter 3 explains insert points more fully.)

Once you've connected a patchbay to a mixer insert point, the mixer's internal signal path is broken because there's a jack permanently plugged into the mixer insert socket. If you didn't do something about this, it would mean that, whenever you didn't have a processor plugged into the patchbay, you'd have to use a patch cable to join the top and bottom sockets simply to complete the circuit. This would need a lot of patch leads and would make for a very congested patchbay, so instead we use so-called normalised patchbays with internal switch contacts to do this for us automatically. When no connection is made to the patchbay, the input jack is connected directly to the output jack.

semi-normalised patchbays

In some circumstances, it can be useful to take a signal from an insert send without breaking the signal path. For example, you might want to split a signal so that you can feed it both through the mixer channel and into a signal processor at the same time. To make this easy, the semi-normalised patchbay was developed. On these, when nothing is plugged in, the patchbay output (insert send) is connected back to its input (insert return) via the normalising contacts. However, by fitting normalising contacts only to the input (lower socket), whenever a jack is plugged into the output socket only, the input still remains connected to the output and the signal flow isn't interrupted. Conversely, whenever a jack is plugged into the input (lower socket), the signal path is broken. By using this type of patchbay, you can plug into the top socket on its own to split the signal or you can plug into both to connect a signal processor to the console's insert point.

The term "sniff and break" is sometimes used to describe this type of patchbay; plugging into the patchbay output socket allows you to "sniff" the signal without affecting the existing signal flow, while plugging into the patchbay input breaks the signal flow. Semi-normalised sniff-and-break operation is now almost universal, even when the patchbay is said to be normalised, and there's no obvious advantage in using a fully normalised patchbay connection scheme. Most commercial patchbays include some form of link or some other simple switching system to allow them to be configured for either semi-normalised or non-normalised operation. Figure 6.4 shows how both non-normalised and semi-normalised patchbays are wired, and if you only need a few patch points you could copy this wiring arrangement to build your own.

balancing

Most home studios use unbalanced patching systems, simply because most synths and pre-amps have unbalanced outputs. Insert points are also unbalanced on all but the very top-end pro studio consoles. However, if you want to use a patchbay to provide access points between

Front panel

Ground connected to cable screen

Output

Normalised

Link (normalised when in place, non-normalised when removed)

Input

Console insert send

Console insert return

Rear sockets

Front panel

Output

Non-normalised

Link (normalised when in place, non-normalised when removed)

Input

Signal output on console or external device

Signal input on console or external device

Rear sockets

Ground connected to cable screen

Figure 6.4: Semi-normalised patchbay

the balanced outputs of a mixer and the balanced inputs of a multitrack recorder, it's probably worth using a balanced patchbay for this application. This will require stereo jack patch leads, although most systems will allow you to use unbalanced mono jacks to feed unbalanced signals into a balanced input.

what to connect

It's always a good idea to bring out all of your console insert points to a semi-normalised patchbay, including the group inserts and the master (stereo output) inserts. If you don't want to wire up all of the channel inserts, decide which channels you're likely to use for microphones and take their inserts to the patchbay so that you can patch in compressors when recording.

In more sophisticated systems, it may be useful to connect a normalised patchbay between your mixer group outs and multitrack inputs, thus allowing you – for example – to route a DI box or mic pre-amp directly to tape without having to pass the signal through the mixer. Similarly, you might want to use a semi-normalised patchbay to bring the multitrack returns back into the line inputs of the mixer, especially if your console has no Line/Tape switch.

As stated earlier, non-normalised patchbays are simple extension leads, and they're useful for bringing out the console line inputs, effects sends and effects returns and direct channel outputs. Similarly, you could bring the inputs and outputs of all of your effects, processors and MIDI instruments to a non-normalised patchbay. Other uses for non-normalised patchbays include line-level "tie lines" (screened cables running from your patchbay to a wall box in the studio), which may be used for any type of general-purpose connection. For example, you might want to play a guitar in the control room but have it plugged into an amp in the studio. Similarly, you might have synths in the studio area that you want to plug into the mixer in the control room.

logistics

Plan the location of your patchbay to minimise the wiring between it and the rest of your studio equipment. As most patching involves the mixer and the effects rack, it pays to keep them and the patchbay as close together as possible. Use good-quality screened cable to wire everything up and keep the leads as short as possible. In the case of insert Y-leads, with stereo TRS jack at one end and two mono jacks at the other, consider buying ready-made moulded ones if you don't want to solder up your own.

For the patch leads, choose a soft, non-kinking cable or buy ready-made patch leads, and ensure that they're long enough to reach between the two furthermost sockets on your patchbay system. Coloured leads or plugs help you to keep track of what's patched where.

chapter 7

miking techniques

The first secret of miking up an instrument is that the instrument must sound good in the first place. Not only should the instrument be properly maintained, properly tuned and properly played, it should also, where possible, be played in a sympathetic acoustic environment. If something sounds good played in a room, there's no reason why a good mic placed in the room shouldn't capture that sound quality for you. If the room you have isn't suitable, use a long mic lead and try another room!

With most acoustic instruments, capacitor mics capture the most accurate sound, although you can also get excellent results by using back-electret mics or the budget Tandy/Radio Shack PZMs. Dynamic mics can be used to make acceptable recordings, although their lack of sensitivity may cause noise problems when recording quiet instruments. Furthermore, because capacitor mics tend to work much better than dynamic mics at the high end of the audio spectrum, bright or detailed sounds are invariably captured more accurately by capacitor mics. Even if you only have access to dynamic mics, you should still try out the following techniques, because you'll still learn a lot, and in most cases the results will be quite good enough for demo work.

distance

Now that you've got your instrument sounding right in the room, the next question is, how far away do you put the mic? There are textbook mic positions for most instruments, but it must be stressed that these are just starting points, and that the longer you're prepared to experiment, the more successful your recording is likely to be. For example, the acoustic guitar is normally recorded from the front, but I've also miked it successfully from above, over the player's shoulder, working on the theory that if it sounds good to the player then it should also sound good to the mic! All of the techniques described here are based on cardioid-pattern mics, because that's what most people working at home have access to.

universal mic theory

A real instrument is not a point source of sound – what we hear is a blend of an infinite number of sounds emanating from all parts of the instrument. This means that, if the mic is too close to the instrument, only part of the sound is captured; on the other hand, if you put the mic too far away, not only will you be struggling for level but you'll also pick up more reflected room sound than you do direct sound. In some rooms, this can sound good, but in most cases you end up with a boxy, distant sound lacking in detail and presence.

A good compromise is to space the mic away from the instrument by a distance similar to the longest dimension of the instrument. In the case of a guitar, you can say that the sound-producing part of the instrument is just the body (not strictly true) and put the mic around 400mm from the body, or you could accept that some sound comes directly from the strings and neck and put the mic at up to 800mm from the guitar. If you're working on a drum kit or some other collection of percussion instruments and you want to record them with a single mic or stereo pair, again you could treat the whole thing as one instrument and space the mic accordingly. In the case of a typical drum kit, the mics would be placed 1-1.5m or so in front of the kit. Although this rule isn't perfect, it will usually get you in the right ballpark very quickly, and it's come in very handy when I've been asked to record unusual instruments for which no textbook method exists.

vocals

There's no great mystery to recording vocals, but you do need to pick a location where wall reflections are at a minimum. If necessary, deaden the area by improvising screens with thick blankets or quilts. Set up a cardioid mic so that it points roughly at the singer's nose and use at a distance of around 200mm. Even the best vocal mics are prone to picking up popping on B and P sounds, so use a pop shield midway between the mic and the singer. Although you can buy pop shields, a piece of stocking material stretched over a wire frame or wooden hoop works just as well. The diameter should be around 150-200mm.

If you have a compressor, try applying it gently to the vocals during recording, then add more as you mix – this will avoid over-compression. Figure 7.1 shows a typical vocal miking position.

drums

Although pro studios tend to mic drum kits using lots of microphones, it's useful to look at the alternative approaches for recording drums, which can vary from one mic per drum to a single mic for the whole kit.

Mesh pop
shield

Cardioid
microphone

Mic between 150mm
and 300mm from mouth

Figure 7.1: Typical vocal miking position

A good drum sound starts with a good-sounding kit, played well. That means having a kit fitted with good heads that have been properly tuned and a drummer who knows how to hit them to get a happening sound. If the room is too dead, you might also get better results by putting sheets of hardboard beneath the kit and around the walls.

If a drum rings too much, or if the toms resonate every time you hit the bass drum, pads of folded cloth can be taped to the edges of the heads, but don't kill the sound with too much damping – what might sound like a lot of ring in isolation might be completely hidden in a full mix.

It's possible to get a good drum sound by setting up a pair of mics a few feet in front of the kit, and because this produces a very live sound this approach has become very fashionable as an alternative to the close-miked drum sound of the '80s and the clinical precision of drum machines. Position the two mics (known in the trade as *overheads*) between one and two metres from the kit (either in front or above), depending on the acoustic of the room, and space the mics about 1-1.5m apart. As a rule, the more reflective the room, the more exciting the sound will be. Capacitor or back-electret mics are good for this simple approach, and you can also get a good sound from budget PZMs by taping them to the wall behind the kit or by placing them on the floor in front of the kit.

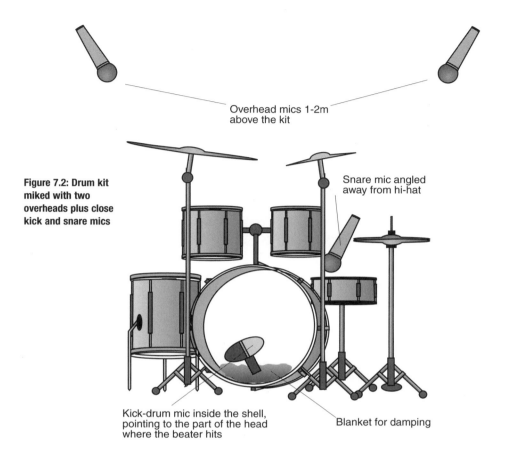

Overhead mics 1-2m
above the kit

**Figure 7.2: Drum kit
miked with two
overheads plus close
kick and snare mics**

Snare mic angled
away from hi-hat

Kick-drum mic inside the shell,
pointing to the part of the head
where the beater hits

Blanket for damping

close mics

If the kick drum and snare drum seem to be getting lost, use additional close dynamic mics and bring up their levels underneath the stereo mics until you hear a good balance. Mic the bass drum through a hole cut in the front head and place a folded blanket or feather pillow inside the shell to provide some damping. The mic should be about 200mm from the beater and suspended inside the drum shell on a boom stand that isn't physically touching any part of the drum shell. Figure 7.2 shows a drum kit miked with two overheads plus close kick and snare mics.

For the snare, use a dynamic mic around 50mm from the edge of the drum and about 50mm above the head. Try to arrange it so that the mic is pointing away from the hi-hat, or you might find that the hi-hat overpowers everything. Some engineers like to add a second mic to the snare pointing at the snare head from underneath. I've never had great results doing this, but if you want to give it a try then I suggest that you switch the bottom mic out of phase with the top, or the two mics will be trying to cancel each other out.

multiple mics

Most commercial pop recordings are made by miking all of the drums separately, in which case the toms may be miked in exactly the same way as the snare drum, using a single dynamic mic close above the head. If the hi-hats need more prominence, a capacitor or back-electret mic can be set up around 200mm above (or below) and a little to one side of the hi-hat, as long as you take care not to angle directly at the edges of the hi-hats, or you'll risk picking up the wind noise as the hi-hats close. However you set up the mics, try to make sure that they're somewhere that the drummer isn't likely to hit them.

If you're short of tape tracks, try at least to keep the overhead mics on separate tracks, because the way in which these are mixed in with the close mics has a profound effect on the final drum sound. For example, to get a tight, close-miked drum sound, you first have to get the drums balanced using the close mics and then bring in just a little of the overheads to add air and definition to the cymbals. For a more live sound, on the other hand, start off with the stereo overheads and then use just a little of the close-miked sounds to fine-tune the balance between the various drums.

Close-miked drums usually need some EQ for the sound to be just right, and if you have to mix some of the drums as you record then you may have to EQ during recording. If you have the luxury of keeping the drum sounds separate, however, try to save the EQ until you mix.

bass guitars

Most people now record the bass guitar using a DI box or recording pre-amp, but I've yet to find one that produces the authority and punch of the real thing. While the bass guitar isn't an acoustic instrument, the bass amplifier/speaker can be considered in exactly the same way as any other instrument.

The best miked bass sounds are usually achieved by putting a good dynamic mic 200-300mm from the speaker grille and playing normally. If the cabinet has more than one speaker, listen to them all, and if one is better than the others then put the mic close to that speaker. The choice of mic can have a big effect on the sound, and if you want a really deep bass sound then you should try using a bass drum mic rather than a vocal mic. One tip when recording either electric guitar or bass is to put the amp and mic in a separate room from the one in which you're monitoring so that you can hear what the recorded sound is going to be like over the studio monitors.

Try adding the output from a second mic placed further away in the room. It's also worth trying to mic the sides or rear of the cabinet to find out what different sounds can be achieved

Mic pointed directly at the speaker from a position very close to the grille cloth

Figure 7.3: Miking a guitar combo

electric guitars

At one time, no serious engineer would record the electric guitar any other way than with a mic, but now guitar pre-amps seem to be just as popular. Even so, there's a real difference in the resulting sound, and miking the amp usually produces the best rock or blues sounds.

When you mic an amp, you'll notice that the sound changes as you move the mic closer to the speakers, and it also gets more mellow as you move away from the centre of the speaker. For rock sounds, put a dynamic mic right up against the grille and, as with the bass guitar, see if any one speaker sounds better than the others. Try to record without additional EQ so that your options are still open when you come to mix. As with recording bass, try to monitor the to-tape sound in the control room, because you'll invariably find that the miked sound is a lot brighter than the perceived sound of the amp. I'd recommend that you adjust the tone controls on the amp prior to recording so that the monitored sound is correct, rather than simply accepting what you get and then trying to EQ it afterwards.

If you have the facilities, try combining the outputs from two mics, one close and the other further away. It's also worth experimenting by moving the second mic around the sides of the guitar amp, or even behind it. If your mixer has a phase switch, listen to determine what difference reversing the phase of the distant mic makes. Figure 7.3 shows how a guitar amp may be miked.

acoustic guitars

Acoustic guitars – especially steel-strung models – cover a very wide frequency range, so you'll need to use a fairly sensitive mic with a good high-frequency response if you're to do them justice. You can produce usable results from a good dynamic mic, but a capacitor or back-electret model is far preferable. I always used to mic my acoustic guitars in stereo, but the image always seemed to lack solidarity. I've now come to the conclusion that, if you're going to add stereo reverb anyway, you might as well record the guitar with a single mic and rely on the reverb to give it space. Again, if you're short on tracks, you'll need to record in mono anyway.

Position the mic at around 400mm from the guitar and aim it either at the point at which the neck joins the body or at the bridge. Some people aim the mic at the soundhole, because that's where most of the sound comes from, but in practice this usually results in a boomy or boxy sound that needs a lot of EQ to salvage it. The only exception is if you're working with a small-scale guitar or one that has a very thin sound, in which case working closer to the soundhole may help fatten up the sound. If you want to try recording in stereo, try pointing a second mic at the centre of the neck from 300mm or 400mm away. Because this isn't a "true" way to record accurate stereo, it doesn't really matter if the two mics are different types, although for all proper stereo applications it's important to make sure that the two mics are identical.

A live acoustic environment is essential for a good acoustic guitar sound, so if your studio is too dead, place a piece of hardboard on the floor or against the wall to reflect some of the sound, just as was suggested in the section on recording drums. Figure 7.4 shows an acoustic guitar miked with a single microphone.

Figure 7.4: Miking the acoustic guitar

Try various positions on the guitar body, but avoid pointing the mic directly at the soundhole to avoid booming. If you want to try miking in stereo, try the miking arrangement shown, or move the right hand mic so that it's pointing at the centre of the neck

Place hardboard on the floor to give a more live sound if the room has a carpet

keyboards

Keyboards, drum machines and samplers may be recorded by plugging them directly into the line inputs of your mixer, but miking an amp can sometimes produce a warmer sound that could be used to take the edge off digital instruments. In general, keyboard amps are miked a little further back than guitar amps so that the sound from the tweeter is also captured, although, for raunchy rock sounds, you can use a guitar amp to add overdrive to the sound and then mic up the amp in exactly the same way as you would for the guitar.

Miking up keyboards is now the exception rather than the rule, although if you're using a Leslie cabinet you'll need to use mics to capture the sound. There are many documented ways of miking the Leslie cabinet, but the trick seems to be to work in stereo, with one mic on each side of the cabinet, facing the speaker grilles, and not set up too close. (Otherwise you'll pick up wind noise from the rotors and lose the benefit of room reflections.) An initial distance of 300-400 mm should get you in the ballpark.

wind instruments

Most wind instruments can be successfully recorded by positioning a mic around half a metre in front of the instrument, angled down from above so that it isn't pointing directly down the bell or mouth of the instrument. If you're not sure which is the best mic position, go back to the universal mic rule and start from there. I've used this simple rule to make successful recordings of many different instruments, including accordions (it's best to use a mic on each side of these) and Irish pipes. I've even recorded the didgeridoo in the same way, but with this instrument, because most of the sound does come out of the end of the pipe and not through the sides, you can afford to get as close as 200mm.

Loud wind instruments, such as saxes, respond well to both capacitor and dynamic mics, while flutes seem to sound more open and natural when recorded with a capacitor or back-electret mic. In a pop context, you may find that the more punchy, less toppy sound produced by a dynamic mic cuts through a mix better than the more accurate sound of a capacitor mic, so once again it's a matter of picking what works best on a subjective level.

stereo miking

A successful stereo microphone technique must emulate the way in which we utilise our own two ears to experience sound in a three-dimensional space, and logic might suggest that using two microphones in place of our own ears would be the nearest we could get. This can be tested using a piece of equipment known as a *dummy head*. If sound is picked up from microphones placed within the ears of a dummy head, it must be reproduced by loudspeakers in the same physical position as the microphones in order to maintain any degree of accuracy, and the nearest we can get to this in real life is to use headphones, as unfortunately the technique doesn't work nearly as well when the sound is replayed via loudspeakers. This is because, when we listen to stereo loudspeakers, some of the sound from the left speaker reaches the right ear, and vice versa. This introduces a new set of conditions, and different microphone techniques are required. In real life, sound arrives from all directions, but with speakers all of the sound comes from just two locations. Sophisticated though the human hearing system is, it appears to be quite forgiving when it comes to stereophonic sound, and although no man-made recording equals the experience of the live event, even a relatively crude stereo recording can provide a satisfying and pleasurable listening experience.

coincident or XY pair

Possibly the most popular method of stereo miking is the coincident or XY pair. This set-up comprises two identical high-quality cardioid or figure-of-eight mics mounted at approximately 90° to each other and with their capsules as close to each other as is physically possible. As directional microphones are used, one will tend to pick up sound mainly from one side of the soundstage and the other from the opposite side. Figure-of-eight mics will also capture the left and right sound from the rear of the room, including audience noise and room reverberation, although, as far as the recording is concerned, these rear sounds will also appear to emanate from the front.

Mics arranged in the XY way provide the necessary change in level from left to right but make no attempt to account for the masking effect of the human head or the time-delay effects caused by the distance between one ear and the other. However, because cardioids often have a less-than-perfect high-frequency response when presented with off-axis sounds, the high-frequency attenuation caused by the presence of the human head may, to a degree, be simulated quite by accident!

Because the two microphone capsules are so close to each other that they can be considered coincident (ie occupying the same space at the same time), all sounds arrive at both capsules at the same time, regardless of their direction, and consequently there are no phase problems that might destroy mono compatibility. However, there are also negative aspects to this arrangement.

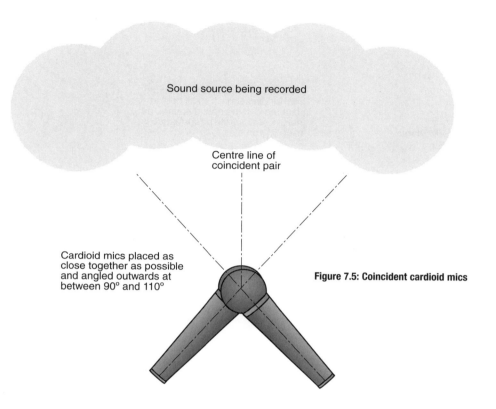

Sound source being recorded

Centre line of
coincident pair

Cardioid mics placed as
close together as possible
and angled outwards at
between 90° and 110°

Figure 7.5: Coincident cardioid mics

The lack of phase information means that some of the auditory clues we rely on in nature are missing, which results in a "dilution" of the stereo image. When the two microphones are summed together to provide a mono signal, the lack of phase errors ensures that no significant compatibility problems exist, other than those caused by the small physical separation between the capsules. Figure 7.5 shows a coincident pair of cardioid mics.

spaced techniques

So far, we know that coincident miking systems create a difference in level between left and right sounds, but no account is taken of the time delay caused by the distance between the ears. We could space apart the microphones of a coincident pair by a few inches and thus create an additional sense of space. In this case, however, the phase cancellations that occur when the signal is summed to mono cause a degree of coloration, due to the inevitable comb-filtering effects brought about by the different arrival times of off-axis sounds.

Sound source

Although omni mics pick up sound
from all directions, it's still best to
point them at the sound source, as
their most accurate performance is
invariably on axis

**Figure 7.6: Spaced
omni mics**

Omni mics

In professional circles, a more common approach is to use spaced omni microphones as, although the spacing still causes problems with mono compatibility, the comb-filtering effects seem to be less pronounced. Such a microphone arrangement is known as an *AB pair*, and is extensively used for recordings that are destined to be replayed over loudspeakers.

The distance of the microphones from the performers must be carefully adjusted so that the desired balance of direct and reverberant sound is being picked up. If the sound is too ambient, the mics need to be brought closer to the performers. Conversely, if the sound is too dry, the microphones may be moved further away. Excellent budget recordings may also be made by using inexpensive Tandy PZM microphones in place of conventional omni-pattern microphones. Figure 7.6 shows how spaced omni mics might be arranged.

direct-to-stereo recording

If you're working with limited equipment, the simplest way to make a home recording is to use just two microphones to record a complete live performance directly onto a stereo cassette or open-reel recorder. This may sound unsophisticated, but it's just about the most accurate way of recording anything. All of the best classical recordings are made in this way because, by using just a single stereo pair of microphones, we can most closely approach what a person would actually experience when listening to a live performance.

Of course, there are difficulties – the performers have to get the song right all the way through, and the balance between the instruments can't be changed after the recording has been made. Even so, most early records were made in this way – many in mono with no EQ! – and they still sound good today.

acoustic music

In the case of acoustic music, such as piano or guitar recitals, choirs, chamber music or even folk bands, the direct-to-stereo approach using a single stereo microphone pair can yield excellent results, even when recorded onto a domestic hi-fi cassette recorder. The microphones may be coincident or spaced unidirectional models, or even a pair of PZMs fixed to sheets of plywood approximately one metre square.

Given the modest equipment requirements, it's well worth exploring the basic stereo techniques described in this chapter before spending even more money on a multitrack system. Good microphones will always be useful, and if you have to buy a decent cassette deck or digital mastering machine especially for the purpose, this can still be used in your multitrack studio for mastering or producing stereo copies.

acoustic environments

The first thing that you have to get right is the actual sound of the musicians, so you'll need to have them all playing in an acoustically sympathetic room with all tuning and maintenance problems taken care of before the session starts. Choirs tend to sound better in reverberant rooms or halls, as do string quartets and suchlike, so check your neighbourhood for suitable community halls that don't suffer from excessive outside noise.

Most other instruments also need a live environment to sound their best, but a shorter reverberation time is more normal. For example, to record an acoustic guitar, it may be sufficient to place a sheet of hardboard beneath the player to reflect back some of the sound that would normally be absorbed by the carpet. For home recording purposes, it's worth checking out different rooms to find the one with the best sound, and if you can roll up the carpet in your recording room then so much the better.

balance

If there are several musicians playing together and there is a problem with one being louder than the others, your only recourse is to change the position of the musicians relative to the microphones so that the loudest ones are further away. Of course, there may be some element of compromise involved, because the players will probably want to maintain eye contact with each other to help them with their performance. They'll also need to be spread out from left to right in order to produce the required stereo picture. As a rule, keep any bass instruments or rhythmic percussion close to the centre.

In the case of a singer/guitarist, the balance between the voice and the guitar can usually be fine-tuned by changing the height of the microphones so that they favour either the voice or the instrument as necessary. After each change in position, make a short test recording to check the balance and overall sound quality.

mic distance

The amount of reverberation that the room contributes to the recording will be dictated largely by the distance of the microphones from the performers. The closer you get, the more direct sound you'll pick up relative to the room ambience. Conversely, working at a greater distance will give a more reverberant sound, but the performance may lose intimacy.

Unless the room has a good live sound, you'll invariably be better off miking fairly close to the instruments to exclude the room sound. If after recording you feel that more ambience would have benefited the performance, you can always copy the tape via a stereo reverb unit to add a little artificial ambience, but take care not to over-process it.

In finalising the microphone positions when working with ensembles, listen to the musicians run through their performance, close your eyes and concentrate on the sound being produced. Check out different places in the room and see if you can identify sweet spots (ie areas in which the music seems to sound better than elsewhere), especially if you're recording in a large room or concert hall. Ultimately, if you can find a spot where the performance sounds good to you, it should also sound good to a microphone. If you have access to a good set of enclosed headphones, you can plug these into your recorder to check out the sound that's actually being picked up. In this way you'll be able to hear the results of any changes in microphone positioning as you make them.

other considerations

Aside from the distance of the microphones from the performers, you also have to decide how far to position them from the floor. Ideally, the microphones should be higher than the musicians, looking down towards them; by arranging them in this way, you'll avoid picking up strong sound reflections from the floor that might adversely colour the sound of your recording.

If you're recording a live concert, you'll also have to find a position that doesn't pick up too much audience noise. Some audience noise will add to the atmosphere of the recording, but the last thing you want is to pick up the conversation of the people sitting closest to the mics. Again, you can use height to your advantage, and you may even be able to suspend the microphones from the ceiling so that your stands don't obstruct the audience's view.

You'll also need to consider the angle between the microphones, because if it's too large you may end up with a stereo image that's all left and right, with very little in the centre. Conversely, if the angle is too small, the sound will be narrow, almost like mono. As a rule, the mics should point roughly between the centre of the stage and the performers at the outside of the group. This same general rule applies if you decide to use spaced microphones rather than a coincident pair. Even so, every recording is different, so don't be afraid to use your ears and move the mics around until you're happy with the result. Figure 7.7 illustrates a typical spaced mic arrangement for recording an ensemble.

multi-mic methods

Pop and rock music is less easy to record with just two microphones, because the balance between the instruments isn't a natural one – after all, the unamplified human voice could never compete with a drum kit. Likewise, many instruments – such as electric guitars and basses or electronic keyboards – are only designed to be used with amplification. Certainly, it's possible to balance the levels of all of the different instrument amplifiers and then record the result, but the main problem is that amplified vocals are rarely of sufficient quality to record. Nevertheless, if you have a decent-sounding PA system, by all means give it a try – the experience will always be worthwhile, and the results may be quite adequate to use as a demo.

A better solution is to use a small mixer and several different microphones so that the various elements of the performance can be

Sound source being recorded

Omni mics pick up sound from all directions, so the amount of room sound being picked up can be altered by adjusting the distance between the mics and the performers

Mics placed so that each half of the sound source is covered fairly equally by each mic. This usually means bringing the mics between a quarter and a third of the way in from each end of the sound stage

Omni mics

Figure 7.7: Ensemble recording using a spaced pair

balanced prior to recording. You'll need to use a number of mics on the drums – a minimum of two overheads, but ideally close mics on the snare and kick drum, too. Some of the sound from the other instruments will inevitably get into the drum mics, but this needn't be too serious. In the event that the players are packed close together because of space constraints, it's advantageous to improvise acoustic screens in order to separate the drums and amplifiers from each other by draping heavy blankets or sleeping bags over clothes-drying frames, microphone stands or other similar impromptu structures. This won't cure sound spillage completely, but it may make the difference between a situation that is viable and one that isn't.

vintage recordings

Harking back to the old days of direct-to-stereo pop recording, this was achieved by using a simple mixing console similar to the ones used for small live performances today. Separate microphones would be used for the main instruments or groups of instruments, and their levels would then be balanced at the mixer. The singer would also sing into a microphone plugged into the mixer, and a headphone mix would be provided for monitoring.

These early mixers had no EQ, and so, if the engineer wanted to change the tone of something, he'd have to move the mic around or even try a different type of microphone. Reverb was usually created using specially-built live rooms, and to multitrack an instrument several players would be hired in to play the same part at the same time. Obviously, the fact that the mixers available to us have all got some form of equalisation and the availability of inexpensive effects units provides us with quite an advantage over these pioneers.

If you want to try multi-mic recording for yourself, with the minimum of equipment, I'd recommend that you close-mike the instruments in the band but have the singer in a totally separate room monitoring the sound going to tape via headphones, preferably the fully enclosed type that don't allow much sound to leak out. (This method requires the band to learn the song well enough to play it without hearing the vocals or even seeing the vocalist, but that should be no problem for competent players.) The engineer, the mixer and the stereo recorder can then be located in a third room, so that the engineer can hear the performance as it sounds over monitor speakers or headphones without interference from the performance itself.

Because modern mixers allow us the luxury of stereo panning, it's possible to create some kind of stereo picture, but be sure to keep all of the bass sounds – such as bass guitar and bass drum – near the centre of the mix. Failure to do this will result in a less powerful sound, and the uneven left/right balance rarely sounds artistically pleasing. For a full description on setting up a musically-pleasing balance, refer to Chapter 12 on "Mixing".

adding effects

If any effects are required, these must be added at the mixer before the recording takes place, although you can probably get away with just a little reverb on the vocals. The effects would be patched into the effects send/return circuit, just as they would be for a live performance. If you

Figure 7.8: Live recording to stereo

have more sophisticated signal processing at your disposal, such as a reasonable compressor, it would be a good idea to use this to keep the vocal level even by patching it into the insert point of the channel handling the lead vocal mic. Compressors are discussed in more detail in the following chapter.

Because the recording can't be changed at all once it's complete, the players must be made aware that mistakes or balance problems can't be corrected afterwards, and they should also be cautioned to stay quiet after the recording has finished. Solos should also be worked out, at least for length, because there will be no way for the guitar player to give a knowing nod to the singer when he feels that he's expressed himself enough.

sequencers

Although this is essentially a chapter on microphones and their application, an interesting variation on the direct-to-stereo theme involves the use of MIDI sequencer. If you're one of those musicians who feels quite at home creating entire backing tracks by using sequenced drum machines, synths and samplers, these can take the place of your live band when you come to do your recording. In other words, you'll be recording live instruments and vocals via mics at the same time as recording the backing from your sequencer. You'll still need to get the vocals right first time, though, and this also goes for any instruments that you intend to add live, but at least you'll know your "band" will deliver perfect performances indefinitely and without complaint until you're happy with the result. I like to think of this method of recording as the modern equivalent of a vintage direct-to-stereo session, where session musicians were used to play the backing.

If you can overcome the attitude that all good recordings must be made by using multitrack, you can achieve first-rate results by going direct to stereo, especially if you have access to an open-reel analogue machine or DAT stereo recorder; it does demand a more disciplined musical approach, but you cut out a whole generation of recording and the loss in quality that this entails. It also does wonders for your musical ability – multitrack recording and computer sequencing have become a crutch for a great many musicians, and their performing ability has suffered because of it.

summary

If you play a musical instrument, you probably practise on a regular basis, and the same should be true of your recording techniques. Don't wait until you have to make a record before you try out new mic techniques – set aside an hour or two and just experiment with a few things to see what different results you can come up with. In particular, try to assess the effect of changing the type and distance of your mics. One way of doing this is to monitor the results via enclosed headphones as you physically move the mic. With just a little persistence, you can maintain more traditional recording skills as well as make the most of what modern synth and sampler technology has to offer.

THE LEARNING CENTRE
TOWER HAMLETS COLLEGE
POPLAR CENTRE
POPLAR HIGH STREET
LONDON E14 0AF

chapter 8

effects and processors

why do we need them?

One of the problems with recording in a home studio is that everything sounds small, because your recording space doesn't have the same acoustic ambience as a concert hall or club. In fact, the same is true of most professional studios, apart from those with large, live rooms, and most pop music is recorded fairly "dry", either in a fairly dead environment or by close miking, after which electronic effects units are used to recreate the desired ambience. The most important effects unit of them all is reverberation, or reverb.

Reverberation occurs naturally when sound is reflected and re-reflected from walls and other obstacles within a large room, and an electronic reverb unit mimics this effect by generating thousands of reflections electronically. Like all modern-day effects, reverb can be used to create the impression of a real room, but it may also be used to create new effects that have no obvious counterpart in nature.

Effects are very powerful tools, but if you try to use them to cover up a poor recording you won't fool anyone. A good mix always starts with a good recording of a good performance.

If you do all of your recording dry, adding effects only when you mix, you have the advantage that you can experiment with different types of effect after the recording has been made. In the professional studio, where there's a big mixer, lots of tape tracks and plenty of different effects units, that's quite feasible; but in a small home studio, it's often more practical to add some effects as you record and others as you mix.

If you're working with a four-track system, for example, you often have to bounce tracks, which means that, if you want the individual sounds to have different effects, you'll have to add these as you bounce. You may also find that your multitrack workstation doesn't have as many effects sends and returns as you need, so it's quite possible that some of the effects will have to be added when you first record the parts.

Guitar effects are usually recorded to tape, because they affect the way in which the guitarist plays. Even so, it helps if you can save putting on the reverb until last – not only does this let you find the right type and balance of effect, but it also enables you to keep the reverb in stereo, which does much to create the feeling of space and depth within a mix. Usually, effects added at the recording stage will be in mono, because you simply can't afford the tape tracks to keep everything in stereo, but if you add a little stereo reverb at the final mixing stage you'll be surprised at how the sound takes on new depth and realism.

main studio effects
reverberation

Reverberation is closely linked with the way in which we perceive sound, and it contains clues which our unconscious mind uses to determine such things as direction, type of acoustic environment and distance.

As touched upon earlier, reverberation occurs naturally when a sound bounces from the surfaces within a room, and its effect is evident as a series of closely spaced echoes following the original sound. If you were to examine the individual reflections that make up natural reverb, you'd discover that, after the initial sound, there's a short pause as the sound travels to the nearest surfaces (walls, floors and ceilings) and then bounces back to the listener. After this, closely spaced reflections or echoes bounce back, although some of these encounter other surfaces and are re-reflected.

As time elapses, the complexity of the reflections builds up rapidly so that the individual echoes are no longer audible, and because natural materials absorb sound as well as reflect it, the intensity of the reflections dies away. With most materials, the high frequencies are absorbed more readily than the low frequencies, so the reverb sounds duller as it decays. Different types of rooms and different materials produce different sounds, which is why modern reverberation units provide settings that imitate a number of types of room and user-adjustable parameters.

The time it takes for reverb to fall in level by 60dB (which effectively means to near silence) is known as the *decay time*, and most musical applications require a fairly short reverb time of between one and three seconds, although digital reverbs can also emulate huge caverns with decay times of

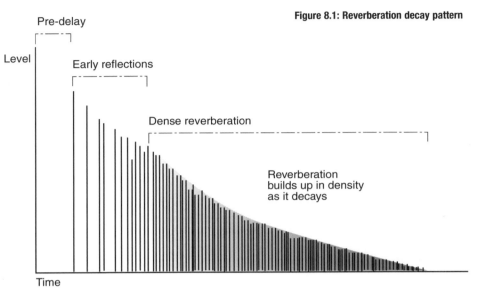

Figure 8.1: Reverberation decay pattern

Pre-delay

Level

Early reflections

Dense reverberation

Reverberation builds up in density as it decays

Time

ten seconds or even more. Plate settings are popular for general use, especially on vocals and drums. (The term *plate* refers to the mechanical reverb plate that was used before digital reverb units were invented.)

In real life, you hear a different pattern of reverb reflections with each ear, and this is what provides the brain with stereo information. Even if the sound source is mono – a single voice or handclap, for example – the reverberation will always be stereo. Digital reverb units process a mono input to produce two different sets of synthetic reflections in order to produce a convincing stereo effect. Figure 8.1 shows the pattern of decaying reflections created by a typical digital reverberation unit.

reverb patching

Effects such as reverb are normally fed from a post-fade send control (effects send), which means that the reverb level will increase and decrease along with the original sound if the channel fader is moved. This is obviously the way that you'd normally want to work, although you can drive a reverb unit from a pre-fade send if you want to fade out the dry signal while still leaving the reverb audible – something you may want to do to create an unusual or special effect.

The advantage of the aux send system is that it allows the same effects device to be shared among all of the mixer channels while still allowing you to have different amounts of effect on each channel. For example, you might be able to use the same reverb setting on both drums and vocals, but you may want to use more on the vocals than on the drums.

To maintain a stereo effect while mixing, the reverb left and right outputs should be panned hard left and right in the mix. A multitrack workstation with stereo effects returns will automatically pan the effects return signals left and right, but if you're using spare input channels then you'll have to remember to do this manually. The effects unit mix output parameter or control is then set for effect only – no dry signal. If you use input channels as returns, ensure that the corresponding aux send is turned off completely on those channels, or some of the reverb will be fed back to its own input, causing feedback or tonal coloration.

To make sure that your reverb unit (or multi-effects processor) works as quietly as possible (remember gain structure?), set the aux sends on the channels you want to effect to around three quarters full up. The aux send master should also be set to three quarters full up – the input level control on the effects unit itself is used to set the signal level going into the unit so that a healthy meter reading is obtained. You should set the output level of the effects unit to be close to maximum and then adjust the effects return level on the mixer to give you the right subjective level of effect.

To keep unwanted noise to an absolute minimum, it's important to turn down any post-fade aux sends that aren't being used and to de-route any mixer channels that aren't being used in the mix. This doesn't just mean turning the fader down; you should also mute the channel. If you're using a console with routing buttons, also make sure that unused channels aren't routed to the main stereo mix. It's not often realised that a muted channel with the fader down will still contribute a little noise – known as *mix-buss noise* – just from being connected to the stereo mix buss.

If you're using a separate studio mixer and you want to add a specific effect to only one channel, you can take your effects send from the channel's insert send or from the channel's direct output, if it has one, which will remove the contribution of mix-buss noise altogether. Alternatively, you can feed the signal to be treated directly from your multitrack recorder into the effects unit and then feed the effects unit outputs into two adjacent mixer channels panned hard left and right. The effect/mix balance will have to be set on the effects unit.

If all of the effects sends are in use, effects may be connected via insert points, although this limits their use to that one channel only. When working in the aux send/return mode, the dry sound should be turned off on the effects unit. When used via an insert point, the effect/dry balance must be set on the effects unit itself.

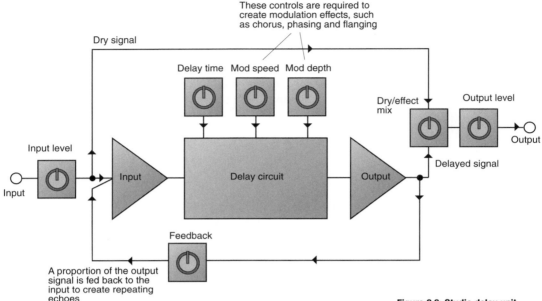

Figure 8.2: Studio delay unit

delay

As the name suggests, delay is a means of delaying an audio signal so as to produce one or more distinct echoes. By feeding some of the delayed sound back to the input, the echoes continue to recirculate and decay, creating multiple echoes. The higher the level of the feedback, the longer the echoes take to decay. The main parameters are delay time and feedback. Figure 8.2 shows the block diagram of a delay unit.

multi-tapped delay

Modern multi-effects units often include multi-tapped delay programs, which generate multiple echoes at different delay times. It may also be possible to pan the individual delays from left to right in the stereo field to create interesting spatial effects.

A popular technique is to set the echo delay time so that the repeats are in time with the tempo of the song, although shorter delays can be used to create a doubling or double-tracking effect. Echo effects were popular back in the '60s and early '70s, when they were often used on lead guitars and vocals. The effect is still popular today, and is used on all types of instrument and voice.

modulation effects

It's surprising how many of the standard studio effects are variations on the digital-delay theme, where the delay time is modulated by an LFO (Low-Frequency Oscillator) to produce chorus, flanging, phasing and vibrato effects. Modulation in this context simply means that the delay time is varied under the control of an LFO. Some modulation effects, such as phasing, use such short delay times that no delay is perceptible, while chorus and ADT use a slightly longer delay time to produce a doubling or thickening effect.

chorus and ADT

Chorus uses a short delay of up to about 70ms to create a slight doubling effect, and the delay time is then modulated to produce a slight wavering in pitch. An equal mix of the delayed and unprocessed sound is used to produce an effect rather like two instruments playing the same part but with slight differences in timing and tuning. This characteristic makes chorus useful for creating ensemble effects from single instruments.

The chorus depth is controlled by the LFO modulation depth, and as a rule the faster the modulation, the less depth is needed. Chorus is often used on string sounds, synthesiser pads, electric guitars and fretless bass guitars.

ADT (Automatic Double Tracking) is similar to chorus but uses a delay time in excess of 70ms to create a more pronounced doubling or "slapback" effect, and the depth of modulation is shallower. ADT is often used to process vocals to make it appear that the same singer has performed the part twice, on different tape tracks, again to obtain a thicker sound. The amount of modulation should be so slight as to be only just noticeable.

flanging

Flanging is closely related to chorus but uses shorter delay times and feedback is added to create an effect similar to classic tape flanging. The higher the feedback setting, the stronger the effect. As with chorus, faster speed should be used with reduced depth. Both chorus and flanging sound best in stereo, if your effects unit has that capability.

Flanging sounds good on vocals, bass, synthesiser and even drums, but because it's such a dramatic effect it's best when it's used sparingly. The more harmonically rich the original sound, the more pronounced the flanging effect.

phasing

Phasing uses shorter delay times than flanging does and little or no feedback to produce a moving comb filter which sounds not unlike mild flanging. Because the effect is more subtle than flanging, it can be used more extensively, and many Pink Floyd tracks feature phasing on the lead guitar.

vibrato

Vibrato is a modulation of pitch similar to that produced manually by a guitar or violin, and is created by using only the delayed sound and none of the original. The delay is kept to just a few milliseconds so as not to significantly affect the timing of the performance, and the modulation depth sets the depth of the vibrato.

pitch shifting

Pitch shifters can change the pitch of the original signal but without changing the speed of the sound, and they usually have a maximum range of at least one octave up and down. Pitch shifting is often found in the modulation section of multi-effects units, but it isn't a modulated delay process at all. Pitch shifting works by breaking the sound into very short segments and sampling them in turn. Each sample is then either looped or truncated, depending on whether the pitch is being moved up or down, and digital algorithms are used to splice the segments back together so as to avoid glitching. Most low-cost pitch shifters impart a strange timbre caused by the regular modulation of the looping and splicing processes, but this side-effect can be disguised if mixed with the original sound. There's also a slight delay due to the sampling and splicing processes, but this can be as short as just a few milliseconds.

Smaller pitch shifts sound very similar to chorus effects but without the regular modulation of chorus. Such "detuning" treatments, combined with a short delay, are often used to double or thicken vocals. Larger shifts can be used to create octaves or parallel harmonies, and so-called intelligent pitch shifters can be set to add musically correct, real-time harmonies to vocal or guitar parts. Interesting effects may also be achieved by pitch shifting percussive sounds to create deep snare and kick-drum sounds.

The newest pitch-shifting feature is *format correction*, whereby the character of a voice can be altered without changing the speed or, alternatively, the pitch of a voice can be changed without the usual Mickey Mouse effect being produced. It's anticipated that future developments in this area will allow singers to change their voices so that they sound more like the artistes that they're covering.

External signal processor

Channel insert point
Insert point is usually a stereo jack,
so that both the insert send and
insert return signal can be sent
through a single socket

Output

Master
fader

Mixer channel

Master section

Connection via insert point

Figure 8.3: Processor and effect signal paths

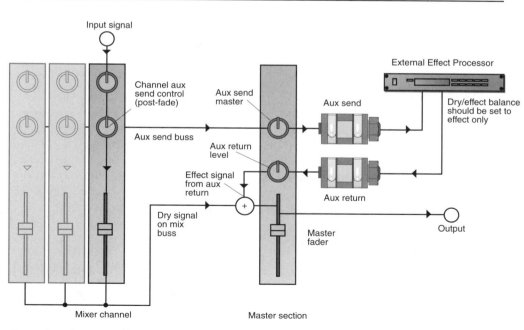

Input signal

Channel aux
send control
(post-fade)

Aux send
master

Aux send

External Effect Processor

Dry/effect balance
should be set to
effect only

Aux send buss

Aux return
level

Effect signal
from aux
return

Aux return

Dry signal
on mix
buss

Master
fader

Output

Mixer channel

Master section

Connection via aux send/return

aux sends and inserts

Delay- or reverb-type effects can be connected to either an aux send or an insert point, but there are other processing devices which don't have the same flexibility when it comes to patching. Reverb and delay effects are usually added to the original signal, so that you hear both together, but when you put a signal though an equaliser the whole signal is affected – no untreated sound is heard at all. To avoid confusion, it helps if you mentally divide your outboard devices into two categories: "effects" should be reserved to describe those devices that rely on some form of delay circuitry to make them operate, while the other category, "processors", describes the type of device that processes the entire signal, changing it either tonally or in level. Another clue, when deciding which device belongs in which category, is that effects usually have some form of dry/effect balance control, whereas processors (with the possible exception of exciters) don't. Processors should only be connected via insert points or between the line output of one piece of equipment and the line input of another, whereas effects can be connected via both insert points and aux sends.

Effects based on delay circuitry include reverb, delay, echo, chorus, flanging, vibrato and pitch shift. When used in the aux send system of a mixing console, the dry signal level should be turned right down at the effects unit and the effect level set to maximum. The amount of effect added to each mixer channel is then determined by the channel aux send control.

If insert points are used to connect effects, the dry/effect balance must be set at the effects unit.

processors

Those devices categorised as processors include exciters, equalisers, compressors, limiters, gates, expanders and auto-panners. These change either the level or the tonal quality of the signal passing through them, and you wouldn't normally add a dry signal to the output of one of these units. Because aux sends are used to add the output from an effect to the dry signal, it isn't normal to connect a processor via an aux send. Figure 8.3 shows the difference in the signal paths of a processor and an effect.

compressors/limiters

Compressors are used to "even out" excessive peaks in signal level that occur in vocal or instrumental performances, and they do this by changing the gain of the signal path depending on the level of the signal passing through. Just as an engineer might pull down a fader if the level gets too

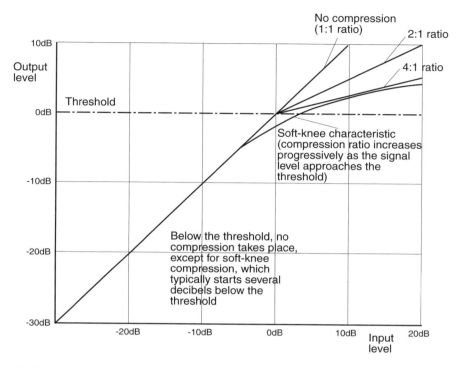

Figure 8.4: Compressor ratio graph

high, so a compressor will turn down the level if it exceeds a threshold set by the user, while signals falling below the threshold level remain unchanged. The degree of gain reduction applied is set by the Compression Ratio control setting, as shown in the graph in Figure 8.4.

When the ratio is very high, the compressor's maximum output is maintained at the threshold level and is effectively prevented from going beyond it. This sets a limit on the maximum signal level, regardless of the input, and a compressor used with a high ratio setting is often described as a *limiter*, hence the term "compressor/limiter". As a rule, high compression ratios are used in conjunction with high threshold settings, so that only the signal peaks are affected. Lower ratios may be used with lower threshold settings to provide gain levelling over a greater dynamic range.

The compressor's Attack control determines how quickly the circuitry responds once a signal has exceeded the threshold, while Release sets the time for the gain to return to normal once the input has dropped back below the threshold. Some compressors have auto-attack and -release settings that respond to the dynamic character of the input signal. Auto mode is very useful for processing signals with constantly changing characteristics, such as vocals, slap/pull bass guitar or complete mixes.

Most two-channel compressors have a Stereo Link switch so that stereo signals can be processed. In Link mode, both channels are compressed by the same amount, which prevents the image from appearing to move to one side or the other when a loud sound appears on only one side of the mix.

The maximum gain of a compressor occurs when the input signal is below the threshold, which can sometimes lead to background noise being boosted during quiet passages or pauses. To combat this problem, some compressors are provided with built-in gates so that the signal may be silenced during pauses.

Compressors are most often used to keep instrument and vocal levels at an even volume during a mix, although they may also be used to add sustain to guitars. Setting a deliberately long attack time can also help emphasise the attack of a sound such as the slap of a bass guitar.

Limiting is used in circumstances where it would be undesirable for a signal to exceed a specific level – for example, to prevent clipping on a digital recorder.

gates

Whereas compressors control the levels of signals that exceed a threshold, gates control the levels of signals that fall below a threshold. The aim is to silence the signal during pauses, when any background noise won't be masked by the presence of a signal. If the gate threshold level is set just above the background noise, the gate will operate whenever there is a pause in the signal.

Gates are used for muting the spill from other instruments as well as for tackling straightforward noise or hiss problems, and they're regularly used when miking drum kits – for example, to prevent the bass drum mic from picking up the other drums in the kit. They're also often used with electric guitars to combat the high level of noise and hum generated by a typical guitar amplifier when the guitarist isn't actually playing. Vocals may be gated to hide any rustling of clothing or audible breathing.

It must be understood that gates only remove noise when there's a pause in the wanted signal – they can't help with noise that's audible over the top of the programme material. Even so, using gates on all of the noisy tracks in a multitrack recording can help to produce a much cleaner-sounding

Figure 8.5: Operation of a gate

recording. Expanders are very similar to gates, except that they close down gently, more like a compressor in reverse. Figure 8.5 shows how a gate reacts when the signal level falls below the threshold.

equalisers

Equalisers are essentially tone controls, and the different types available are described in Chapter 5, on "Equalisation". Most mixers have EQ built in, but it's often useful to have a better-quality external equaliser that can be patched in via an insert point for those occasions when more precise control is required. Parametric equalisers are the most versatile, but they're also the most time consuming to set up properly.

exciters

Also known as enhancers, exciters are devices that add synthesised high-frequency harmonics to a signal to make it sound brighter and more intimate than it did originally. The process was developed and patented by Aphex and is different to equalisation, which only redistributes the harmonics that already exist. Exciters are used to push sounds to the front of a mix or to create clarity and space in a crowded mix. They can be used on whole mixes or just on individual tracks, and they may also be used to brighten stereo mixes destined to be masters used for cassette copying, in order to help compensate for the loss of high-frequency content that cassette duplication often entails. Enhancers that work on slightly different principles are available from other manufacturers.

autopanners

An autopanner is simply a device that automatically pans a mono signal from left to right in a mix, usually under the control of a low-frequency oscillator or external trigger. Used in time with the tempo of a track, panning can be quite subtle. Many multi-effects units include a panning facility as well as a rotary speaker emulator, designed to simulate Leslie speakers and similar systems that employ rotating baffles to add vibrato to organ sounds. Most rotary-speaker sounds combine panning with chorus, and they often have two speeds, with delayed "speed up" and "slow down" functions to mimic the mechanical inertia of the real thing.

patching

Patching effects can be confusing to newcomers, so I've included this list of key points for reference:

• Insert points are invariably presented as stereo jacks wired to carry both the send and return signal, so if you don't have a patchbay you'll need a Y-lead with a stereo jack on one end and two monos on the other;

• Processors must always be used "in line" with a signal and not in the effects send/return loop, unless you really know exactly what you're doing and why you're doing it;

• Most processors work at line level, so you can't plug a mic directly into them. The correct way to compress a mic signal, for example, is to patch the compressor into the insert point of the mic channel. In this way, the mixer's mic amp brings the mic signal up to line level before feeding it to the compressor;

• If an effect is used via the aux/send return system, it's normal to set the effect unit's dry/effect balance to Effect Only so as to allow the console's aux send controls to control the effect balance;

- Some effects – such as phasing and flanging – rely on a precise effect/dry balance, which may be better accomplished in the effects unit itself. In this case, either patch the effect unit into an insert point or, if you must use the aux/send system, you can either de-route the channel from the stereo mix to kill the dry signal or feed the effects unit from a pre-fade (foldback) send and turn the channel fader right down;

- To use a mono-in/stereo-out effect unit (such as reverb or stereo delay) via insert points, simply route one output of the unit to the insert return of the channel feeding it and the other to the insert return of an adjacent channel. Match the levels and pan one track hard left and the other hard right for maximum stereo effect;

- To use a stereo-in/stereo-out effect unit via insert points, use two adjacent mixer channels panned hard left and right;

- To treat a whole mix with, say, EQ or compression, patch your processor into the master insert points. This places your unit in the signal path just before the master stereo faders, which means that, if you're using a compressor, it won't try to fight you if you do a fade-out. Similarly, any noise generated by the processor will also be faded as you pull the faders down;

- If you don't have master insert points, you can patch a processor between the mixer's stereo out and the input to your stereo mastering recorder. However, if you want to do fades with a compressor patched in, you'll need to do them using the Input Level control on the tape machine rather than on the desk.

summary

Effects are essential to modern recording, with reverberation being the most important effect of all. Fortunately, good multi-effects units are now relatively cheap, but if one unit is all that you can afford then make sure that it can deliver smooth, natural reverb as well as the more dramatic effects. Poor-quality reverb units tend to have a metallic ring to them when percussive sounds – such as snare drums – are being treated.

chapter 9

introducing MIDI

MIDI is an integral part of contemporary music making, but I remember that, when I first encountered it, I thought that it was very much more complicated than actually turned out to be the case. Of course, there's no need to use MIDI at all if you're only recording conventional instruments, but in practice the majority of commercial recordings use both MIDI and "real" sound sources. MIDI will be covered more thoroughly in another book in this series, but the following chapter should provide you with enough background information to get started.

Part of the problem with MIDI is the jargon that goes with it. Also, some people harbour a suspicion that MIDI and computers mean handing over the musical process to a machine. On top of that, it's not always made clear exactly what MIDI can do for the musician. To tackle the first question first, though, is MIDI really complicated?

MIDI is complicated in the same way that a car engine or a telephone exchange is complicated, but you don't have to be a car mechanic to drive a car or an electronics engineer to use a telephone. MIDI is just another creative tool, and you can use it either simply or to perform complex tasks – you're in control.

what does MIDI do?

MIDI is often defined as a communication protocol for use with musical instruments, but that definition is of little help to the newcomer. What this really means is that MIDI is a common electronic protocol that enables two or more MIDI-equipped electronic instruments to be linked together in such a way that musical information can pass from one to the other. (I'll come onto the definition of musical information shortly.) MIDI stands for Musical Instrument Digital Interface, but you don't have to know anything about digital electronics to use it. In fact, from the user's point of view, MIDI has more in common with telephones and TV remote controls.

MIDI instruments, and other MIDI devices, are equipped with five-pin DIN sockets to handle the MIDI data, and on a typical unit you'll see sockets marked MIDI In, MIDI Out and MIDI Thru. These sockets are connected using standard MIDI cables, but there are a few simple rules governing what should be plugged in where, and I'll cover these a little later.

First of all, I'd like to elaborate on this mysterious information that is passed from one device to another via MIDI. There are many types of MIDI message, so I'll start by covering the most obvious ones first. MIDI instruments are electronic, which means that the sound you hear is created electronically rather than by a mechanical action, as with a piano or guitar. In other words, the keys on an electronic instrument are little more than switches that generate electronic signals to tell the instrument's circuitry what note to play and how loud to play it. Whenever a key is pressed on a MIDI synthesiser, a signal known as a Note On message is sent, and when the key is released a second message is sent, known as a Note Off. The pitch of the note being played is generally related to which key you hit, just as it is on a piano, and the faster or harder you hit the key, the louder the sound. Because playing "hardness" is really the same thing as speed, as far as the key is concerned, we call the hardness of playing *velocity*. This is an often-used piece of MIDI jargon, so it's worth remembering it.

Time for a quick recap. So far, we know that a musical note transmitted over MIDI comprises a Note On message, the pitch of the note, the loudness of the note and a Note Off message. There are other things that you can do to a note, such as bending the pitch or adding vibrato, but the main thing to grasp at the moment is that, every time you press down a key on a MIDI keyboard, information is generated that defines the note, its duration and its loudness.

The next conceptual leap is to take this electronic pitch, Note On, Note Off and velocity information and send it down a MIDI cable so that it can control a remote MIDI instrument that may be on the other side of the room. This may not seem particularly useful just yet, but this concept is the basis of MIDI and its applications.

MIDI isn't a means of transmitting sounds directly; it's a system for transmitting instructions concerning what's happening on the master keyboard. One analogy is the written musical score – this only tells the performer what notes to play and when to play them; it can't affect the sound of the instrument or even the instrument on which you decide to play that music.

MIDI connections

To make a basic MIDI connection, plug the MIDI Out of the keyboard (the instrument you're actually playing) into the MIDI In socket of a second MIDI instrument, known as the slave, as shown in Figure 9.1. Now, when you play

Provided that the two instruments are set to the same MIDI channel, notes played on the master will also be played on the slave

Master

MIDI cable

Slave

Figure 9.1: Basic MIDI connection

a note on the master keyboard, the slave instrument will also play, provided that both instruments are set to the same MIDI channel.

MIDI channels

To connect more MIDI instruments together, the MIDI Thru of the first slave is connected to the MIDI In of the second slave, and so on. In such a system, all of the modules receive the same MIDI information at the same time. However, most of the time, we want the MIDI data to be played back by only one of several modules in the system, which is why MIDI channels are needed.

There are 16 MIDI channels, and they work in a very similar way to TV channels, inasmuch as all TV channels are picked up by the same aerial and yet we can still switch channels to watch just the one we want. With MIDI, information can be sent on any one of 16 channels (something you can select on the master keyboard), and the sound modules making up the rest of the system may each be set to receive any one of the 16 channels. (Most modules have a MIDI mode called Omni, which allows them to respond to

Provided that the two instruments are set to the same MIDI channel, notes played on the master will also be played on the slave

MIDI Out

MIDI In   MIDI Thru   MIDI Out

Master

MIDI cable

Slave module 1

MIDI In   MIDI Thru

Provided that all of the instruments are set to the same MIDI channel, anything played on the master keyboard will also be played by the slaves

Slave module 2

MIDI In   MIDI Thru

Slave module 3

MIDI In

Figure 9.2: Master keyboard with three slaves

all 16 MIDI channels at once, but this is of little use in normal situations.)

If the master keyboard is set to transmit on MIDI channel 1 and is connected to two different MIDI modules set to receive on channels 1 and 2, only the module set to channel 1 will respond (provided that module 2 hasn't been accidentally set to Omni mode). Both modules still receive the information, but, unless the MIDI transmit and receive channels are the same, it will be ignored. You could put two or more modules on the same MIDI channel in order to layer sounds, but in most systems each sound module would be set to a different MIDI channel.

By selecting different channels on the master keyboard, up to 16 different modules – each set to their own MIDI channels – can be controlled individually. Figure 9.2 shows a master keyboard connected to three slaves.

sound modules

A MIDI sound module is really just a MIDI instrument without a keyboard, but most modern instruments and modules can play several different sounds at once, each on their own MIDI channels. In other words, you might find that the box you've bought isn't just one musical instrument but as many as 16 different MIDI instruments all sharing the same box. A MIDI module or keyboard that can behave as several different instruments at the same time is said to be *multitimbral*. However, the different instruments inside the box aren't usually totally independent; they invariably share the same set of front-panel controls, and the sound outputs may be internally mixed so that everything comes out via a single stereo pair of output sockets.

On more expensive instruments, there may be more outputs to which the individual musical parts can be directed, but few instruments have more than eight separate outputs. You can change the relative levels and pan positions of the various parts using the front-panel controls, so having everything mixed to one stereo output isn't as big a restriction as it might at first appear.

sequencers

If until now you've been a live performer, you might wonder why you need 16 different instruments in one box, because surely you can only play one at a time, given the limitation of a single pair of hands? Well, you could split your keyboard and have something like a bass instrument on the bottom two octaves and maybe a piano on the rest. However, even this doesn't need 16-part multitimbrality.

The answer, of course, is the MIDI sequencer, which can play all 16 parts together with no effort. When using a sequencer, just one multitimbral module can provide you with a complete backing track, including the drums. Before MIDI, few people could compose a symphony – or a pop song, for that matter – and ever expect to hear it performed, but now almost anyone can turn their musical ideas into a performance by using affordable technology.

The traditional way of creating music is to compose a score and then, once this is completed, hiring an orchestra and getting them to play what you've written. As with the orchestral composer, sequencer-based work usually starts at the keyboard, but this time the keyboard is a MIDI instrument connected to a MIDI sequencer. Instead of writing down a score, the composer will record sections of the music into the sequencer against an electronic metronome set to the desired tempo, and instead of scanning a score to verify what's been done it's a simple matter to play back the recording to hear exactly what has been recorded. Best of all, you don't have to hire in an orchestra, because a relatively inexpensive multitimbral synthesiser will provide all of the sounds for you; each "part" of the multitimbral synth plays one line of your electronic score. If the end result isn't quite right, you can make changes without having to hire the orchestra again to confirm that your changes are okay. To make changes, you simply erase or move the unwanted notes and add new ones.

It's often convenient to visualise a sequencer as being something like a multitrack tape recorder, which is fine as long as you don't go back to thinking about recording sounds – MIDI is all about data, or instructions that tell your instruments what to play. Just as a musical score is a series of instructions to the musicians, a MIDI sequence holds a series of instructions which tell your synths what to play.

In some ways, the sequencer is better than the written score, because it can play back a part exactly as you played it in the first place – it doesn't have to "quantise" everything to equal subdivisions of a musical bar like the written score does.

In reality, MIDI does have a finite timing resolution, because the computer has to work to an internal timing routine based on an electronic clock. In practice, however, MIDI is far more accurate than a typical human performer and is capable of resolving a bar of music into at least 960 time divisions, and frequently more.

Some software sequencer packages include sophisticated score-writing facilities, which enable you to print out sheet music for your compositions, in which case you'll need a printer which is compatible with both your computer and the software package. However, some musical literacy is useful, because the computer doesn't always interpret what you play in the same way that a trained score-writer would.

sequencer set-up

In a typical set-up, a MIDI master keyboard is connected to a sequencer via a MIDI cable so that, when the sequencer is set to Record, any notes played on the keyboard are recorded as MIDI data, and, like the multitrack tape machine, a sequencer has multiple tracks on which to record the various musical parts of your composition. You might have 16 MIDI tracks set up so that each is on a different MIDI channel for use with a 16-part multitimbral module, enabling you to play back all 16 tracks at once; but if you only have an eight-part multitimbral module, you can only play back eight different musical parts at once, regardless of how many tracks your sequencer has.

It would be tedious to have to change the MIDI channel on which your master keyboard transmits every time you wanted to record a new track, so modern sequencers invariably convert the incoming MIDI data to the appropriate channel for you. In this way, once a track is finished, you simply move onto the next one and keep playing with the new sound.

sequence editing

In many ways, a MIDI sequencer is like a word processor – you can delete or replace wrong musical notes, you can use the same phrase more than once by copying it or you can move sections about. In some ways, a better analogy might be the "player piano", or pianola, where a punched paper roll holds the instructions that make the piano play, except that, with MIDI, you have a multitrack, virtual "paper roll" capable of controlling many instruments at the same time.

In Edit mode, you can change the value, timing and velocity of any note or even build up entire compositions by entering the notes manually. A number of editing options are usually available, including the ability to transpose your music, either as you play or after recording, and you have the ability to make the music louder or softer by adjusting the overall note-velocity values.

On some systems, you can even compress the dynamic range of your MIDI data to even out the difference between the louder notes and the softer ones, and you can delay or advance tracks relative to each other. This is frequently achieved by recalculating the note data during playback, but the real data isn't changed, so you can always revert to your original performance data.

quantisation

One important feature common to both hardware and software sequencers is the ability to quantise data after recording. When you quantise something, the timing is changed so as to push each note you've recorded to the nearest exact subdivision of a bar. For example, if you're working in 4/4 time and you select 16 as your quantise value, everything moves so that it falls on the nearest 16th of a bar. Over-quantising will ruin the feel of some types of music, but in dance music, where precise timing is essential, the quantise feature is routinely used.

A sequencer will record just about any MIDI data you send it (with the exception of MIDI Clock), and unless you deliberately filter out certain types of MIDI data you can record Note On/Off, pitch, velocity, aftertouch and controller information as well as MIDI Program Changes and even system-exclusive (Sysex) data, which is what you get if you do a patch dump from your instrument.

A MIDI Program-Change message recorded during the count-in period of a track will ensure that the connected synth switches to the correct patch before playing commences, and then, when your sequence is played back, the sequencer transmits the MIDI information to the receiving synth in exactly the same order and with the same timing as you originally played it. Because MIDI is only data, you can change the tempo after recording without affecting the pitch (unlike a tape recorder, where you're dealing with sound rather than MIDI data).

types of sequencer

MIDI sequencers are all really based on computer technology, but you can choose a software-based system that runs on a desktop computer, such as an Apple Macintosh/PowerMac, IBM PC or Atari, or instead you can go for a one-box dedicated solution, where everything you need is in one portable package. The main difference between the two types is the way in which the recorded information is displayed, as the hardware models don't have the benefit of having a large screen.

Whichever type you use, it's very important to save your work to disk at regular intervals. Most hardware sequencers have a built-in disk drive, allowing songs to be saved as files on floppy disks, although some models use battery-backed-up memory instead of disks.

MIDI interface

If you're not using an Atari ST, which has an integral MIDI interface, you'll need to buy an external MIDI interface, unless one of your synths or modules has a built-in computer interface. Figure 9.3 shows a basic sequencing set-up. This diagram shows a MIDI master keyboard, but if you're using a synth as a master keyboard you should select Local Off on the master keyboard and connect the MIDI In of your master synth to one of the outputs of your MIDI Thru box.

As the Record and Playback controls of a typical sequencer are designed to look similar to tape-recorder transport buttons, there will be a means of examining your stored MIDI data and make changes to it if necessary.

MIDI troubleshooting

In a typical MIDI system, the MIDI data originates at the master keyboard, which is connected via its MIDI Out to the MIDI In of your sequencer. As mentioned earlier, if your keyboard includes a synth section, activate Local Off and patch a MIDI cable from the sequencer's MIDI Out (or from your

Master keyboard should be set to Local Off mode to prevent creating a MIDI feedback loop. If no Local On/Off facility is provided, set the master keyboard to transmit on MIDI channel 1 and set the sequencer Thru to Off on channel 1

Figure 9.3: Basic sequencing system

Thru box) to the keyboard's MIDI In. Up to three modules can normally be chained from Thru to In without problems, but longer chains may suffer stuck or missed notes. If you have more than three MIDI devices, a Thru box is highly recommended.

If you've connected up your system as described but no sound comes out, here are a few things to check:

• Make sure that your amplification system and all of your MIDI units are switched on and the volumes are turned up to a reasonable level;

• Make sure that your synth modules are set to Multi or Sequencer mode as appropriate;

- Check your MIDI cable connections. If one of the modules has a combined MIDI Out/Thru socket, make sure that MIDI Thru is enabled. Most sequencers have an indicator to show that they're receiving MIDI data;

- Check the MIDI channels on your modules. If two or more instruments play the same part, check whether more than one module is set to the same MIDI channel. Alternatively, something may still be in Omni mode;

- If your master keyboard plays its own sounds when you're trying to record using another module, check that Local Off is activated;

- If playing a single note results in a burst of notes, if you get stuck notes or if the polyphony seems less than it should be, you probably have a MIDI loop, where data generated by the master keyboard is passing through the sequencer and getting back to the input of the master keyboard. Here it goes around the system again and again, choking the system with unnecessary and unwanted data. This usually happens when you have a keyboard synth as your master keyboard and Local Off is accidentally switched to Local On.

MIDI sound sources

MIDI sequencers can be used to control synthesisers, MIDI electronic pianos or organs, samplers or drum machines, but there's a limit to the number of notes that a sound module or synthesiser can play at once, and this is known as the *maximum polyphony*. If you try to play more notes than this, one of the notes already sounding will be cut off. In a multitimbral instrument, the polyphony is shared between the various instruments so that, if the piano isn't playing, for example, the string part can use more notes before you run out of polyphony. Different instruments have different systems for sharing their polyphony, but you'll need to look in your instrument handbooks to find out how your own instrument is likely to behave.

drum machines

Technically speaking, drum machines are also synthesisers of a sort – they're simply MIDI modules with their own rhythm sequencer built in, and the drum sounds may be played over MIDI exactly like conventional synth notes, However, instead of each key giving you a new pitch of the same drum sound, drum machines are organised so that you get a different drum sound for each key played. A drum machine with no internal rhythm sequencer is known as a *drum module*. Most people who use drum machines with sequencers ignore the drum machine's internal sequencer and instead use the drum machine in the same way as they would any other sound module. New drum parts are then recorded directly from the keyboard (usually in two or three passes, to make things simpler).

samplers

A MIDI sampler is very similar to a synthesiser, expect that, instead of having built-in sounds, you can record your own sounds and then play them back at any pitch. The sounds might be musical instruments, but you can also turn household objects, such as pans or bottles, into new instruments. For example, tap a bottle, sample it, then play it back at different pitches from the keyboard and you have your own xylophone. Libraries of ready-made sample sounds are available on both audio CD and CD-ROM.

MIDI connections

Earlier, we learned that MIDI instruments have three MIDI sockets, labelled In, Out and Thru, although some models actually have a combined MIDI Out and Thru connection. The master instrument in a system always sends information from its MIDI Out socket, which is connected to the MIDI In socket of the first slave. (If you want a longer chain, I've already explained that you can take the MIDI Thru of the slave and connect it to the MIDI In of the next slave.) However, you can't chain instruments together indefinitely, because the MIDI signal gets slightly distorted every time it passes through another unit, and eventually there comes a point where the system becomes unreliable and some of the slaves start missing notes or, worse still, playing notes and forgetting to turn them off again!

MIDI thru boxes

Unless you have a very simple MIDI system, you should use a MIDI Thru box, as shown in Figure 9.4. This is fed from the MIDI Out of the sequencer and has several MIDI Thru outputs, each of which can be connected to a different MIDI slave module.

You may have noticed that so far the only MIDI Out that's been used is on the master synth or keyboard – the MIDI Outs of the slave units have been left unconnected. The reason modules have MIDI Outs is that, if they're being edited with software and a computer with a MIDI interface, the MIDI Out is required to transfer information about the module and the sounds it contains back to the computer.

MIDI In

MIDI Out

MIDI IN   MIDI THRU   MIDI OUT

Master

Using a MIDI Thru box
avoids data corruption
caused by excessively
long MIDI chains

MIDI In

MIDI Sequencer   MIDI Out

MIDI Out

MIDI Out   MIDI In

MIDI Out

MIDI In

MIDI Out

MIDI module 1

MIDI Thru box

MIDI In

MIDI module 2

MIDI In

MIDI module 3

Figure 9.4: MIDI Thru box

program-change messages

There's a great deal more useful information than can be transmitted over MIDI than musical notes. Most MIDI synthesisers are programmable and have the ability to store a great number of different sounds, which can be recalled almost instantly. One way to recall sounds is to use the front panel buttons, but you can also do it via MIDI. MIDI provides direct access for up to 128 sound patches, and when you change the patch on your master keyboard using the front panel controls a Program Change command is transmitted from the MIDI

Out (unless this function has been deliberately disabled via a software option). Program-Change messages may also be used to select the effects patches on a MIDI effects unit or to switch drum kits on a drum sound module.

bank-change messages

Some MIDI instruments provide far more than 128 different sounds, in which case these have to be stored in banks, where each bank contains up to 128 different patches or programs. MIDI Bank-Change commands may then be sent to switch from one bank to another, although at the moment there are several non-standard Bank-Change message formats in use, so you may need to consult the manual that came with your module.

real-time control

There's more to playing a synthesiser than simply hitting the right notes on the keyboard – there are performance controls, such as the pitch-bend and modulation wheels, which add interest and life to a performance. As you might imagine, the effect of moving these wheels may also be transmitted via MIDI.

MIDI instruments can often be "scaled" so that the maximum travel of the pitch-bend wheel causes a pitch shift of anywhere between one semitone and a full octave in either direction from a spring-loaded centre position. Most people use a default setting of two semitones over the full travel of the wheel, but whatever scale you choose it's important that any instruments likely to play at the same time are set with the same scaling values. The same is true when you're working with a sequencer, and it's generally advisable to set up all of your instruments to the same pitch-bend range.

MIDI volume

On a master instrument that sends master volume information, turning up the master volume slider will send the appropriate control information over MIDI and the receiving instrument will respond to it. Some older instruments don't respond to MIDI volume control, but most modern instruments do.

MIDI controllers

If you look in the manual for your synthesiser or module, you'll find that a number of other performance controls are also supported by MIDI, including sustain pedals, joysticks, *sostenuto*, pan and many more. These so-called MIDI controllers are divided into two main types: those that are either on or off, and those that can be varied in fine increments. The latter are known as *continuous controllers*. A sustain pedal has a simple on/off function, whereas pan or volume are continuous controllers. Most things in MIDI – including controllers – have a maximum value of 128, which in computer terms equates to a seven-bit message.

MIDI modes

As mentioned at the start of this chapter, the majority of MIDI instruments can be set to work on any of the 16 MIDI channels, and I mentioned that there is also an Omni mode, which allows the unit to respond to all incoming data, regardless of the channel it's on. It is also possible to tell an instrument to play either polyphonically or monophonically, and while polyphonic operation is the most common, mono operation has certain applications when playing bass lines and analogue-style lead lines, or for use with guitar synths, where each string transmits on its own MIDI channel and needs to be allocated its own monophonic synthesiser, in effect, in order to work properly.

The four possible combinations of Omni On/Off and Poly/Mono are known as the four MIDI modes and they are defined as follows:

Mode 1: Omni On/Poly
Mode 2: Omni On/Mono
Mode 3: Omni Off/Poly
Mode 4: Omni Off/Mono

Mode 1 allows the instrument to play polyphonically, but it will attempt to play all incoming data, regardless of the channel it was sent on.

Mode 2 is widely held to be a mistake, and I can't recall anyone finding a valid use for it. Many instruments don't include Mode 2 for that reason.

Mode 3 is the most common mode, as it allows the instrument to respond to individual MIDI channels and to play polyphonically.

Mode 4 turns a multitimbral synth into several monophonic synths, each on its own MIDI channel. Mode 4 is used mainly when playing mono-style melodies or bass lines for use with guitar synths.

MIDI and tempo

Drum machines have built-in sequencers that allow them to create and play back drum patterns at different tempi. Both drum machines and MIDI sequencers send and receive MIDI Clock data, which is like a series of metronome pulses, but instead of getting four to the bar you get 96 per crotchet/quarter note, or 384 pulses per 4/4 bar. These pulses do much the same job as the sprocket holes used to guide cine film through the projector – they keep it in sync.

MIDI Clock makes it possible to sync two or more MIDI devices together, where one device is again the master and the other the slave. In this way, you can connect two drum machines so that they both run together at precisely the same tempo, or you can slave a sequencer to a drum machine or vice versa. Even when the master machine isn't playing, it's still sending out MIDI Clock data at the current tempo, which means that any connected slave device will know exactly what tempo to start at when it receives a Start command. The MIDI commands for starting and stopping drum machines and sequencers are known as MIDI Real-Time messages.

real-time MIDI

The Stop command will cause both the master and slave machines to stop running, while a Continue command forces the machines to continue playing from the point at which they were stopped. A Start message always forces the master and slave to start from the beginning of the song. The master is always switched to its Internal Clock mode, while the slave machine must be switched to External Clock mode. Figure 9.5 shows how a MIDI master/slave system is linked for clock sync.

MIDI Out

Sequencer

A sequencer will always transmit MIDI Clock as well as MIDI Start, Stop and Continue commands. To make the drum machine follow the sequencer, it should be set to External MIDI Clock mode, sometimes abbreviated to Ext Sync. Drum machines may also include settings to enable or disable their ability to respond to incoming MIDI notes. If you find that the drum machine is playing back parts intended for other sequenced instruments, disable incoming MIDI notes. Look in the MIDI Utilities menu for these settings

MIDI In

Drum machine

Figure 9.5: MIDI Clock sync

sequencer syncing

MIDI instruments provide a huge range of sounds, and MIDI sequencers let you record and replay multitrack compositions involving lots of instruments, but you can't record audio onto a conventional MIDI sequencer. If you want to have both audio and MIDI-controlled sounds in a mix, and you don't have a sequencer with an integral hard-disk audio recording system, you need a means of getting your tape recorder and your sequencer working as a team.

You could create a complete backing track using your sequencer and your synths, samplers and drum machines and then mix this onto your multitrack tape machine, leaving two tracks free for vocals or acoustic instruments, but there's a better way to work. For this, all you need is some way of getting the sequencer to run in sync with your multitracker and you have the best of both worlds. Working in this way, all of the sequenced sounds can run directly into the final mix in perfect sync with the vocals or acoustic sounds recorded on tape. And because your synth sounds are never recorded onto multitrack, the sound quality is limited only by the type of mastering machine you use. But how can you sync your sequencer to your tape machine?

MIDI sync

Both sequencers and drum machines can be synchronised to tape recorders, and the normal way to do this is to have the tape recorder working as a master and the drum machine or sequencer as a slave. Because tape machines don't output MIDI directly, an interface box or sync unit is needed to enable the MIDI timing data to be recorded onto one track of the tape. However, there are several possible systems, the main points of which are summarised below.

simple FSK

This system requires a MIDI-Clock-to-tape sync box and works by recording a timing track derived from MIDI Clock onto one of the multitrack machine's tracks (usually the highest-numbered one). When the tape is relayed, this information starts the sequencer and sends it MIDI Clock timing pulses to keep it synchronised. Such systems are tedious to use, though, because every time the tape is stopped partway through a song it has to be started from the beginning again to restore sync.

smart FSK

Smart FSK is similar to the above but it works with another piece of hidden MIDI information, known as MIDI Song Position Pointers, or SPPs. Most modern equipment generates and recognises these, and everything is

MIDI Out

Smart FSK sync box

MIDI In   Sync In

Stripe   Play

MIDI Out   Sync Out

Sequencer set to internal
sync and playing back the
song to be worked on,
complete with any tempo
changes

Input to sync track
(usually the
highest-numbered
tape track)

Multitrack recorder

Set-up for striping tape with code

MIDI Out from keyboard merges
with the sync signal allowing
new MIDI parts to be recorded
while synced to tape

MIDI In   MIDI Thru   MIDI Out

MIDI In

MIDI In   Sync In

Stripe   Play

MIDI Out   Sync Out

Sequencer set to
External MIDI
Sync mode

Smart FSK sync box

Output from
sync track

Multitrack recorder

Set-up for syncing sequencer to tape

Figure 9.6: Connecting a Smart FSK sync box

transparent to the user – there's no set-up to worry about. Provided that your sync box uses smart FSK, you can start the tape anywhere in the song and the sequencer will lock up within a couple of seconds.

A big advantage of MIDI-Clock-based sync systems is that the tempo of the music is contained within the sync code, so any tempo changes in the original sequence will be followed faithfully and automatically when the tape is run.

Smart FSK tape-to-MIDI sync boxes with built-in MIDI Merge facilities are best, because these allow new sequencer parts to be recorded while the sequencer is synced to tape. Figure 9.6 shows how a smart FSK box is connected.

SMPTE

SMPTE is a professional time code borrowed from the film industry and is unnecessarily complicated for syncing MIDI sequencers to tape machines. However, some MIDI sequencers have dedicated SMPTE sync boxes that are still easy to use, because the sequencer program looks after tempo mapping automatically. If you have such a sequencer, SMPTE sync is worth considering, although MTC is a more popular standard for contemporary equipment.

SMPTE code contains only elapsed-time information, which is subdivided into hours, minutes, seconds and frames of film or TV picture, so a conversion has to be done in order to calculate the tempo. Tempo information – including any tempo changes – must be stored in a tempo map, which is usually stored as part of the MIDI sequence. If this is handled by your sequencer, it's all quite straightforward, but if not then smart FSK is a lot simpler. SMPTE comes in several frame formats, depending on whether it's being used for film or television. The most popular formats are 30fps (feet per second) for US TV, 25fps for European TV and 24fps for film. The format is usually selectable in software, and if you're not doing film or TV work then the local TV frame rate is normally adopted.

MTC

MTC (MIDI Time Code) is the direct MIDI equivalent of SMPTE, and most modern sequencers read and generate it. MTC contains the same embedded timing information as SMPTE, including the choice of frame rates, but once again, if your sequencer doesn't handle the tempo maps for you, smart FSK is still a simpler option. However, the majority of modern sequencers support MTC automatically, making it a very practical option. To use MTC with tape, an MTC-to-tape sync interface box is required. Many of the larger multiport MIDI interfaces include full SMPTE and MTC support.

General MIDI

General MIDI is another stage of standardisation, and has been added to the existing MIDI protocol in order to enable manufacturers to build synthesisers and synth modules that exhibit a specified degree of compatibility in certain areas. General MIDI sets out strict rules for patch mapping, drum-note mapping, multitimbrality and polyphony, and the aim is to allow a MIDI sequence recorded using one GM module to be played back on any other GM module without the need to remap patches, move drum-note allocations or worry about running out of parts or polyphony. This doesn't mean that all GM synths have to sound exactly the same, but it does mean that, for example, a piano preset on one machine must be in the same patch location as a similar piano preset on any other GM machine.

pre-GM compatibility

Sequencer users often insert Patch-Change commands at the start of a piece and at any subsequent locations in the piece where a sound is required to change. In this way, whenever the sequence is played back on the same instruments and modules, the correct sounds are automatically called up. However, if you were to play the sequence back on a friend's MIDI system, you may well find that all of the sounds are completely wrong, because not only are the patches completely different in sound but any that are suitable are also stored in different patch locations. In the case of programmable instruments, this kind of chaos is difficult to avoid, because most users have their own systems for storing their edited sounds. Furthermore, the factory presets that come with most MIDI instruments weren't stored in any particular order prior to the introduction of GM.

Another potential stumbling block is the drum and percussion part. Is your friend's system set up with the drum part on the same MIDI channel? If so, are the drum sounds mapped to the same notes?

Let's say you're lucky and you get all of the sounds mapped out. There's still a good chance that you'll come unstuck when it comes to controller information; perhaps one of the modules doesn't respond to controller 7 (master volume), or perhaps the pitch-bend ranges are set differently to those on your own system.

General MIDI philosophy

General MIDI was devised to be used in situations where a high degree of compatibility is essential – for example, when replaying pre-recorded MIDI song files. Using GM, musicians can play each other's GM song files and be confident that they'll sound more or less the way they should, even though there are subtle subjective differences between one manufacturer's GM machine and another. This has opened up the market for commercially available MIDI song files. Although these hold little attraction for the serious composer, they are very effective as live backings and may also be used to gain experience in recording, mixing and effects processing.

polyphony and multitimbrality

The problem with polyphony and multitimbrality is that you can never have enough of it! GM instruments provide the ability to play back 16 parts on 16 MIDI channels, with a minimum of 24-note polyphony. However, where a synth uses two voices to make up a sound, the actual polyphony is further reduced, which means that a GM song file written for one GM machine could still come unstuck if played back using a different GM module whose manufacturers claim that number of voices and polyphony mean the same thing.

Roland's GS format

Much of the present GM format owes its existence to Roland's own protocols, so it's hardly surprising that Roland have gone one step further and devised an enhanced version of General MIDI, which they call GS. Realising that many users wouldn't be satisfied with 128 preset sounds, Roland have designed their GS machines to offer several alternative banks of sounds, the basic GM set (capital tones) being the first bank (Bank 0). There are up to seven "variation tones", based on each of the capital tones, and these are arranged so as to have the same Program Change numbers as the tones from which they are derived. In other words, all the variation tones of a piano capital tone will still be pianos, although they will all be subtly different. Further banks are provided for sounds known as sub-capital tones, which are less obviously related to the capital tones.

A Bank-Change facility (in Roland's case, based on controller zero) allows the user to switch between the various banks. Conventional Program-Change commands are then used to select the sounds within each bank – a neat way of getting around MIDI's limitation of being able to directly address only 128 patches. Yamaha have their own extended GM system, which they call XG. The major difference, as far as the user is concerned, is that Yamaha's XG system uses different Bank-Change commands to GS. At the time of writing, GS looks set to remain the adopted standard.

General MIDI overview

General MIDI aims to define a minimum set of MIDI capabilities with which all GM MIDI devices must comply. The main points are as follows:

- A GM instrument must support all 16 MIDI channels simultaneously in order to provide 16-part multitimbrality;

- Percussion parts must be on MIDI channel 10. A minimum set of 47 standard sound types – including the most common drum and Latin percussion sounds – must be provided, and these must all be mapped in accordance with the GM standard. This mapping owes a lot to Roland's original mapping system;

- GM instruments must be capable of 24-note polyphony and notes must be allocated dynamically. However, the specification allows eight notes to be reserved for percussion, leaving 16 for the other instruments;

- All 128 preset sounds are defined according to their type and patch location. Although there is some variation in sound between one module and another, the instrument type and even playing style (in the case of basses, for example) for each patch location is quite rigidly defined, right down to the dog barks and gun shots in the special effects section. Some of the sounds – such as pads – are a little more flexible, but they must still be of a roughly similar tone and style.

- All GM instruments must respond to the same set of MIDI controllers. The MIDI controller implementation includes the ability to change the master tuning and pitch-bend wheel range via MIDI, to Reset All Controllers (which resets all MIDI controllers to their default values) and to turn All Notes Off. All GM machines must also respond to pitch bend and aftertouch.

chapter 10

using a submixer

assette multitrackers are a useful compromise between flexibility and cost, and for better audio quality there are also MiniDisc and hard-disk alternatives available. However, unless your requirements are fairly modest, you'll eventually run out of input channels. For example, if you plan to work with a MIDI system, or you need the flexibility to handle multi-mic recording sessions, you'll need a large number of input channels, either for recording or for mixing. One cost-effective way around this is to add an external mixer which can handle the appropriate number of microphones or MIDI instruments.

track outputs

If you have a large MIDI system, the external mixer may be used to combine the outputs from the various MIDI modules down to stereo. Then the stereo output of the mixer can be plugged into two spare input channels of your multitracker, or even into a pair of aux returns, to be added to the off-tape mix. Alternatively, the multitracker outputs can feed two channels of your external mixer, as shown in Figure 10.1.

Better still, if your multitracker has separate track outputs, you can feed each of these into channels of your external mixer, so as to make use of the better facilities that external mixers invariably have to offer.

If you're syncing to MIDI and don't have separate track outputs, a useful tip is to pan tracks 1 and 2 hard left and right respectively and then pull down the fader on track 3 and use the pre-fade (foldback) aux send to route channel 3 to the foldback output jack. Now you have three separate outputs – track 1 is on the left buss, track 2 is on the right buss and track 3 is on the foldback output jack. These can be fed to three mixer channels for external mixing. Track 4 will contain time code, and this has its own output on all but the most rudimentary multitrackers.

You could simply record the "MIDI mix" onto a pair of tracks in your multitrack recording, but a great many musicians prefer to sync their MIDI

Tip: if the multitracker has no dedicated sync output or separate track outputs, turn the fader down on track 4, turn up the pre-fade aux send and take code from the foldback (pre-fade send) output jack. Disable noise reduction if it causes the sync code to read unreliably

MIDI tape sync box

MIDI synthesisers and sound modules

Multitracker

Direct track outputs are connected to the mixer line inputs

Track 4 used for sync code

MIDI connection

MIDI In Out

MIDI In

MIDI sequencer

Stereo Mixer

Effects unit connected to aux send/returns

Note: if the multitracker doesn't have separate track outputs, its main stereo output may be connected to two mixer line inputs with the channels panned hard left and right. In this case, it's probably better to use the effects unit on the aux sends/returns of the multitracker so as to allow different amounts of treatment to be added to each track. This will leave the main mixer without effects, but most MIDI instruments have on-board effects which may be used instead. If you have two effects units, you could use one on the multitracker and one on the main stereo mixer

Stereo mastering deck

Figure 10.1: Mixing multitracker and MIDI instruments

sequencers to their multitrackers so as to bypass the need to record the MIDI instruments onto multitrack tape at all. In this case, the MIDI contribution to the mix runs "live" as you mix and is combined with the recorded tracks from tape. Admittedly you lose one tape track for recording the time code necessary to sync the audio and MIDI, but the benefit of having separate control over all of the MIDI instruments outweighs this

Vocals and miked amplifiers

Bass guitars may be DI'd

Guitars can be recorded using a dedicated pre-amp/effects unit

DI box

Guitar processor

Keyboards may be DI'd

Stereo mixer

Effects unit connected to aux sends/returns

Optional compressor/limiter, useful to prevent overloading on unexpected signal peaks. This may be connected via the mixer's stereo insert points, if fitted. Otherwise, it may be connected between the mixer and master recorder, as shown

Mix monitored over headphones. If a compressor/limiter is connected between the mixer and the recorder, it's better to monitor from the headphone socket of the recorder so that the effect of the compressor/limiter can be heard

Stereo mastering deck

Figure 10.2: Live recording using a stereo mixer

disadvantage. Because the sequencer is synced to the tape machine, the two parts always run in perfect time with each other.

live recording

For live recording, a simple stereo mixer can be used to mix a number of mics into stereo to be recorded onto two tracks of your multitracker, while the remaining two tracks are conventionally used to record, for example, the lead vocal and the lead guitar. Figure 10.2 shows the use of a simple stereo mixer in live recording.

chapter 11

the recording session

Before you start work, you'll need to make sure that you have something worth recording. Also, because the project-studio owner is more often than not recording his or her own material, this means having good songs, rehearsing them thoroughly and making sure that all of your instruments play properly and stay in tune.

Step one is to make sure that you have some good material to record, and if you play live on a regular basis you must have a fair idea of which songs go down best with your audience. Even so, on some numbers it may just be your visual stage act that gets the applause – on tape, you can only be heard, not seen, so your preparations should start right back in the rehearsal room. When you're working on songs, it's a good idea to tape absolutely everything to help you spot weaknesses more effectively. By the same token, if you're thinking of recording an unfamiliar band in your home studio, make sure that they send you a tape first.

Another advantage of making rough recordings is that you'll be able to hear if there's anything about the arrangement that doesn't quite work on record. Solos might need shortening; intros and links might need cutting down – if something isn't in there for a reason, shorten it or cut it out altogether. It usually helps if you play the tapes to a friend who isn't as familiar with the material as you are – you'll learn a lot from his reaction.

fine tuning

After sorting out the arrangements, you'll need to rehearse – every detail must be correct or every mistake will stick out like a sore thumb. What's more, you often need to learn the song well enough to be able to play it without the vocals or the guitar solo, because vocals and guitar are usually added afterwards.

Even if you've rehearsed your parts and feel confident about performing for the microphone, poor tuning and timing can still let you down. When working on pop music that incorporates sequenced MIDI tracks, it's common practice to play along with a click track when recording, and I know that some drummers find this particularly difficult to get used to. If this is a problem, it helps to have the drummer practise by playing along to a drum machine before the recording session.

If you're working on a pop or dance track and using a MIDI sequencer, consider using some drums sequenced and some live. For example, you could program the bass drum and snare to get a really tight feel and then overdub live toms and hi-hats to put the humanity back into it. This is often done on rock recordings as well as on pop music.

tuning blues

Guitars should be fitted with new strings before a session, ideally the night before, and the instrument should be taken out of its case and allowed to acclimatise for as long as possible before tuning up. Take just two or three turns of the string around the tuning peg and give all of the strings a good pull to make sure that there's no stretch left in them. In this way, you shouldn't have tuning problems, even with freshly changed strings. However, use an electronic guitar tuner to check that every instrument is in tune before every take and every overdub. Tuning has a habit of drifting as the temperature or humidity changes, and if your instrument has intonation problems or rogue buzzes then it's best to get it sorted out before attempting to record.

drum tuning

A certain amount of expertise and experience is needed to tune a drum kit for the studio, but a good drum sound starts with a kit that's in good condition. Worn heads produce a dreadful sound that no amount of trying to "fix it in the mix" will put right, and if you don't have particularly good cymbals you should borrow or hire some. Watch out for rattling fittings and squeaking stools or pedals and fix these before the session – it helps to keep a can of WD40 handy to cure squeaks.

A final tip on drum tuning is to avoid overdamping them. Some people stick so much tape on a drum that it sounds like you're hitting a suitcase, but most of the ring will get lost in the mix. Err on the side of minimal damping by using small pads of tissue or cloth and tape.

session planning

How long should you allow if you're recording an outside band rather than your own material? How much you can get done in a day depends on the proficiency of the artistes, the complexity of the music and whether or not you're producing demos or masters. For example, you wouldn't normally expect to get more than three or four demo tracks finished in one day, whereas a well-recorded single could take you several days to perfect. Even for demo work, you should allow a couple of hours to get all of the mics set up and to get the basic sound right. You'll also need time to mix, which could take anything from half an hour per song for a simple demo to a day or more for a single or album track.

With analogue open-reel or cassette-tape machines, you should always use new, good-quality tape – anything else is false economy. Also, clean the heads with a cotton bud dipped in isopropyl alcohol at the start of each session and again after every three or four hours.

This method of cleaning applies only to traditional analogue recorders – digital tape machines have special cleaning tapes, while tapeless systems based on computer-style hard-disk drives require no cleaning at all. Similarly, make sure that your instruments are working properly and that you aren't plagued with faulty leads or mysterious hums and buzzes. Fit new strings to any guitars that you're using and ensure that drum heads are in good condition. This may sound obvious, but you'd be surprised at how many people turn up for professional recording sessions with instruments that are virtually unplayable through general lack of basic maintenance.

monitoring

Although some vocalists have problems working with headphones, it's something that they'll have to learn to live with if they want to make records. It's important to minimise the amount of sound leakage from the headphones to the vocal mic, so enclosed headphones are preferred. Vocalists, in particular, often benefit from having reverb added to the headphone mix, as it encourages a good performance and generally makes them feel more relaxed.

recording order

In a typical pop mix, it's quite common to record at least the bass, drums and guitar at the same time, as it helps to maintain the feel of musicians playing together. This forms the basic backing track over which additional instrumentation and vocals can be overdubbed. Because there are no vocals recorded at this stage, it can help to have the singer record a rough guide vocal part onto a spare track of tape, but if you have no tracks to spare then have the singer use a mic and sing along into the headphone monitoring system so that everyone knows where they are. Most people play better if there's a guide vocal to listen to, even if they can find their way through a song without it.

On stage, it's quite normal for a guitarist in a one-guitar band to stop playing chords and go into a solo, but in the studio you can always hear where the rhythm stops playing. It's usually better to record the rhythm part all the way through the song, including the solo section, when you first put down the backing track, and then to add the solo as a separate overdub. This also provides more chance for getting the solo just right. Make sure that you know exactly when the solo will end, and get the singer to dictate cues on the guide track, if need be.

If you're recording a vocal or acoustic instrument part that may need patching up with a few punch-ins, ask the players to stay where they are after they've finished recording. If they come out to listen to the recording, the chances are that they'll never return to exactly the same position relative to the microphone, and you'll probably hear a slight change in level or tone whenever you punch in.

keeping records

Always make a chart or track sheet of what instruments will be recorded on what tracks; otherwise, you might get half way through a song and find that you've run out of tracks. This is particularly important if you're working with only four or eight tracks, as you'll almost certainly have to bounce something to make everything fit. If the song needs an intro that will be recorded after the main backing track has gone down, get the drummer to record the correct number of bars of clicks. For example, if you need a 16-bar intro, record a 17-bar click count-in.

demos

If you're recording demos, don't spend too much time over-producing them. If they're too fussy, it makes it more difficult for an A&R man to visualise alternative ways of approaching the song. If the vocal is well sung and you have a good melody, you're more than halfway to a good demo.

getting the sounds

When performing a soundcheck, only the musician whose sound you're working on should play. If everyone insists on playing all the time, you'll waste a lot of time, your patience will become worn and you'll probably end up with a less-than-ideal sound. Hide the drummer's sticks, if you have to!

counting in

A tip is to get the drummer to count in each song by tapping out the first three beats of the count-in on the hi-hat, leaving the fourth beat silent. In this way, when you come to tidy up the start of the song at the mix, it'll be a lot easier to get a clean run into the first beat.

When you get around to the actual recording, everybody will probably be a little excited, but remind them to stay dead silent during the count-in and, more importantly, at the end of each song. Many a perfect ending has been spoiled by somebody yelling, "Yeah, that's the one!" over the decay of the final chord, or by the drummer dumping his sticks on his kit. Wait a good ten seconds until all sound has ceased before you even breathe. Similarly, make sure that you have no unduly noisy clothing or jewellery – you'd be surprised at what finds its way into the mic.

Be ruthless about tuning and double-check guitars and basses before every take – even the best guitars have a habit of drifting out of pitch as the room warms up. Modern keyboards don't have this problem, but old analogue synths should be switched on at least an hour before you start to record, and even then you should check them at regular intervals. If you don't already have an electronic tuner, buy one!

track discipline

Most project studios are based around four- or eight-track systems, which don't leave a lot of leeway for bouncing. To avoid wasting tracks, any live band recordings should be done with most if not all of the members playing together, and you might find it helpful to put down a guide vocal as you play.

Instrumental solos, lead vocals and backing vocals can be added later, so that you can record as many takes as you need to get them right. Also, because of the disparity in levels, acoustic instruments should also be overdubbed.

Because solos often come in between vocal verses, you can sometimes get away with recording your solo on the vocal track. You just have to be careful to drop out of Record before the vocals come back in, or you'll wipe over them.

If you have to bounce any tracks during the course of the session, try to bounce things that aren't main components of the mix. For example, you can usually get away with bouncing backing vocals or pad keyboard parts, but bouncing drums or main vocals is to be avoided where possible. If you do have to bounce an important part, try to do so no more than once, and consider adding a hint of top boost as you bounce to make up for any clarity that's lost in the process.

no second best

Don't let any mistakes get by, either musical or technical. I've said this before, on numerous occasions, but it really is very important to understand that you can't just "fix it in the mix" – no matter how many effects or sound effects you heap on a mistake, you'll still hear it, so do what you have to do and replace any sub-standard work before you even think about mixing. Listen to your recordings for bad notes, bad timing, distortion and noises that shouldn't be there, such as clicking drum sticks or excessive guitar finger noise. These kinds of problems are most audible when listening over a pair of headphones.

chapter 12

mixing

T he mixing stage is the point in the proceedings at which you get to balance the individual sounds that you've recorded, modify their tonality and add effects. For me, mixing is the most creative part of the whole process – it's where all of your hard work comes together to produce the end result. While in professional circles there's invariably a producer looking over the engineer's shoulder and calling the shots, most of us have to double as engineer and producer, and quite often as the artist, too, and this means that we have to know something about music production as well as engineering.

A good mix starts with getting good sounds onto tape (or disk) in the first place – attempting to fix things in the mix really is an uphill struggle and rarely entirely successful. No matter what system you're using for multitracking, you need to use the best possible mastering format in order to preserve your work to the highest possible quality. The most popular budget choice for use with cassette multitrackers is a good-quality hi-fi cassette deck, but DAT, DCC or MiniDisc are significantly better for more serious work. Good-quality results may also be achieved by mixing onto a hi-fi video recorder, as pointed out earlier in this book.

before mixing

The mixing session starts once the recording has stopped, and ideally after a suitable break. At this point, you should have track sheets describing what's on the various tape tracks, any notes taken during the recording and all of the mixer EQ, level and routing controls set to neutral ready for a clean start. (The only exception to this latter condition is if you've been setting up your mix as you record, in which case it's simply a matter of checking that nothing is routed that shouldn't be.) If you have a separate mixer, ensure that, if any channels are redundant, they're not routed either to the groups or to the left/right buss. On channels where EQ won't be needed, bypass it and mute any unused monitor inputs.

If you have a multitrack mixer with routing, it helps to separate logical groups of sounds into subgroups so that the mix can be handled with fewer faders. For example, if the recording includes real drums, these are likely to occupy several tracks, so it makes sense to assign them to a single stereo subgroup. Other candidates for subgrouping are backing vocals and multi-layered keyboard parts.

start in mono

I find it helpful to set up a balance in mono to start with so that you can hear how well the separate sounds blend together. Unless the quality of the original recording leaves something to be desired, it should be possible to set up a workable balance fairly quickly, without resorting to EQ. Don't worry about panning the sounds until a reasonably good balance has been achieved. After this, you can then think about adding EQ and effects. Whatever you do, don't get too bogged down trying to EQ individual tracks, because they'll almost certainly sound quite different once the rest of the mix is up and running.

If MIDI instruments are to be a part of the mix, these may be fed into any spare input channels, or even into spare aux returns, but if you don't have enough spare channels then the best option is to patch in a submixer. Sync signals shouldn't be fed via the mixer because of the danger of crosstalk where high-level sync codes are used. It's always best to use separate, external cables to route the time-code track from the tape machine to the synchroniser.

setting a balance

On mixers with PFL buttons, the PFL metering system should be used for each input channel in turn to optimise the gain setting – the PFL meter should go just into the red on signal peaks. It's often easiest to balance the drums and bass first and then, once the rhythm section is working, to add the lead vocal followed by the other parts of the mix, always being aware that you must leave space for the vocal. I invariably add some compression to vocals while mixing to even out the level, and if noise is in any way a problem I'll also gate the vocals before the compressor. A useful compressor setting is to choose a fast attack combined with a release time of half a second or so and a ratio of between 4:1 and 12:1, depending on whether you want to hear the compressor working or not. If you're experiencing sibilance problems, try a less bright reverb setting or add a little EQ cut at around 6kHz.

panning

Once the mix starts to sound good in mono, you can work on the stereo panning. Bass drums, bass guitars and lead vocals should be left in the centre, because these sounds carry most of the energy of a mix, and when they're reproduced over a stereo system it's best to have both speakers sharing the load. Try not to monitor too loudly, as this will affect your judgement and may eventually damage your hearing. The most logical monitoring level would be that at which the end user is likely to be listening – in other words, a sensible domestic listening volume.

Other instruments, backing vocals and effects can be spread out to create an illusion of space. Reverb should almost always be added in stereo, as this gives the mix a sense of space and reality. Most digital reverberation units have a mono input and a stereo output. The ones with stereo inputs tend to use a mono mix of the left and right inputs to create the reverb, with only the original sound being passed through in stereo. This means that, no matter where in the mix the original signal is panned, its reverb will come equally from both sides.

localisation

On the face of it, the fact that the reverb level is equal in the left and right channels tends to "dilute" the effect of using panning to localise the original sound, but it helps when thinking through this type of situation to compare the outcome with what happens in a real-life situation, such as when music is played in a concert hall. Take the example of a violin playing at one side of the stage; the direct sound will appear to come from the violin, because our ears analyse the relative levels heard by the left and right ears and the phase relationship between these two sounds to establish direction. However, the room reverberation resulting from the performance will come from everywhere at once, because the sound is continually bouncing off all of the hard surfaces in the room. In other words, we have a direct parallel to the digital reverb situation, in which the direct sound appears to come from whatever point we've panned it to in a mix, while the reverb comes from both sides. This does tend to dilute the stereo positioning of the original sound, but no more so than in real life.

Reverberant sound produces the illusion of space and depth, so the pragmatic way to look at it is that, by adding reverb, you trade off a degree of stereo localisation for a sense of stereo space. Adding a short reverb to a panned mono sound is probably the most effective way of making it sound as though it exists in a natural environment.

performance panning

Very often we try to set up pan positions that correspond to the way in which performers might be arranged on a stage. This means placing the main vocals in the centre, along with the bass guitar, bass drum and very often the snare drum, too. The guitars and keyboards can be panned to either side, as can backing vocals, while the output from a stereo reverb unit is invariably panned to the left and right extremes.

If you're attempting to create the illusion of a live performance, there are pitfalls of which you should be aware. For example, it's very tempting to spread things out in the stereo mix simply because the opportunity is there, but this can lead to an unnatural, even uncomfortable sound; if you pan the various drums in a kit – or the high and low notes on a piano – hard left and right, you can end up with the illusion of a 30-feet-wide instrument! The same is true of stereo keyboard synthesisers; although it's tempting to spread them from ear to ear, it might be better to pan one side to the left or right extreme and the other to the centre of the mix, for example, as this will maintain some illusion of stereo spread but will confine it to just half of the soundstage.

Don't worry that you're not making full use of your stereo-mixing capabilities simply because so many of your sounds are located at or near the centre of the mix; you only need to move a couple of sounds out to the sides to create a sense of space, and the addition of stereo reverb will greatly add to the sense of width.

perspective

Real music doesn't just exist along an imaginary line drawn from left to right, and yet when we pan a sound between two loudspeakers this is exactly what we're working with. The dimensions of height and depth are missing from the equation, so we have to simulate them using other techniques. Recent work has indicated that the early reflections produced when a sound occurs in an enclosed space have a profound influence on how near or far the sound appears to be from the listener. Intuitively, it seems logical that a more distant sound will contain a greater proportion of reverberant sound than a near one, but the spacing and rate of build-up of these reflections also appears to be important. If you have a reverb device which allows you to create early reflection patterns, it's worth experimenting with the various options and making notes of any settings that produce a definite sense of closeness or distance. Small-room or closely-spaced reflection patterns seem to create a sense of closeness or intimacy, but much more work has to be done in this area before we can dispense with trial and error.

stereo checklist

• Pan bass instruments and bass drums to the centre of the mix. Snare drums also tend to work best when panned near the centre, but the toms and cymbals may be spread from left to right (although not too widely).

• Keep the lead vocals close to the centre of the mix, as they are the focus of the performance, but experiment with positioning backing vocals to the sides.

- When you pan an instrument away from the centre of the mix, don't always feel that you have to set it hard left or right. Try to paint a picture, with your sounds spreading across the stereo stage in interesting ways and the main sounds nearest the centre.

- Take care not to pan stereo mics or the outputs from a stereo instrument (such as a piano or drum kit) so wide that you produce the illusion of an instrument that's as wide as the stage!

- Unless you're specifically trying to create a special effect, pan the outputs from your stereo reverb unit hard left and right and ensure they're at the same levels in the mix.

- Use your discretion when panning the outputs from stereo effects units, such as delays and chorus units. Consider panning them over just half of the stereo soundstage – for example, between dead centre and hard left.

problems?

Recording problems can be broken down into many types, some clearly defined and others less so. The most obvious technical problems relate to things like noise, distortion, EQ and spill, while the more artistic considerations include the wrong choice of sounds, poor timing, out-of-tune notes or just plain wrong ones.

Probably the most common technical problem is noise, which includes tape hiss, instrument amplifier hiss, amplifier hum and general digital noise from budget synths and effects units. You can attack noise on several different levels, and if the contamination is serious you may need to use two or more of the following processes in combination.

A noise gate is a very effective way of removing noise during the pauses between sounds, and you'd be surprised at how much you can clean up a mix by gating any channels containing parts that aren't playing all the way through the mix. For example, if the lead guitar solo only pops up in the middle of the song, you don't want any background noise on that track contributing to the mix the rest of the time, so bang a gate on it. It's also often worth gating vocals, because there are usually pauses between words or phrases where nothing useful is happening. However, don't feel that you have to gate out traces of breath noise, or the vocal track may well end up sounding unnatural.

With any slowly decaying sounds, make sure that you set an appropriately long gate-release time. Even if some gated sounds appear to be slightly unnatural, there's a good chance that they'll sound okay when you add reverb, especially when the rest of the mix is playing.

corrective EQ

Changing the EQ of a signal is obviously going to have some effect on the overall sound of that signal, but quite often you'll find that your mix includes sounds that occupy only a limited part of the audio spectrum. For example, the overdriven electric guitar contains no really deep bass, and the top end rolls off very quickly above 4kHz or so, because of the limited response of a guitar speaker. With this being the case, you can apply a sharp top cut above 4kHz and a low cut below 100Hz without changing the sound significantly. You'll have to experiment to find the exactly frequencies, but you'll find this technique very useful, not only with guitars (including bass guitars) but also with warm synth pads from cheap or vintage instruments. Careful use of EQ may also help to reduce the effect of finger noise on stringed instruments.

the wrong sound

Sometimes you'll find that you've made a technically good recording but that the sound just doesn't seem to work in the context of the mix. If EQ doesn't bring results, the tape tracks containing instruments such as electric guitars, bass guitars or organs may be played back through guitar combos and remiked. In this way, the speakers will act as filters, while the amp EQ will also give you a chance to polish up the basic tone.

The same technique can be used with distorted synth sounds, and just occasionally you'll find that you can hide unwanted distortion by applying even more distortion to the whole track. Admittedly, this is more likely to work on an artistic level when used on guitars and synths than it is on, say, vocals or piano!

cases for treatment

While I seldom advocate the use of radical amounts of EQ for acoustic instruments or natural sounds, bass and electric guitars can often benefit from quite assertive equalisation. However, it's little use working on a bass-guitar sound in isolation, because it will seem totally different when you add the rest of the band. What seems like a wonderfully rich bass sound when solo'd can easily dissolve into an indistinct mess when you bring up the rest of the mix. A better way to work is to set up a nominal mix balance and then EQ the bass in context so that it cuts through properly.

Mid range is very important when creating bass guitar sounds, and you may have to apply quite a lot of boost somewhere between 2kHz and 4kHz to get the right edge on the sound. If you boost much higher up, you're into fret-noise and string-buzz territory, and if you've recorded without a speaker simulator you might want to roll off some top at the same time.

At the bass end, you can add boost at between 70Hz and 120Hz to fatten up the sound, and using a good sweep equaliser – or, better still, a parametric model – will help a lot. A simple low shelving EQ will emphasise the bass but may leave you with a poorly defined, muddy bass end. Although most mixing consoles these days have pretty good EQ sections, a quality parametric equaliser is a lot more flexible, and every serious studio should use at least one.

guitars

A great electric guitar sound starts out with good playing technique, and the better the player, the simpler the recording technique you can get away with. Interestingly, the most aggressive lead sounds come through when the amount of distortion is turned down rather than up. If you use too much overdrive, you end up with a wall of fizz that loses almost the whole of the character of the instrument. Picking intensity and vibrato are very important, as is string bending.

If you've close-miked a guitar amp, you'll still have to add reverb, either using the spring reverb in the amp itself or during the mix using a digital reverb unit. However, try to choose a short ambient setting rather than a long wash, unless the track demands that kind of treatment. You can also experiment with a little slap-back echo to give the sound a clubby, intimate feel. The size of the sound coming off the tape has little to do with the physical size or power of your set-up, and many classic rock albums have been made using small valve combos.

Chorus, phasing and flanging all work well on guitar, but as a general rule, the more dramatic the effect, the less you need to use it. For example, extreme flanging might work for a couple of bars, whereas gentle chorus can be used all the way through a song.

Guitar players need certain effects to be able to perform properly. Overdrive, wah-wah and chorus are examples of commonly-used guitar effects, but if you have a spare track then it might pay to make a duplicate DI recording straight from the guitar at the same time. In this way, if the sound on your main track doesn't work out, you can take the clean DI'd sound from your extra track and feed it back through an amp or effect unit to create a new guitar sound without having to get the part played again.

vocals

For a natural vocal sound, try to get away with as little EQ as possible, and if you do need EQ then try to get hold of a good-quality parametric model rather than rely on the EQ in your mixer.

Other than a little compression to keep the level even, and maybe a touch of EQ, all that you need to make your vocal sit properly in the track is reverb. Usually, the main vocal will be panned to the centre, with the stereo reverb outputs panned hard left and right to create the illusion of space. Listen carefully to professional records and try to hear the type of reverb they're using – is it long or short? bright or warm? You'll often find that they're using less reverb than you think, and many demos sound cluttered simply because there's too much reverb on everything.

In pop music, you're after a hard-hitting sound most of the time, so be sparing in your use of reverb or the impact will be lost. (This, incidentally, applies just as much to backing instruments as it does to vocals.) Bright reverb sounds are popular on vocals but they also tend to emphasise any sibilance present in the recording, so again use your ears and choose a warmer reverb sound if you detect any problems.

stubborn mixes

Occasionally, you'll find a mix that defies all of your attempts to balance it satisfactorily, perhaps because the song hasn't been arranged in a way that leaves space for all of the important parts. If you find yourself in this situation, here are a few tricks you can try. Work through the following points and you should end up with something usable.

- Set up a rough mix, in mono, with no EQ or effects, and see how it sounds.

- If the mix seems too busy, ask yourself if all of the parts are really necessary, or if you can lose something. What matters most in the majority of pop songs is the rhythm and the vocals – the rest is decoration. If you can't lose something completely, try mixing it so low that you only notice it if you turn it off, or "squeeze" it with EQ so that it occupies a narrower part of the audio spectrum. Double-checking on headphones can also help you sort out what's clashing with what.

- If the mid-range sounds are fighting with the bass sounds, again try using EQ to thin out some of them by taking some bottom end out of the pad synth, backing vocal or acoustic guitar parts.

- Still no luck? In that case, go back to the basic rhythm section plus vocals and see if that's working. If not, is it too late to try a different drum or bass sound? Similarly, if you're working with a sequencer, you could try picking thinner pad keyboard sounds or brighter bass sounds.

- Don't overdo effects – reverb creates the illusion of distance and space, yet often you want something to stand out in front. Try using less reverb on up-front sounds to make them drier.

- If things are improving, try panning the instruments and effects to their desired positions, as this will further improve the separation between sounds.

- Although exciters shouldn't be thought of as a means of salvaging poor recordings, the extra separation that they create can make the difference between an OK mix and a good one. Use only when you've got everything as good as it can be without it.

- Perhaps the mix sounds fine but just lacks cohesion or punch. In this case, try a little overall compression. A soft-knee compressor will usually provide the most transparent results, but try whatever you have and let your ears be the judge. Start out with a low ratio of around 2:1 and lower the threshold until you get between 5dB and 10dB of gain reduction. Use a 20ms attack time and around a 200ms release time to start with, and then adjust by ear, making sure that you don't squeeze the life out of the track.

the door test

When the mix finally starts to happen, it helps to take a break, have a cup of tea, listen to a few records and then come back to it. I like to listen to my final mix from the next room with the adjoining door left open, because then anything that's too loud or too quiet in the mix is instantly obvious. (Strangely, you can miss quite large-level discrepancies when you're sitting right in front of the monitors, especially if you're a little tired.) Also, play some commercial recordings through your studio system before you mix and listen to these from both inside and outside the room – this should provide an idea of the sort of sound balance for which you should be aiming. Some people also like to complete a rough mix and then check how it sounds on a car stereo or a ghetto blaster.

Level adjustments are often necessary during the mix – for example, guitars might have to come up slightly during solos and vocal levels may need a little extra "riding" to keep them under control. However, try to avoid changing the levels of the drums or the bass. If the mix is set up correctly, there probably won't be too much to change; but if things get difficult, get a friend in to help and use a wax pencil to mark where the faders should be at different points in the song. Gates or expanders may be used to clean up tape tracks or the outputs from noisy synths, although care must be taken to ensure that the release time of a gate is long enough to prevent slowly-decaying sounds from being cut short.

mix compression

It sometimes helps to compress an otherwise finished mix in order to create the illusion of greater energy, and the best place to patch a compressor is between the multitracker stereo outputs and the input of your stereo tape machine. If you have a separate mixer, patch the compressor into the mixer's main left/right insert points. Overall compression of this kind causes an overall increase in musical energy, which works well on rock, pop and dance material. Some engineers like to add further processing to the stereo mix, including EQ or some kind of harmonic exciter.

using EQ

Using EQ could be the subject of a book in its own right, but the real secret lies in knowing when not to use it. If in doubt, use as little as you can to get the job done, and always use the best outboard EQ you can afford – there's a huge subjective difference between budget models and the high-end boxes that the pros use.

Equalising the whole mix can improve the sound by helping to compensate for limitations in the recording chain, which is especially true if you're using a cassette multitrack format. A subtle high-frequency boost helps to create a more "digital" sound, and you can do this by boosting between 6kHz and 12kHz by using either an external graphic or parametric EQ. Add the EQ sparingly, and if you have access to a parametric model then use a low-to-medium Q value.

using reverb

Digital reverberation creates the illusion of stereo by synthesising different sets of pseudo-random delays for the left and right channels, which makes the reverb patterns slightly different between the left and right outputs. This makes it possible to take a mono tape track and give it both a stereo identity and a sense of being somewhere rather than existing in a void. Even if no obvious reverb is needed, a sound can still be given substance and width by adding a very short reverb, ambience or a pattern of early reflections to it. When you consider that most pop instruments and voices are recorded in mono, reverb's ability to simulate a real acoustic space is invaluable in completing the illusion.

For drum and vocal tracks, where a longer reverb time is often chosen for artistic reasons, try to pick a setting that doesn't fill up all of the space and stifle the mix. It may help to add a pre-delay of around 50ms or so, and if the reverb makes the mix sound muddy you can feed it back through a channel with EQ and roll off some of the bottom end. Alternatively, if the reverb is diluting the stereo image of a sound too much, try panning the sound and its reverb to the same point in the mix. This will kill the stereo-width effect, but it can be effective when a sound needs to come from a precise location.

Avoid putting more than the barest hint of reverb on bass drums or bass instruments, unless the mix has loads of empty space to allow the reverb to breathe without clouding the overall picture. Short early-reflection or ambience patches seem to work the best.

effects with delay

Try panning a signal to one side of the mix with a delayed version (5-50ms) panned to the other side. The sound will appear to be coming from the speaker carrying the unprocessed sound, even if the delay is as loud as the original signal. (Although the psychoacoustic reasons why this is so are rather too complex to go into here, it does provide another way of adding space to a sound.) If the delay is then modulated to produce a chorus sound, an illusion of movement is created, and when you listen in stereo you really can't tell that one channel is carrying a dry sound and the other a processed version – the movement seems to occupy the whole of the space between the speakers.

Of course, delay can be used to create more conventional echo and doubling effects, and it has become fashionable to set up delay times that are multiples of the tempo of the song. For example, if a song is running at 120bpm, each beat is 60 divided by two seconds long, which is half a second. Therefore, a delay of 500ms (half a second), 250ms or 125ms will always create echoes that are in time with the music. You can also divide up the beat time into threes and create echoes that occur in triplet time.

fades

If a track requires a fade-out ending, make sure that you start to fade at least 20 seconds before the recorded material runs out, and don't rush the tail-end of the fade, or it will sound unnatural. If the album is going to be compiled on a hard-disk editing system, leave off the fade and do it as part of the editing process. This will be smoother, and the fade will taper off into true silence.

Once you've recorded your master tape, check it on as many different sound systems as you can to ensure that the balance is OK. Listening to it in the car or on a portable stereo is always a good test.

mastering levels

If you're mastering to cassette, adjust the record level on your mastering cassette recorder so that the loudest signal peaks push the meters around +4dB into the red. I prefer to work without Dolby noise reduction on the mastering recorder, but this is largely a matter of personal preference. If you're working with open-reel analogue tape, you can probably afford to push the levels a couple of decibels further still, but if you're using one of the digital mastering formats then don't allow the peaks to hit the 0VU mark at all. Often the meters on semi-professional DAT and cassette decks won't agree with the meters on the mixer, so for mastering purposes you should always go by the meter on the tape machine rather than the meters on the desk. It's safest to leave around 30 seconds of unrecorded tape at the beginning of an analogue or DAT cassette in order to avoid drop-outs and to store the finished master in a safe place away from dust, excessive heat, moisture or strong magnetic fields.

Analogue multitrackers, stereo cassette decks and open-reel analogue machines should be cleaned before every mixing session, as well as before every recording session. Clean the heads and any other metal parts in the tape path with isopropyl alcohol and cotton buds. Keep cleaning until the cotton bud comes away clean and then allow the machine to dry for a minute or so before replacing the tape.

coda

Mixing is an acquired skill, so don't be put off if your first attempts don't come up to scratch. You can learn a lot by listening to the production techniques employed on commercial records, and it's also useful to get together with other musicians to swap ideas. Provided that you have a clear idea of what you want to achieve, there's no reason why you shouldn't employ the techniques discussed in this book to produce first-class demos or even master recordings.

When it comes to choosing equipment, always buy the best that you can afford, and as a rule, if it comes down to a choice between sound quality and features, put sound quality first. In reality, you can make a good-sounding recording with just a basic recorder, a mixer, a reverb unit and a couple of nice mics – the rest can be added when your budget allows. Good luck!

chapter 13

digital recording

The vast majority of modern recording equipment is digital, but to understand its strengths and weaknesses it's necessary to take a closer look at traditional analogue recording. Analogue tape recording has been with us for many years, but digital recording is still a relatively recent development, and is often misunderstood. In some ways, digitising sound is the audio equivalent to cine film, on which the constant motion of real life is represented by a series of still frames shown consecutively. As long as there are enough frames per second, the human eye is deceived into perceiving continuous motion. When a sound is digitised, it too is broken up into a series of frozen images but, whereas cinema can be made to work with just 24 frames of film per second, audio needs to be sampled (with an analogue-to-digital converter) at over 40,000 times per second in order to convey full-bandwidth audio. Each sample is really just an instantaneous measurement of the voltage of the audio signal, as shown in Figure 13.1.

sample rates

Physics dictates that audio must be sampled at a rate at least twice that of the maximum frequency to be stored, which for 20kHz audio means a sampling rate of at least 40kHz. In practice, however, we need to sample at a slightly higher rate to allow for the filters used to exclude audio frequencies above 20kHz. The CD format is based on a sampling rate of 44.1kHz, although some audio applications also sample at 48kHz. Sampling at a lower frequency means limiting the audio bandwidth to less than the 20kHz required by professional audio, but less demanding multimedia applications may sample at 32kHz or less to minimise the amount of data that needs to be stored.

bits

The sample rate determines the highest frequency that we can digitise, but the accuracy of the process also depends on how precisely we can measure each of the tiny slices, or *samples*. As a rule, the more "bits" used to represent each sample, the less noise and distortion there will be. CDs are sampled with 16-bit resolution, resulting in a possible signal-to-noise ratio of

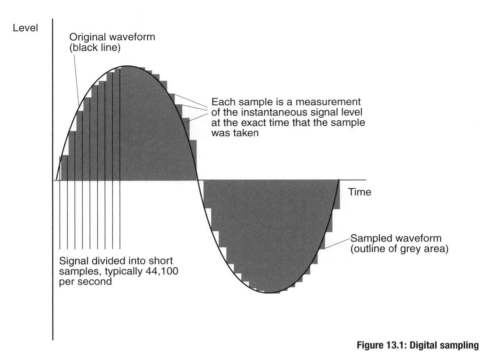

Level

Original waveform
(black line)

Each sample is a measurement
of the instantaneous signal level
at the exact time that the sample
was taken

Time

Sampled waveform
(outline of grey area)

Signal divided into short
samples, typically 44,100
per second

Figure 13.1: Digital sampling

around 96dB – significantly better than analogue tape. Once again, though, for less demanding multimedia applications, such as lo-fi computer games, eight-bit sampling may give acceptable results, although the signal-to-noise ratio will be reduced to a rather poor 48dB, at best.

Future professional audio formats are likely to require between 18- and 24-bit sampling, with the possibility of even higher sample rates. At the moment, though, the CD format sets the standard at a sample rate of 44.1kHz/16 bits. DAT machines usually offer playback at both 44.1kHz and 48kHz sample rates, although the low-cost domestic models that find their way into home studios may only record at the 48kHz sample rate. In theory, a 48kHz sample rate should produce a slightly improved frequency response, but in reality there's no perceptible difference – at least, not on consumer machines.

evolving digital

Analogue tape recording is unique, in that it was developed from the ground up as an audio recording medium, whereas most of the digital formats borrow technology from other market areas, such as the computer, video and hi-fi industries. This makes mass-manufacture commercially viable, because of the economies of scale. Analogue recording has been refined over the past few decades to a point at which it's unlikely that any further significant improvements will be made, and Dolby SR noise reduction may well be the last hardware breakthrough. By using the latest generation of high-energy tapes along with Dolby SR noise reduction, analogue recorders can provide a dynamic range approaching that of 16-bit digital recorders; and, unlike other noise-reduction systems, Dolby SR has virtually no audible side-effects.

tape saturation

Analogue tape exhibits a magnetic saturation effect when overloaded, which has the result of causing a progressive increase in distortion at higher recording levels. This is rather more friendly than the hard clipping that occurs when digital systems overload, and indeed analogue tape saturation is used deliberately to create "warm"-sounding recordings. Analogue multitrack obviously still has a lot going for it, and even in this digital age many people still seek out well-maintained analogue machines specifically for their sound. Ironically, a number of digital processors and software packages are available which set out to process digital data in a way that emulates analogue tape-saturation effects.

magnetic tape

All tape recorders suffer from the inherent disadvantage that the tape is in physical contact with the heads and guides of the machine, and this translates into wear, both for the tape itself and for the metal parts of the recorder. The other obvious disadvantage of a tape-based recording system is that winding the tape from one spool to another takes time.

Accepting the aforementioned limitations, and acknowledging that analogue recorders can sound exceptionally good, the actual results obtained are dependent on the electronic design of the recorder, the mechanics of the transport and the quality of the tape being used. If the tape isn't moved across the heads at a perfectly constant speed, audible effects such as "wow" and "flutter" result. (Solo piano is a good instrument on which to test for wow and flutter, because it has no natural vibrato.) Analogue machines also suffer from modulation noise caused by the way in which the tape moves over the surface of the head, and although this isn't usually audible when you're recording music, if you try recording a pure sine wave and then play it back, the chances are that it will sound so jittery that you'll think the machine is faulty. When you compare this with the same test done on a digital machine, you'll wonder why analogue sounds as good as it does.

sound quality

Given a well-set-up, properly-designed analogue tape machine, the most significant factors affecting sound quality are tape speed and track width. As pointed out in the early chapters of this book, the faster the tape passes over the heads and the wider the tracks (the tape width itself is immaterial), the better the sound quality. An analogue recording is made by magnetising millions of tiny particles of oxide as they pass over the record head, so the recording can be considered as the statistical summation of the magnetic charge of however many of these tiny magnets is passing over the head at any one time. The faster the tape or the wider the tracks, the more particles per second pass over the heads and the more accurate the recording. (Photographers will recognise a close analogy between tape noise and film graininess as a function of film speed.)

Narrow-format open-reel machines and cassette multitrack systems don't pass enough oxide over the heads each second to produce an adequately low noise floor, so noise-reduction systems have to be employed, and all noise-reduction systems cause a deterioration in some other aspect of the sound quality, to a greater or lesser extent. Professionals tend to prefer working with two-inch tape running at 30ips (inches per second) without noise reduction. Where noise reduction must be used, Dolby SR is the system of choice for professionals, while for the home user Dolby S is generally regarded to be the best. Cassette multitrackers are often designed to run at double the normal tape speed so that the noise-reduction system chosen doesn't have to work so hard, but even a double-speed cassette runs at least four times slower, and has far narrower tracks, than a professional 15ips open-reel recorder.

Copying a recording from one tape track to another – as you do when bouncing – causes a loss of quality. Every time an analogue recording is copied, more noise is added and a little more clarity is lost. There can also be problems when playing back tapes recorded on different machines due to small differences in mechanical-head alignment, causing a loss of high frequencies.

analogue benefits

Having identified some of the weaknesses of the analogue regime, it's only fair to look at the benefits. Analogue tape recorders have been around for a long time; they work, they're not too difficult to maintain and tape itself is relatively cheap. Tape can be spliced, which makes editing easy, and recordings can be kept for many years with minimal deterioration, provided that they're stored in a suitable environment.

Because you can overdrive analogue tape without running into hard clipping, you can be a little more casual about recording levels than you have to be with digital systems. When overloaded, digital systems simply clip, and unless the periods of clipping are extremely short the result is generally audible as a crackle or glitch. You can also varispeed analogue tape over a very large range, turn the tape over to create reverse effects and even use two analogue machines to create flanging effects by using your hand as a brake on one or other of the machine's tape reels. If the worst comes to the worst, and you do have a problem with an analogue tape, such as a drop-out (usually caused by faulty tape or large pieces of foreign material on the heads), you can hear the problem straight away and then either redo the recording on a new tape or try to patch in a piece copied from elsewhere in the song.

Deterioration caused by inappropriate storage is usually gradual and generally involves an overall loss of quality rather than a drastic and complete failure. For all of its operational crudities, most audio professionals still seem to feel that analogue tape has the best sound, on an artistic level, and there's also more confidence in its reliability than there is in digital tape and other digital, tapeless alternatives.

digital tape

There's a lot of rhetoric spoken about the way in which digital recordings sound, but ultimately most serious music listening is done via compact disc, which is a 16-bit/44.1kHz digital format with a theoretical maximum dynamic range of 96dB. Even though this is a better dynamic range than you can get from analogue tape used with noise reduction, you have to keep in mind that digital systems have no headroom at all above 0VU – there's no soft clipping as there is with analogue tape. For this reason, when working with digital multitrack, it may be necessary to set the nominal record level at around -12dB on the recorder's own meters, and even then you'll still need to keep an eye on the peaks. Once you've allowed a suitable safety margin (headroom), a 16-bit digital system may have little more usable dynamic range than a good analogue recorder working with Dolby SR, so why is everyone going digital? Perhaps digital systems produce less distortion?

more on sampling

As touched on at the beginning of this chapter, digital recording systems work by sampling the instantaneous level of the input signal – usually at either 44,100 or 48,000 times a second – and then storing these samples as binary numbers. The number of bits defines the precision with which each

HOME RECORDING made easy

sample can be taken, and because every sample can only be measured to the nearest whole bit the digital representation of an analogue waveform is really a series of tiny steps, as shown in Figure 13.1. In the case of a 16-bit system, a full-scale signal would occupy two to the power of 16 (65,536) steps, and if the signal being recorded is large it will use most of the available bits and so be adequately accurate. However, smaller signals will be represented by fewer bits, so the lower the signal level, the higher the percentage of distortion. Analogue tape machines work the other way around – the distortion increases as the level increases.

Another benefit of digital systems is that no noise-reduction system is required to achieve in excess of a 90dB signal-to-noise ratio, and because digital machines are driven from a very accurate, crystal-controlled clock, there's no mechanism by which the recording rate can drift, as there is with analogue, where an imperfect capstan shaft or worn pinch roller can compromise the performance. Even with a budget digital system, wow and flutter are effectively eliminated, because the digital data goes to and from tape via a crystal-clocked memory buffer.

by the numbers

Once a recording is in the digital domain, it's really just a catalogue of numbers, rather like storing a piece of line art as a precision join-the-dots drawing. Because we're dealing with absolute numbers, it's possible to copy the data from one digital machine to another, or from one track to another, simply by duplicating these numbers. The result is a perfect copy, with no loss in quality.

error correction

In the real world, the numbers occasionally get lost or altered when a transfer takes place, but digital recorders use a very powerful error-correction system to enable them to reconstruct small amounts of damaged data, so loss of accuracy is only a problem when something is seriously wrong with either the hardware or the tape. This error correction is absolutely necessary in order to offset the destructive effects of particles of dirt on the tape's surface and to compensate for minor tape drop-outs.

The ability to make a perfectly accurate clone of digital data is of immense value when mastering to DAT, or when multitracking on something like the Alesis ADAT or Tascam DA-88, because a second machine will allow you to make safety copies just in case anything should happen to the original version.

184

what can go wrong?

Both analogue and digital tape formats are fine when they're working properly, but what happens when a tape becomes worn or a machine goes out of alignment? With an analogue machine, alignment errors usually lead to a fall-off in the high-frequency response of the recording, while a damaged tape may result in momentary drop-outs (brief but audible drops in level and/or high-end frequency response). Digital machines, on the other hand, deal with absolute numbers, and because some errors are inevitable – due to dust on the tape, head wear and imperfections on the surface of the tape – their error-correction systems are constantly checking for and repairing corrupted data. A system of recording redundant data enables the machine to verify the integrity of the data by means of checksums, and small errors can be repaired completely by using the redundant data to reconstruct the original data. This is made possible because the recording process distributes the data on tape in such a way that a brief drop-out causes a multitude of small errors over a short period of time rather than a large cluster of adjacent errors. If the data were to be recorded in a linear fashion, a single drop-out would be unrecoverable, because all of the errors would be in one place.

error concealment

Errors involving a greater amount of data corruption may not leave sufficient information remaining for the error-correction system to reconstruct the original. It's rather like jabbing a number of small holes in the page of a newspaper; if there are only a few holes, you can work out the missing letters from the context of the undamaged text surrounding the holes, but as the number of holes increases you'll eventually get to a point where you don't have enough undamaged text to be sure about what's missing. You may still be able to guess, but at some point even guessing will become impossible.

When this happens to audio data, the system moves from error-correction to error-concealment mode. In effect, the software looks at the data on each side of the problem section and uses interpolation to construct a plausible replacement for the missing data. Technically, this will cause a brief rise in distortion, but this is usually too brief to be audible. If longer errors occur, the system won't even be able to hazard a rough guess as to what's missing, so it mutes the audio output until more good data comes along. Only at this point will you notice that something's wrong.

While error correction is a wonderful ally, it prevents us from seeing problems developing until it's too late, unless the equipment concerned has some form of error-readout system. Sadly, most home studio equipment has little or no error-readout facility, and the first you know about anything going wrong is when you hear a drop-out. Because head wear or recorder misalignment can cause data corruption or misreading problems, it's very important to have digital tape machines serviced on a regular basis, even if no problems are apparent. Most DAT and digital multitrack tape machines should be serviced every 500 hours.

Digital tape can't be edited with razor blades, like analogue tape. Instead, editing can be achieved by cloning data from one digital machine to another, but this is a time-consuming process and not everyone has access to two machines. In fact, the only really satisfactory way of editing digital material is to use a hard-disk editing system, and these are described later in the chapter.

For routine work where little or no editing is needed, analogue tape is still probably the easiest medium to use, and it has fewer complications. Digital tape recording is a seductive concept, but inexperienced users might find that their recordings are just as noisy as they ever were, because the major source of noise isn't usually the recording system – it's the material being fed into it. However, digital tape has the benefit that recordings can be cloned, there's no wow or flutter and the media is inexpensive.

DCC

Before leaving digital tape recording systems, it's appropriate to mention the Philips DCC (Digital Compact Cassette) format. This was a less-than-successful consumer system that used data-reduction algorithms to simplify the digitised audio signal to the extent that it could be recorded onto tape by means of a stationary, multi-channel head. The result is technically inferior to DAT and CD inasmuch as data reduction can be shown to have audible side-effects on some types of material, although to put it into perspective, the side-effects are less serious than those arising from most types of semi-pro (and indeed most professional) analogue tape noise-reduction systems. The vast majority of people are unable to differentiate between DCC and CD on commercial pop music, but classical music may show up a lack of detail or a reduction in the sense of space or stereo imaging.

Because DCC lost its battle with MiniDisc, DCC machines (where still available) are being sold very cheaply, which makes them a viable – and far superior – option to analogue cassette in a home-studio environment. Portable versions are also available for location sound gathering and for recording samples. The digital data from a DCC machine can be transferred to DAT or to a soundcard with an S/PDIF input, but DCC can't be used for backing up digital data from hard-disk recorders, because of the data-reduction algorithms used. For mastering purposes in a home studio, DCC works acceptably well, but as the format is now officially obsolete you should ensure that blank tapes are still available before you buy a machine

MiniDisc

Like DCC, MiniDisc – or MD, as it's commonly known – relies on a data-compression system that reduces the size of an audio file by approximately 4:1. Without getting too technical, it achieves this by discarding information that would normally be inaudible to humans, because of the masking effect from stronger signal components at similar frequencies. The psychoacoustic algorithms that decide what is and isn't audible are very sophisticated, and work amazingly well, considering the degree of data reduction that can be realised.

While those with good ears can detect the difference between MD and uncompressed CDs on good equipment and with the right choice of material, the audio quality is more than adequate for mastering serious demo recordings, and it has been known for commercial releases to be made from MD masters. Furthermore, the recording hardware is relatively inexpensive, although it's important to be aware that most of the portable models don't have mic pre-amps suitable for location recording with serious microphones. Professional models with balanced, phantom-powered mic inputs are available, but these tend to be considerably more expensive than consumer models.

hard-disk recording

Even as recently as the early '90s, tapeless recording was too expensive for most home recording enthusiasts to contemplate, but now the cost of the hardware has fallen to the point at which it's probably the cheapest way to get into multitrack recording, other than buying a basic cassette multitracker. Using a computer such as a Macintosh G3/G4 or a Pentium III PC fitted with a suitable soundcard and a large-capacity hard drive, you can experiment with tapeless recording and editing for very little more than the cost of the computer and some software. (Knowing how quickly computers are replaced by faster models, I expect that these models will start to look outdated very quickly.) If you're planning to buy a PC system, but you aren't sure what to go for, check out the FAQ (Frequently Asked Question) sections on the various music web sites, including the extensive FAQ section in the Forum of the *Sound On Sound* site at www.sospubs.co.uk. Simply picking a high-powered machine from a general-purpose computer store is no guarantee that you'll end up with good results when you use it to work with audio.

All hard-disk recording systems require a significant amount of computational power to process audio data, and the more real-time virtual effects and instruments you wish to use, the more processing power is required. Some card-based systems allow you to add more DSP power in the form of additional cards, which are either fitted inside the computer or to an expansion chassis. Nevertheless, such systems tend to be expensive, and specially-written effects plug-ins are required, as the common types can't be supported in their usual Mac and PC VST forms. Format-specific plug-ins for DSP-based systems invariably cost more than their VST counterparts, and as computers continue to get more powerful so the necessity for such DSP assistance should continue to diminish.

hardware recorders

An alternative to computers are stand-alone, hard-disk-based digital workstations, which offer upwards of eight tracks, with 16-track recorders currently being the most popular configuration. These combine multitrack tapeless recording, mixing and effects within one box, and are very compact and simple to set up. Some even offer CD-burning facilities via an optional CD writer, making the desktop-studio dream a reality. These integrated systems are both powerful and cost-effective, but they're more limited than their computer-based counterparts inasmuch as they're closed systems, with few options for expandability, and they can't run software plug-ins. Those working with MIDI may also find the integration of their sequencers and their digital workstations a little clumsy, although some of the major manufacturers have co-operated to provide direct support from within some of the more popular MIDI sequencing software packages. This support sometime extends to providing improved editing facilities, as well as access to audio and MIDI, within a common environment.

A little further up the scale there are stand-alone tapeless recorders (designed to be used with separate mixers), which generally come in 16- or 24-track configurations, and if more tracks are required they usually provide the option to sync multiple machines. These recorders are designed to offer a familiar tape-recorder-like environment, but they often have additional built-in data-processing and editing functions. The most flexible of these can be used in conjunction with a separate monitor display or computer to provide audio waveform displays during the editing process. Hard-disk recorders that conform to the tape-machine-operation paradigm are often more appropriate for traditional multisource recording than most computer-based systems, as they can record multiple tracks simultaneously and facilitate punching in and out, just like an analogue tape machine. They also have one physical output for each recorded track, thus allowing all tracks to be mixed conventionally, using an external mixer. Backing up recorded data is always a concern with such machines, however, and solutions range from CD-Recordable and DVD-Recordable to removable magneto-optical drives and EIDE hard drives in removable trays.

The reasons why the cost of tapeless recording has fallen so significantly is that, unlike analogue recording, the hardware used in these systems is based on the same components that are used elsewhere in the computer industry (notably high-capacity hard drives and computer chips) and because the demands of multimedia keep on pushing the price down and the performance up. However, the downside of this trend is that the audio industry is guided to a large extent by what the computer industry is doing. It's not cost-effective to try and develop a radically new technology specifically for audio applications.

integrated tapeless workstations

The other option is to choose a hardware-based audio workstation that combines tapeless recording, mixing and effects. These tend to have fewer features than their computer-based cousins, but they're invariably more straightforward to use, and the usual minefield of computer problems and conflicts is neatly avoided. More importantly, if it stops working, you know exactly where the blame lies, whereas if a computer system gives you problems then the fault could be in either the hardware or the software.

Currently, cassette based multitrackers are being superseded by Data MiniDisc-based four- and eight-track machines, and although four tracks may not seem like much to play with, once a MIDI sequencer is locked to such a machine via MIDI Time Code (MTC), there's a lot of creative potential. What's more, Data MiniDiscs are a cost-effective way of archiving material – you can treat them much like cassette tapes. MiniDisc uses an aggressive data-compression system to maximise the recording time available from a disk but, as stated earlier, the side-effects of data compression are far less serious than those that were caused by the analogue tape noise-reduction systems that were used previously. While uncompressed audio remains the preferred choice for professional applications, formats like MiniDisc provide an affordable, good-sounding alternative for the private studio owner or recording musician. If you need only a few tracks of audio, and you'd rather not deal with the potential complexities of an audio-plus-MIDI sequencer, syncing an MD multitracker to a MIDI sequencer of some kind is a very practical proposition. You should note, however, than cut-and-paste editing is far more clumsy on a typical MD multitracker than it is on a desktop computer.

Other integrated systems combine traditional fixed hard-drive recording facilities with mixers and hardware effects, often with some form of mixer automation. Although these are limited in expandability, they are compact and require little wiring or additional hardware, other than a monitoring system and a microphone. Virtually all models can generate MTC to sync a MIDI sequencer and offer all of the essential cut, copy, paste and move editing tools. However, few hardware recording systems rival computer-based systems when it comes to in-depth editing or for working on audio and MIDI in a common environment.

tapeless quality

16-bit hard-disk recording can provide the same audio quality as CD, and indeed the quality should be better than digital tape because, unlike tape, hard-disk error-correction systems always reconstruct the original data – guesswork isn't in their nature! However, audio fidelity is mainly dictated by the quality of the analogue-to-digital and digital-to-analogue converters used in the product. For example, high-quality converters in an external rack box or fitted to a professional-quality audio card are likely to sound every bit as good as CD, while budget converters residing in a computer – either as part of the basic hardware or as a consumer-type soundcard – tend to offer poorer resolution and impart higher noise levels. As with other aspects of digital systems, converters are improving at an impressive rate, and so even relatively inexpensive hardware can produce good results, as long as it's carefully chosen. Most serious hardware also supports 24-bit recording, which provides even better resolution, translating into a greater dynamic range and a lower noise floor. Few home studios are electrically quiet enough to take advantage of the full resolution of 24-bit audio, but its most practical advantage is that it allows you the luxury of leaving a few extra decibels of safety headroom while you're recording in order to accommodate any unexpected peaks.

hard drives

Tapeless multitrack recorders usually store data onto computer hard drives or onto some form of removable disk. Although not all hard-disk drives are suitable for recording multitrack audio, most recent models are designed for AV (Audio-Visual) use for when data needs to be read in a continuous stream. Some older computer drives take short breaks in order to recalibrate themselves and to offset the effects of temperature changes, and while the computer's buffer memory may be large enough to ensure that this doesn't interrupt the data flow, if you're recording or playing back more than a handful of tracks, you may hear breaks or dropouts in the audio. Also, the more buffering you use, the greater the latency figure. (See the explanation of latency later in this chapter.) The more tracks you intend to play back at once, the more serious the problem becomes, which is why AV drives were originally developed. These have intelligent thermal recalibration systems that avoid interrupting the data flow when the disk is reading or writing data, which makes them a better choice for multitrack work. Unless you're working with an old drive, or one with a capacity of under 1GB (which these days is very unlikely), it's unlikely that thermal recalibration will be a problem.

There are two main types of drive, and the one that's used will depend on the system to which it's connected. Computers tend to come fitted with low-cost EIDE drives (also called Ultra DMA), which – although fast enough to handle reliably upwards of 16 tracks of audio – aren't as fast as Ultra SCSI (pronounced "scuzzi") drives, which may be able to provide more than 48 tracks of playback or recording. SCSI drives need to be connected via a special SCSI adaptor card, and as there are so many variants of SCSI available it's important that you consult with your computer audio dealer to find out which SCSI card and drive are best for your own particular needs. As a rule, the drives with the fastest spindle speeds provide the best rates of continuous data transfer, which is important for multitrack audio work. Regardless of which type of drive you use, it's always best to use a second hard drive for storing your audio files, as this makes it a lot easier to manage them and to defragment the drive.

A further type of interface, known as FireWire, was introduced along with the new-style Mac computers (G3 onwards), and some PCs are also offering FireWire connectivity. FireWire is a high-speed bussing system for connecting multiple devices to a computer, such as hard drives, scanners, digital cameras, audio interfaces, MIDI interfaces and so on. Yamaha are also pushing a specially-adapted version of FireWire called mLan for audio-specific applications, which they hope will become an industry standard. If this goes ahead, one FireWire link will be able to handle all of the audio, MIDI and sync data required by a typical sequencer, which will make it easier to connect high-speed peripherals. Currently, many FireWire drives are still no as fast as the best SCSI drives. (In fact, many are actually SCSI drives equipped with adaptor hardware.) However, this should change within a relatively short period of time. Your software manufacturer's web site should also provide a list of recommended drives, once support is available.

random access

Computer hard drives can access any piece of data within a few milliseconds, which is a great benefit for audio users. For one thing, random access means that you don't have to wait for a tape to wind on to the right position, but the advantages of random access go much further than that. By using RAM as a buffer, audio can be read onto and from a disk in a continuous, uninterrupted stream, even when the audio is located in different places on the disk's surface, which opens up all kinds of interesting editing possibilities. For example, because you can access any section of recorded audio data in any order, it's easy to rearrange sections into a new order and then play back your new arrangement without gaps or glitches.

destructive or non-destructive?

Being able to rearrange, copy or move material without altering the original data file is known as *non-destructive editing*, and there's a lot you can do to a recording without changing the original data in any way. Nevertheless, there are times when you may want a change to become permanent – when silencing the noise immediately prior to the start of a song, for example, or when implementing some kind of time- or pitch-manipulation process. On a desktop-computer-based system, you may even be able to zoom in on a tiny section of the audio waveform and then use special software tools to erase an annoying guitar squeak or to get rid of a click. Permanent changes made to an audio file are said to be *destructive*. (Both destructive and non-destructive editing will be covered in more detail in the section on "Editing".)

The main editing tricks that can be performed with digital systems are based around rearranging your material in a different order (ie cutting, copying, pasting and moving), but you can also normalise signal levels to bring the peaks up to 0dB, apply digital EQ, reverse sections of sound, create fade-ins and -outs and perform a number of other functions that would have been difficult or impossible using tape.

disk fragmentation

Computer drives don't necessarily record audio in one continuous stream. If many files have been written onto a drive and then erased or edited, the drive becomes fragmented. A fragmented drive tends to have sections of different files scattered around in different places, and although it generally manages to join them up seamlessly the overall disk operation can slow down noticeably, which results in a reduction in the maximum number of audio tracks that can be played back at the same time without glitching or drop-outs occurring.

The solution is not only to use a separate audio drive for storing your audio files but also to defragment it fairly regularly using a program such as Norton Utilities. (Windows has a built-in defragment option.) It may also help to clear the drive occasionally (after backing up all your data onto a CD-R, or whatever your favourite back-up medium is) and then reformat it.

media costs

Currently, hard drives are comparably priced (in terms of tracks/minutes) to two-inch analogue tape, although it's only a matter of time before suitable high-capacity drives become cheap enough to enable project-studio owners to archive material on removable hard drives. One minute of mono audio at 16-bit/48kHz audio requires around 5MB of drive space, although correspondingly more space is required for 24-bit audio or material made at a sampling rate of 96kHz. Where it isn't practical to archive to fixed-disk drives in the same way as it is tape, it's possible to use a tape-based data back-up system, such as Exobyte or Data DAT. These systems are considerably cheaper than removable-disk media, but with these backing up to and reloading from digital tape is obviously very slow. Currently, CD-Rs are widely used in project studios for backing up, as both audio files and MIDI song files can be saved together. Blank CD-Rs are exceptionally cheap, and rewritable discs (CD-RWs) cost only around twice as much as write-once discs. Recordable DVD is also an option.

connecting MIDI interfaces

As stated earlier in the book, you'll need a MIDI interface (unless you're using only soundcard or software synths, or a hardware synth with a "to-host" connection) as well as suitable sequencing software that supports both your MIDI and your audio hardware. MIDI interfaces may connect via PC serial ports, USB ports or parallel ports, depending on the model and the support software that comes with it, while older Macs (ie those that came out before the coloured G3 iMacs) use the serial printer or modem ports. Newer Macs use USB, although there are third-party serial-interface adaptor cards available for use with legacy hardware. Not all of these work with MIDI, however, so check out the software manufacturer's web site for more information before you buy.

As a rule, if you intend to use external synth modules, you should choose a MIDI interface with at least six output ports – you always end up acquiring more synths than you think you're going to. If you're using USB for MIDI, I recommend one of the more sophisticated interfaces that uses intelligent buffering to avoid MIDI timing problems. Steinberg have their own interface optimised for Cubase, whereas eMagic make the AMT-8 and Unitor 8 MkII for use with Logic. Mark Of The Unicorn also produce a range of interfaces that work with most leading brands of sequencing software, although Opcode's OMS (Open MIDI System) is generally needed when working with Mac USB interfaces that aren't designed specifially to work with the host software.

combining audio with MIDI

Recording audio directly onto the hard drive of an ordinary computer gets really exciting when you combine it with MIDI. All of the leading sequencer manufacturers now produce software packages that integrate the recording and editing of MIDI data with the recording, editing and mixing of audio. Any audio that's recorded can be accessed and arranged in much the same way as sequenced MIDI patterns are arranged – from the same Arrange page on a sequencer. Because both audio and MIDI are displayed in the same environment, you therefore don't have to keep changing your mental outlook as you switch from working with MIDI data to audio data. Furthermore, MIDI/audio sequencers also tend to support both effects plug-ins and virtual instruments, with the latter encompassing software-based synthesisers, drum machines and samplers. All of these virtual effects and instruments demand their share of computer processing power, but – given the power of modern computers and the rate at which this power is increasing – it's becoming increasingly feasible that hardware effects and instruments can be dispensed with altogether.

If you're already working with MIDI, adding a few tracks of direct-to-disk audio is a very practical and flexible way of installing a complete recording studio on your desktop. Little additional hardware is needed – the audio is automatically synchronised to the MIDI data – and "virtual" effects can be added in real time, provided that you have the right software and a reasonably powerful computer. A system like this will also have room to expand, if required, with the addition of a small mixer, a few synth modules and one or two hardware effects boxes. (Hardware reverb still sounds better than even the best software reverb plug-ins, and it doesn't hog computing power.) Because a typical MIDI composition may only include a little audio data, removable drives or CD-Rs are already quite cost-effective as storage media.

high sample rates

Most serious audio hardware is now able to record at 24-bit resolution as well as at 16-bit, which is a good idea for critical projects, even though it reduces recording time and plug-in capacity by a third. Even when the final result will be a 16-bit CD quality, working at 24 bits helps to avoid any loss of resolution when further processes or mixing functions are applied to the data.

Sampling audio at 96kHz is a different matter, however, as few people can hear the difference between 48kHz and 96kHz sampling. Maybe world-class equipment in a world-class studio would show up a difference, but it's pretty irrelevant in the project studio at the moment. Even so, it pays to be aware that 96kHz audio may become the standard hi-fi format if and when DVD becomes widely adopted as a medium for audio delivery. Most serious audio equipment is now 24-bit/96kHz compatible, whether you need that resolution or not, and as storage capacity rises and processors become more powerful there will be less concern about conserving resources by working at 16-bit/44.1kHz resolution. Already, RAM and computer hard drives are orders of magnitude cheaper than they were a few years ago, so data storage is no longer the major cost concern it once was. However, we're still pushing computers pretty hard, when it comes to processing, and as high resolution 24-bit/96kHz audio takes around three times as much processor power per minute as CD quality 16-bit/44.1kHz, you should expect a dramatic drop in the number of tracks, plug-ins and virtual-instrument voices that you have at your disposal, should you use it.

hard-disk editors

Hard-disk editors exist specifically to manipulate and rearrange stereo (or, more recently, surround) material, and their most common applications involve compiling individual tracks to produce a production master tape for an album project or to rearrange the sections of a song to create a new version. Such editing systems are often used to create extended remixes, to shorten songs or to fix performance errors and technical blemishes. Sophisticated crossfading algorithms are used to ensure that there are no audible glitches at the edit points, something that isn't always true when editing analogue tape with razor blades. Tapeless editing may also be used to assemble the best parts of several different versions of the same piece of music or dialogue.

While basic cut-and-paste editing is possible on a multitrack hard-disk system, a dedicated stereo-editing system or software package will usually include specialist tools that can be used to edit audio to a much finer degree, although the features of both multitrack systems and editors are now staring to converge. Other software tools include facilities for PQ-coding CD masters (ie adding the pause and cue information used in commercial audio CDs) and for burning CD-Rs to produce one-off CD masters from a DAT original.

computer practicalities

While you can go out and buy a Macintosh computer, install the necessary soundcard, MIDI interface and software and then reasonably expect it to work, the same isn't true of PCs. While PCs are apparently less expensive than Macs and easier to upgrade, there's actually no such thing as a standard PC. There are numerous chipsets, motherboards, processors and graphics cards that can be put together to run a suite of Windows office programs perfectly acceptably, but there's no guarantee that they'll work for music. For this reason, I would strongly advise that anyone considering purchasing a PC-based music system should buy the computer, software and hardware ready-configured from a specialist computer-music company. A music-specific PC may appear to cost more than the equivalent PC superstore bargain, but you could offset this in discount by buying everything from the same source. In any event, buying everything from one source will give you legal redress if the system doesn't work as specified, whereas if you buy from separate dealers and then try to get everything working yourself it's unlikely that anyone will take responsibility if you have problems. If the individual components aren't faulty, you have no legal redress if the complete system fails to operate as planned. My own findings are that, if you buy a Mac, you'll learn a lot about making music, whereas if you buy a PC you'll learn a lot about computers! If you must buy a PC, buy a working system and don't use the same machine for games, as these sometimes "hijack" bits of the system that you need for audio work. The same goes for "free" internet software and shareware from magazine cover disks – don't risk it!

lightening the load

Fast and versatile though computers are, both MIDI and audio timing can be optimised by ensuring that your computer isn't doing any unnecessary tasks in the background. Scrolling screen displays usually take up more processing power than those that jump when the cursor gets to the end of the screen, so try turning off scrolling if you think that you're pushing your computer's capabilities. Better still, zoom out so that all of the song fits onto the screen before you play it back, so that there's no scrolling or screen redraw.

Mac users should also consider using the Extensions Manager control panel to disable any system extension that isn't needed for music, and screen savers are definitely something to avoid on any platform. Setting the monitor resolution to 256 colours also reduces the processing burden. You should switch off any energy-conservation system that you may have, or set it to the longest time possible so that the computer doesn't fall asleep during a long recording!

dual drives

With any computer-based audio recording system, it's advisable to use a separate hard drive to store your audio. Audio drives need emptying or defragmenting pretty regularly, particularly if you work with a lot of audio tracks, and this becomes more difficult if you have all of your other software and system files residing on the same drive. With a separate drive, all you need to do is back up finished projects and then erase all of the data on the drive ready for the next session.

Stereo (16-bit) material sampled at 44.1kHz uses around 10MB of disk space per minute, which means that approximately 600MB of disk space is required to record an hour's worth of stereo material. In reality, you need rather more, because if you decide to perform a destructive edit the system usually creates back-up files so that you can undo any changes that don't work out as planned. For this reason, a 2GB drive should be considered the bare minimum for a typical album-editing project, and 10-20GB for multitrack work. As a rule, larger-capacity drives are also faster, which means that you can record and play back more tracks simultaneously on a multitrack system. At the time of writing, drives under 10GB are rather uncommon, although there are countless older 1GB and 3GB SCSI drives around the world that work fine for audio work, as long as their capacity is adequate.

With multitracking, available disk space is shared out between the number of tracks on which you want to record, so it follows that the recording time is halved every time the number of tracks is doubled. Using a 600MB drive, you can expect a maximum of a quarter of an hour of continuous eight-track or less than eight minutes of 16-track recording time. Unlike tape machines, however, tapeless systems usually allow you to use any unused recording time from one track on another, so perhaps the best way of thinking of the available recording time is in "track minutes" rather than in overall recording time. For example, if you only fill half of the available tracks and leave the rest empty, the recording time will double. Similarly, if you only use one track in a 24-track system, the recording time will be 24 times longer than it will be if you record the same length of audio to all 24 tracks.

input/output options

The manner in which audio gets into and out of your system depends on the hardware you're using. Budget soundcards often only have analogue inputs and outputs, while more sophisticated cards may include S/PDIF and/or AES/EBU digital interfaces. Provided that the analogue inputs are of reasonable quality, they'll probably be fine for multitrack work – after all, most of the source material is analogue. However, when editing stereo material, it's generally considered unacceptable to leave the digital domain, unless you specifically need to treat the audio signal by using an analogue processor of some kind.

The audio data to be edited is generally fed in from DAT or some other digital source via the digital I/O (In/Out) connectors, although it's advisable to buy a proper digital transfer cable. While you may get away with using a hi-fi phono lead, you might then end up with inexplicable clicks and glitches, because the cable impedance of these leads is wrong for digital data.

guitars and monitors

Computer monitors – or monitors connected to hardware that has a monitor output – interfere badly with guitar pick-ups, producing a nasty buzz on the recording. Some humbucking pick-ups are reasonably good at rejecting this buzz, provided that you don't sit too close to the monitor while you record, but the level of interference can still be too high if you're working with overdrive effects. The simplest way around this problem is to switch off the monitor just before recording and use keyboard commands to start and stop the recording process.

Although still more costly than glass monitors, flat-screen LCD screens eliminate the electromagnetic interference generated by the scan coils of a typical CRT monitor. If you record a lot of guitar, or are short on space, buying one of these could be a good investment.

fan and drive noise

As computers – and the DSPs (Digital Signal Processors) at the hearts of hardware digital recorders – become more powerful, they require more cooling, and cooling means fan noise. Clearly, when you're miking instruments or voices in the same room as a computer, whirring fans and hard drives are a problem. If possible, you should turn off any unnecessary external drives and CD-ROM burners when recording and set up your mic(s) as far away from the computer/recorder as possible. It also helps to improvise an acoustic screen between the mic and the computer with bedding or blankets. Make sure that the surface at which the mic is pointing is absorptive rather than reflective and work as close to the mic as you can, using a pop shield for vocals.

chapter 14

computers and audio

he most popular form of digital multitrack recording is currently the
computer running audio/MIDI sequencing software such as eMagic's
Logic Audio or Steinberg's Cubase. The reasons for this popularity are
that computers are relatively cheap and yet very powerful, they can be
expanded by both hardware and software, and they provide an integrated
visual environment in which both MIDI and audio can be recorded and
manipulated. Figure 14.1 shows the Arrange page of a typical sequencing
package on which both the audio and MIDI tracks can be viewed and edited.
In addition to recording audio conventionally, such systems are also able to
import audio files from other sources, such as audio CDs or CD-ROMs. Given
that much of modern music relies on ready-made rhythm loops – many of
which are commercially available in audio CD format – this latter
consideration can be important.

Figure 14.1: Sequencer Arrange page showing both audio and MIDI in a common environment

Most computer-based systems also allow you to use real-time, plug-in, software-based effects (the software equivalents of separate signal processors or effects units), such as reverb, delay, compression, stereo enhancement, de-noising, click removal, 3D spatial enhancement and so on. Often, some of these "virtual effects" are provided as part of the software package, but third-party plug-ins – such as the popular VST format – can be purchased separately and used from within your sequencer. You should note, however, that some sequencers use a proprietary plug-in format, so don't buy any plug-ins before making sure that your software can support them. Currently, eMagic and Steinberg support VST plug-ins, while MOTU (Mark Of The Unicorn) Performer has its own plug-in format. In addition to virtual effects and processors, most serious sequencer software will support third-party virtual instrument plug-ins, such as software-driven synths, samplers and drum machines.

Although the ability to record and edit audio alongside MIDI is clearly important, few soundcards or audio interfaces have anything like as many separate physical outputs as the number of audio tracks that the computer can provide. This means that, in order to make meaningful use of all of these audio tracks, there needs to be a way of mixing them via the sequencer software.

the software mixer

A key part of any audio/MIDI sequencing package is the mixer section, which is usually accessed via an on-screen representation of a suitably specified hardware mixer. Most software designers use lavish 3D graphics in an attempt to make their mixers look as much like conventional models as possible, right down to including level faders that can be dragged up or down by using the mouse, and Figure 14.2 shows the Mixer page of a popular sequencer. Rotary controls can usually be adjusted by clicking on them with the pointer and then either moving the mouse left/right, up/down or around in circles. Stereo recordings are usually handled by an adjacent pair of tracks designated as a stereo pair, which in properly-designed software prevents you from accidentally separating the two channels of a stereo pair while editing. Stereo tracks are usually handled by stereo mixer channels that have a single fader for controlling level. If your experience of hardware mixers is limited to simple "something-into-two" models, it's worth revisiting Chapter 3 of this book, "Mixers", where the basics are explained.

The software mixer is mainly concerned with mixing tracks on playback, although some systems also include so-called "live" mixer channels, which allow external sounds patched to the soundcard input to be added to the

Figure 14.2: Sequencer Mixer page

mix. Setting recording levels is achieved by adjusting the level of the source, and in most cases there's little more to do than to set the recording level and arm a track for recording.

When a track is played back through a channel of the virtual mixer, it can be adjusted in level and pan position, just as it can on a hardware mixer. EQ takes processing power, however, so the usual set-up is one which enables the user to activate EQ on only those channels that need it – sometimes on a "per-band" basis. Effects sends can also be set up, and there are insert points provided, but on a virtual mixer the effects accessed via these connections are also likely to be virtual. I say "likely" because, in some systems, it's possible to set up your virtual mixer so that the effects sends feed external processors via spare soundcard inputs and outputs, and there are also DSP-assisted systems available that have onboard hardware-effects-processing capabilities.

The virtual mixers found in the most popular sequencer packages tend to either support third-party plug-in effects – such as VST or some other format – or come with built-in effects. (Logic Audio and Cubase VST both support VST effects, and they also come with built-in dedicated effects.) Also, because you can only adjust one screen fader or knob at a time with a mouse, mix automation is invariably included, and most modern plug-ins can have their parameters automated. This means that, if you want to, you can vary things such as delay time or reverb brightness throughout a song. Something that also mirrors the hardware world is the virtual mixer's ability to route and subgroup, so that, instead of being mixed to a single stereo output, all of the audio tracks can be submixed to as many physical outputs as the card is equipped with. Additionally, groups of tracks may be routed via group channels, which means that their levels can be controlled from a single fader. The facilities and methodologies vary slightly from manufacturer to manufacturer, but it's well worth reading the relevant section of your software manual carefully, paying particular attention to the parts concerning routing, automation and the use of plug-ins.

If you prefer to use hardware knobs or faders to control the levels of mixer channels, pans and so on, there are numerous hardware boxes on the market that allow you to do this by sending the appropriate MIDI controllers to the sequencer. All you need to do is set up the MIDI control messages sent by the hardware to match those expected by your sequencer.

using mix automation

With mix automation, the knobs or faders on your virtual mixer generate MIDI data when they're moved. When the sequencer is set to Write mode for any desired channel or channels, the data produced by moving the on-screen controls is stored by the sequencer in much the same way as any other MIDI data.

It's possible to redo moves or add new sections until automation has been added to all of the tracks that need it, and of course, as with other MIDI information, you can edit mix data after the event, if necessary, by either changing values in an Edit list or (sometimes) by graphical means. The software may also come equipped with an Update or Trim mode, similar to that on a hardware automated console, which will add new fader movements to earlier values rather than replacing them. This is very useful when your original automation pass is mainly OK but you just want to move the levels of certain sections up or down a touch.

graphical automation

One common form of graphical automation display comprises a series of points joined by straight lines. New points occur whenever a control is moved, but you'll be able to edit the mix automation in this mode by adding new points (usually by clicking on the line where you want to create a new point) or by dragging existing points to new positions. This is a very precise way of fine-tuning your automation moves, and in simpler mixes it may provide you with all of the control you need without ever having to resort to recording fader moves. Figure 14.3 shows the Graphical Editing page of a popular sequencer package.

Most automation now extends to level, pan, aux send levels and some effects parameters. In fact, the more advanced packages enable you to automate just about every knob and switch within the virtual mixer or plug-in windows.

Figure 14.3: Graphical edit page

virtual effects

Before patching effects or processors into a mixing console, whether real or virtual, you need to remind yourself of the differences between effects and processors, because this will have implications when you come to route them. The restrictions of both apply just as surely in the virtual world as they do in the hardware world. If you're not sure what the difference is between an effect and a processor, reading Chapter 8 again should clarify things.

Examples of processors include gates, expanders, compressors, limiters, equalisers, enhancers and distortion devices, and all of these are characterised by having no mix control (with the exception of enhancers, on which the mix control determines the depth of the effect produced). Meanwhile, examples of effects include reverberators, digital delay lines, chorus units, flangers, ADT units and pitch shifters. All of these usually have a mix facility, enabling the user to blend the processed and unprocessed sound within the unit.

The main thing to remember is that, under normal circumstances, an effect may be used either in conjunction with an auxiliary send (in which case the strength of the effect is controlled via the mixer and the effect mix control must be set to effect only) or via an insert point (in which case the unit's own mix control is used to determine the strength of the effect). A processor, on the other hand, is normally used only via an insert point. Any attempt to use a processor via the aux send system is likely to yield unpredictable and undesirable results.

using virtual effects

As they're so common, I'll be using VST plug-ins in the following examples, although most proprietary effect plug-ins are deployed in a similar way. Virtual effects, such as VST plug-ins, are accessed from inside the virtual audio mixer section of a sequencer – you may also be able to use the same VST plug-ins in a stereo-editing/-mastering program.

There are three main ways in which plug-in effects can be deployed via a virtual mixer's insert and aux send points. Firstly, and most simply, each channel on a VST-compatible virtual mixer has one or more insert points into which a virtual effect plug-in can be loaded. When more than one plug-in is loaded at the same time, the signal flows through the topmost plug-in first. Normally, these plug-ins are chosen from a pull-down menu that shows all of the virtual effects and processors available. (Note, however, that VST plug-ins may have to be stored in a particular folder before your software

Figure 14.4: Examples of VST effects plug-ins. Top-bottom: Steinberg DeNoiser, Antares Auto-Tune, TC Native CL compressor/limiter

can "see" them.) When you place an effect or a processor in a channel insert point, everything fed through that channel passes through it – although, in the case of effects, there's invariably a dry/effect mix control that can be used to regulate the strength (effect/dry balance) of the effect.

If the same effect is needed elsewhere, you can open another copy of the same plug-in and place it in the insert point of a different channel, although it's important to understand that, even though you may be using the same plug-in, if you use it in two different places it will use twice as much processing power.

Figure 14.5a: Plug-in used in a track

You should also note that plug-ins are available in both mono and stereo versions. Normally, you can only place a mono plug-in into a mono mixer channel, but some software provides a means for you to insert a stereo effect into a mono channel where you may want the added effect to be in stereo. This isn't always as prominently shown in sequencer manuals as it might be, so check out your manual's section on plug-in handling in order to find out how this works for your software. Figure 14.5a shows a plug-in inserted into a mixer track.

A less processor-intensive way of using a plug-in is to deploy it in the insert point of a group and then route any channels that need processing to that group, as shown in Figure 14.5b. (In conventional mixing terms, this equates to creating a subgroup, which may be either in mono or stereo.) The output of the group is then routed to the stereo mix. In this way, you only have to use a plug-in once in order to add an effect to any number of tracks, but you should remember that everything fed via that group will be treated with the same proportion of the plug-in effect.

The third method is to use post-fade aux sends, just as you would on a

Figure 14.5b: Plug-in used in a group

hardware mixing console. While you can use either effects or processors in insert points, aux sends are only suitable for use with effects. In most cases, the aux sends are normally used to add a different amount of the same effect – such as reverb – to the various tracks in a mix, while the effects level for each channel is set by the individual aux send controls on that channel. The way in which these effects sends are set up in a sequencer varies from manufacturer to manufacturer, but they're generally arranged fairly logically and mirror the way in which effects are patched into a hardware mixer. For example, Logic Audio routes each aux send to a buss channel used as an effects return, and any effects that are needed by a particular aux send are then inserted into the buss insert points. The buss output (which is really the aux return) may then be routed as desired, although it would normally be fed into the main stereo mix. Cubase takes a slightly different approach by offering a virtual effects rack, which is fed from up to eight aux sends and returns the individual effect outputs to the main mix. Again, you should refer to the relevant section in your sequencer's operating manual, as understanding how plug-ins are deployed is essential to obtaining professional results.

virtual instruments

Virtual instruments are software equivalents of synths, samplers and drum machines that run on your computer. The most useful of these can be accessed from within your sequencer package, and since the VST Instrument was introduced by Steinberg, and was later supported by eMagic and others, using virtual instruments has become as easy as calling up an effects plug-in.

In order to play a VST instrument from a keyboard, the audio part of your system needs to have a very low latency, or you'll feel the lag between playing and hearing the sound. High latency makes normal playing impossible, especially with sounds that have a fast attack, such as pianos. The only way around the problem (although even then it's not entirely satisfactory) is to record the MIDI part using a regular synth or soundcard, so that there's no latency, and then switch the track to control the VST instrument after you've recorded it. Note that the computing power taken by a VST instrument tends to relate to the number of notes or voices being played at any one time, so your computing-power balancing act has to take into account MIDI sequencing, audio recording and playback, plug-in effects and virtual instruments.

Figure 14.6: eMagic EXS24 virtual sampler

Of all of the virtual instruments I've tried, samplers are the most exciting. Most virtual samplers can read commercial Akai-format CDs (and often other types), and these record the samples and convert them to the required format, after which they're stored on the computer's hard drive. Once they're on the hard drive, they can be loaded almost as fast as synth patches, while parameters such as envelope and filter settings can be set with the same ease as on any other virtual synth.

Many of the better games-type soundcards support a type of sample playback based on something called SoundFonts. Commercial SoundFont CD-ROMs are available relatively cheaply, and they often contain surprisingly high-quality multisamples of instruments, voices and percussion, as well as rhythm loops. Although SoundFonts were originally designed to appeal to the casual computer music user, their quality has now become so high that they can be used for serious composition, so don't write them off just because they're cheap!

monitoring latency

Latency is an issue that's seldom raised in the product's glossy advertising, so it's as well to explain it here before going further. Put simply, latency is a short but musically significant delay between the sound being fed into a computer-based recording system and the same sound emerging via the audio outs. On a well-designed system, this latency may only be a few milliseconds, in which case few people will even notice it. However, if the latency is greater than around 10ms, it can completely upset the timing of any musician trying to perform an overdub. Furthermore, software synths and samplers will exhibit a time lag between the player pressing a key and the note sounding. The effects of latency are compensated for on playback, but this doesn't help you much if it has already thrown your performance out of time. In severe cases, latency also delays the starting and stopping of recording and playback by a small but irritating amount, and it may also interfere with your ability to set up mix automation effectively.

Latency is partly caused by computers needing to use small memory buffers in order to hold enough audio data to keep the signal flowing while the hard drive and/or processor are engaged in other tasks. It's rather like somebody filling a leaky bucket with a cup. Provided that the bucket never runs dry, the leak (our audio) will continue in a steady stream, but if the person with the cup can't keep up, the bucket runs dry and the flow stops. The bigger the memory buffer (the bucket), the less chance there is of a glitch, but in latency terms, the bigger the bucket, the longer the latency between audio going into and coming out of a system. Well-designed software running on a modern computer reduces latency to the point at which it's too small to detect, but some older or less sophisticated systems still cause problems, in which case you need to find a solution.

solutions to latency

There are both hardware and software approaches to minimising latency. Innovations such as Steinberg's ASIO II drivers or eMagic's ESI drivers help on the software side, while soundcards with thru-monitoring help on the hardware side. This thru-monitoring is roughly equivalent to a tape machine monitoring the input signal on the channel being recorded rather than waiting for the signal to be played back a fraction of a second later from the playback head. The original ASIO driver format couldn't help with latency issues, but with ASIO II and a compatible soundcard, when you're recording audio the monitor source (in other words your soundcard or interface audio output) is fed directly from the input signal, not from the input after it's been routed via the CPU and the computer's internal bussing system. You have to use an ASIO-II-compatible soundcard for this to work, but in most cases the monitoring latency should be small enough to be considered negligible. Obviously, because the audio is being routed directly to the soundcard output by the shortest possible route, you can't add any real-time VST effects to the monitored signal, although if you're working with an external mixer and you have a hardware effects unit it's easy enough to add reverb to the monitored signal.

Thru-monitoring of this type doesn't help with virtual instruments, because their sound is generated by the computer itself. Only the use of a fairly fast computer, a suitable soundcard and sympathetically designed software can make these devices respond fast enough to feel natural. In order to give you an idea of what's possible, I've tested an eMagic EXS24 software sampler (only compatible with Logic Audio) using an eMagic AudioWerk 8 soundcard fitted in a modest G3 Macintosh, and the latency was too small to be noticeable.

the hardware latency workaround

If you have a system on which latency can't be reduced to a satisfactory figure by using ASIO II drivers or any other practical means, there's another solution, which relies on you having an external mixer. It's possible to record and monitor via the same mixer, although the set-up is a little simpler to explain if you assume that the recording is being made via a separate voice-channel device.

Figure 14.7: Zero-latency monitoring

First, set up your system so that the output from your recording pre-amp is split to feed both the mixer and the soundcard input. At its simplest, this could be a Y-lead (it's always OK to split signals in this way, although it's important never to mix them), but you'll find that a lot of recording pre-amps have two outputs anyway.

If you don't have a recording pre-amp, try using one of your mixing channels instead, and then use either a direct output, an insert send or a pre-fade aux send to feed your soundcard input (although don't route this channel into the stereo mix or to any of the busses). This will allow you to monitor your overdub directly through the mixer when recording, but you'll need to mute the output from the track being recorded within your software or you'll hear both the direct monitor signal and the delayed (latency-affected) signal. Most sequencer packages have a thru-monitoring on/off switch somewhere in their Set-up pages for this purpose.

Because you're bypassing the computer while monitoring your overdubs, you won't be able to hear the effect of any VST plug-ins until after the track has been recorded, so if you need hardware reverb to help you sing or play then hook it up on the monitoring side of the mixer. The complete set-up for this is shown in Figure 14.7.

If you're attempting a punch-in recording to patch up a mistake, using thru-monitoring as described above means that you won't be able to hear the original track, as it will be turned down or muted. A practical workaround for this problem is to record the punch-in part on a new track and then paste it into the original track once you've got it right.

editing

Edits can be of two types: destructive or non-destructive. Destructive edits change the audio data stored on hard disk, whereas non-destructive edits work via a series of instructions that act on the original file in real time without changing the data in any way. For example, most cut, copy, paste and move actions made in the main Arrange window of a sequencer are non-destructive, but many of the tasks undertaken in the Waveform Edit window are destructive. There's usually one level of undo, after which there's no going back if a destructive edit doesn't work out.

When carried out on the main Arrange page, editing is usually accomplished by cutting audio tracks into sections using a tool resembling a pair of scissors or something similar, after which the newly-created regions can be copied or dragged to new time locations, or even to completely different tracks. These regions are there purely to provide a visual representation of the edits being made – the original audio file remains unchanged, so all of the edits you make are actually handled in real time during playback.

All serious MIDI/audio sequencers include a Waveform Edit page, on which it's possible to view sections of audio as a waveform and perform various operations, usually destructively. The horizontal and vertical scale of the section being viewed may be zoomed over a wide range, sometimes to the level at which individual samples are visible.

The most basic (but also one of the most useful) destructive edit facilities is the ability to select and silence sections of audio – in effect, digital silence is written to the section of audio file selected. Destructive silencing is perfect for removing short-duration noise between sounds. A noise-gate plug-in might enable you to do the same thing, but doing the job manually is often more accurate. What's more, once you've changed the file so that

Figure 14.8: Sequencer Waveform Edit page

the desired sections are silenced, you know that you're not going to get all of that noise back if you accidentally reset a gate or remove a plug-in.

You can use the Silence function to eradicate things like guitar-string squeaks, although it may sound more natural to leave the squeaks intact and instead reduce them in level by between 6dB and 20dB by using the Gain Change function. The same trick may also be used to reduce the level of breath noises without removing them altogether. Gain Change is a very useful destructive function, although if you're cautious you might want to use level automation to achieve the same result. Figure 14.8 shows a typical Waveform Edit page.

Other common destructive functions include fading in and out, pitch or time manipulation, reversing whole sections of audio, physically pasting new data from elsewhere or even using special drawing tools to reconstruct short, damaged sections of waveform, such as clicks or glitches.

editing tricks

Editing audio is an art in itself, but there are a few useful tricks you can learn right away. Firstly, if two sections of audio produce a click or a glitch when joined, use a short crossfade of between 10ms and 50ms to smoothe things out. Marking edit points is generally best done "on the fly", by hitting the appropriate keys as the music is playing, and if you can edit on a drum beat or on a natural gap then you're more likely to get an invisible join than you are if you edit in the middle of a word or a guitar note. If your timing is slightly off, you can fine-tune your edit points while keeping your eye on the waveform display. You might also be able to loop around the edit point and then make small adjustments while you listen to the results.

Editing material that already has reverb or delay added is very tricky, as the effect stops as soon as you make a cut. To get around this, try to record the individual parts dry (ie no effect) and then add reverb and delay when you mix. If there are any edits that aren't as smooth as you'd like, adding the delay or echo afterwards will help disguise the edit points. When you first start editing, you'll probably stick to non-destructive cutting and pasting in the Arrange page, but you'll soon develop your skills to the point at which you can copy a good note from somewhere in a track and past it over a bad one using the destructive capabilities of the Waveform Edit page. You should always make sure that you listen to your edits very critically while you still have the option to undo them, and if you're uncertain whether your editing strategy is going to work out you should make a back-up copy of the original audio file before you start.

audio in arrangements

Unless you're performing surgical waveform-type editing or off-line time stretching, you'll probably spend most of your time in the Arrange window of your sequencer. Here you can split audio sequences, copy and move parts and so on, although you might find a few more useful functions, depending on your sequencing software. One such function is the ability to set up a crossfade between adjoining audio regions. Long crossfades tend to be used for artistic reasons, but shorter crossfades can be used to prevent clicks or glitches, as well as to disguise imperfectly matching sections.

It's important to familiarise yourself with the keyboard commands that will allow you to drag MIDI and audio sections around, and you should also find out how the snap functions (if any) work. These functions effectively quantise the movement of a section of audio, but in some cases you need to be able to bypass this function in order to drag audio without restrictions.

managing CPU resources

It's easy to get carried away and add plug-ins to lots of tracks, but beware of pushing your computer too hard. You'll very often find that you can get a better sound with discrete outboard reverb devices, which won't load your CPU at all. Also, you can compress or EQ signals as you record them and thus save on processing power. Note that a few companies are now building DSP cards that plug into your computer's PCI slots to run specially written plug-ins that can be accessed from within a VST environment. In practice, this means that high-quality reverb algorithms can be used without over-burdening your computer.

Problematic audio timing is one symptom of overtaxing a computer, although that isn't the only cause. Latency is something that many users have to accept when monitoring while recording, but if the problem gets too bad you can get around it by monitoring the input signal via a hardware mixer, as described earlier. However, once the audio has been recorded onto your computer's hard drive, playback timing can still wander around to an unacceptable degree if your computer is short of RAM or simply too slow. As a rule of thumb, double the computer speed and RAM specs that the manufacturers give you as a minimum figure, and you should ideally use a fast, modern computer. (In my experience, the minimum specs usually quoted are often sadly inadequate for any serious work.) Also, you should ensure that the software drivers for your audio card are up to date, as a poorly-written driver may allow the playback latency to vary, which will also cause the audio timing to drift. You may also need to check the settings of your audio driver and adjust the amount of RAM buffering and your playback delay settings in order to get your system behaving properly. Many soundcard manufacturers provide recommended settings for the more common software packages, but sometimes you have to use trial and error.

There may also be problems with audio starting on the first beat of a sequence, such as the first second or two of audio being inaudible. When you press Start on the sequencer, a certain amount of behind-the-scenes activity takes place (buffer-filling and so on) before the audio can start to play back, so it's safest to leave a couple of empty bars after the count-in and before the song starts. The same is true of any MIDI tracks used to play virtual samplers.

audio file management

Clever though sequencers are, they can be pretty dumb when it comes to naming and storing audio files. The safest strategy is to create a new folder on your audio drive and then name it so that it relates to the song on which you're working. Then you can set up the audio record path so that all of your audio files are saved in this folder.

Another bit of organisation relates to extra files of unwanted takes. Some programs have a function that allows you to erase audio files that aren't being used in the song that's currently open, but if yours doesn't then it can help to use the colour capabilities of your software to co-ordinate the audio tracks you're using. In this way, you'll check twice before throwing away anything of the same colour!

audio sync

When a sequencing system is set up properly, the audio and MIDI timing should be adequately solid, although problems may arise if you need to sync your sequencer to a less-than-perfectly-stable outside source, such as a tape recorder. If the master device runs a little slow, the MIDI sequence tempo will drop to match it, but the audio may carry on at its original rate, causing the MIDI and audio to drift apart. Some of the better sequencers compensate for this automatically, but if you experience a problem of this kind, one solution is to chop up the audio tracks into short phrases. Each phrase will be triggered at the correct time relative to the MIDI tracks, and because they're fairly short they won't have time to drift out of sync as a full track-length audio file might.

If you're using multiple soundcards to gain more individual audio outputs, both cards should be linked so that they use the master clock from only one of the cards. This may be as simple as connecting the digital output from one card to the digital input of the other, but you should check the manual that came with your soundcard to find out exactly how to do this.

If you experience any problems for which the manuals offer you no help, you may need to spend some time checking the manufacturer's web site to find the latest drivers and set-up information for your hardware. After ringing the software support helplines, user groups are probably the best place to start looking for answers to any problems you still can't resolve. Again, you should also check out the forums on web sites belonging to specialised audio publications.

making your own CDs

CD recorders – both those that come as hardware and those that take the form of computer peripherals – are now so inexpensive that it's more cost-effective to archive finished mixes on CD-R than on DAT tape. CD-R also allows you to compile your recorded songs onto albums that can be played back on regular CD players. If you have more ambitious aims, many commercial CD-pressing plants are able to work from a properly recorded CD-R, provided that your mastering software is able to produce what's known as a "Red-Book-compatible" CD master.

CDs use a 16-bit/44.1kHz format, so ideally you'll need to get your audio files into that form before you can compile a CD, although many CD recorders offer automatic sample-rate conversion for those working at the 48kHz rate used by most consumer equipment, while computer-based editors often provide software-based sample-rate conversion facilities. The way in which you approach the compiling of your finished album will depend on the equipment that you have at your disposal – computer-based editors are certainly the most flexible, but you can compile individual tracks onto a DAT tape (or MiniDisc) recorder one at a time if you're very careful. This method doesn't give the same degree of timing precision as a computer editor, but it can be close enough.

compiling to DAT

Compiling to DAT simply means copying the source tracks to DAT (ideally in the digital domain, in order to avoid loss of quality), so it's vital that your song mixes all start and end cleanly, as there will be no opportunity to clean these up later if you use a stand-alone CD recorder. When compiling finished songs to DAT, always record past the end of each song by several seconds and then wind the DAT tape back to find the end of the track before putting the recorder into Record/Pause mode ready to capture the next track. This ensures that the DAT subcode track will be continuous, which is important, as the subcode track contains the sample-rate clock as well as the track IDs, and if your aim is to produce a commercial product then it's important not to have any discontinuities in the subcode.

Compiling in this way can be done using any combination of DAT, MiniDisc and DCC. One simple technique is to have the source track cued up and paused before putting the target machine into Record as soon as the previous track has ended and then measuring the length of the gap manually before hitting Start on the source machine. You can't get precise gap lengths this way, but you should be able to work to the nearest second. You should always work in the digital domain, if possible, unless you're using some form of analogue processor to sweeten the mix as you transfer the data. If you're going via analogue, be sure to monitor the record levels, as digital recorders are intolerant of clipping. You can take the digital output of an MD recorder directly into the digital input of a CD recorder, as the MD recorder's output is converted into a conventional 16-bit linear format before it is output.

track timing

As you might expect, there's more to mastering than simply putting all of your tracks in the right order with the right gaps in between them. You also need to think about the relative levels of the tracks on your master tape and the lengths of the pauses between them. Don't just set all of the tracks to reach the same peak level, because the chances are that they'll still sound off balance. The right approach is a mixture of feel and experience, but one tip is to listen in particular to the vocals and the rhythm section.

The voice will normally be reasonably consistent in level from track to track, even if one song is a ballad and the other is a heavy dance track, and a useful technique is to think about whether the vocal sounds closer or further away in comparison with the tracks on either side. You'll know when you've achieved an ideal balance when you can imagine a band on stage moving from one track to the next without the sound appearing to get closer or more distant. If your tracks have been compressed or limited, it will probably mean that the louder tracks show 3dB or 4dB more level than the quieter mixes, but that's fine, as long as they sound even.

If you can get your tracks balanced prior to mastering, so much the better. If you can't, though, one possible method of controlling the gain digitally is to use a digital effects unit fitted with S/PDIF I/O, as it's often possible to rig these up to work purely as digital volume controls. In this case, the processor needs to be set to External Digital Sync and patched between the source and target recorders with a short cable. If you don't have a computer editing system or a suitable digital processor, you may have to copy via the analogue domain as a way of adjusting levels – the resulting loss in quality should be acceptably small.

Setting the right gap length is also a matter of feel, but as a general rule a two- to three-second gap will work after a song that ends with a fade-out or a long reverb decay, whereas a song that ends abruptly may require a slightly longer pause, especially if the following song also starts abruptly. You should also consider the playing order from an artistic point of view; it's customary to maintain dynamics by mixing musical styles rather than by grouping all of the slow songs together. The first and last tracks are particularly important – the first track should win over the listener as quickly as possible, while the last track should leave them wanting more.

CD-R burners

Before recording to a stand-alone CD-R burner, check all of the start IDs on your DAT. Obviously, every track should have its own start ID, but there may be occasions where you've crossfaded two tracks and you need to add a start ID during the crossfade at the point where the DAT machine didn't add it automatically. This is easy to do by hand.

Most DAT machines create their start IDs in accordance with the level of signal, so strictly speaking the IDs are all slightly late, as the sound has to start before an ID can be created. The delay is small, but in CD Sync mode some CD-R machines take a second or so after the first ID is recognised before they start recording, so it's a good idea to place the very first ID a second or two before the audio starts. This involves first erasing the old ID and then writing a new one, a simple technique which should be explained in the manual for your DAT machine. When both erasing and writing IDs, it's important to leave the tape running until the Start ID indicator in the DAT display stops blinking, as IDs are several seconds long. If you don't do this, you may end up adding incomplete IDs or leaving parts of an old ID intact. Commercial CD players may also take a fraction of a second to pick up when a new track is selected, so to be on the safe side I usually move all of the remaining track IDs a quarter of a second or so back, to a point before the actual track starts.

If SCMS is preventing you from compiling your DAT, or if the CD-R burner says that the master DAT is copy protected, you have two main alternatives: you could either go via the analogue connections (which affects the sound less than you might think) or you could use a processor with an SCMS stripper built in. If you have equipment with AES/EBU digital interfaces, you'll find that these strip out SCMS data, although they also remove track IDs, so you may have to put these in manually in real time as you record your master CD. When doing this, you should write down the precise times of the track IDs to make sure that you don't miss any. This is a task that takes a lot of concentration, so take the phone off the hook before you start! You'll also need to make copies in the analogue domain if your source recorder runs at some frequency other than 44.1kHz and if your CD-R burner doesn't include sample-rate conversion.

silence detection

You're now almost ready to burn your CD-R. However, before you do so, take time to check the manual to see how your CD-R burner reacts to silent passages, such as the gaps between tracks. Some stand-alone machines have a silence-detecting auto-stop function that can't be overridden. The purpose of this is to stop the recording process at around ten seconds after the album has ended, but it does make life very difficult if you need to include a long pause or a section of silence for some reason. You may also find that some machines interpret very quiet classical passages as silence.

burning the CD

Firstly, use good-quality, branded discs, as they will probably have lower error rates than the cheap, unbranded discs available from the computer store. Always handle blank CD-Rs with care, and never touch the recording surface. A can of compressed air (which can be obtained from photographic stores) is useful for removing dust from the recording surface of the disc prior to burning it.

To burn your CD-R, use CD Sync mode (Multiple Tracks as opposed to Single Track, Then Stop mode!) so that your DAT IDs are automatically converted to track-start IDs. If the disc is to be used as a master for commercial production, it's also important to burn the entire album in one go rather than pause or stop between tracks. Pausing causes the laser to switch off and, because this takes a finite amount of time, errors tend to be generated during these gaps. The error correction on a commercial CD player will hide these, but the equipment at the CD-pressing plant may consider them to be too serious to allow through the system.

quality control

Once you've got your album on CD-R, listen very carefully for clicks, glitches or other errors before making any further copies. (This is doubly important if you're tooling up for mass production.) Check the sound on as many sound systems as you can, and jot down accurate track timings to use on your sleeve notes. (You should be able to read these directly from your CD player as the album plays through.) When you're happy that the album is as near perfect as it's going to get, make further copies by taking the digital output of a regular CD player directly into the CD-R recorder. This is the easiest way of making backups, and it saves wearing out your DAT master. If you want to label your CDs, buy branded discs with an unprinted white or silver label side so that the brand name doesn't show through the label. Alternatively, commercial labelling kits are also inexpensive and easy to use, and they often come with layout templates which allow you to print your own labels by using a computer and inkjet printer, although if they don't it's easy to make your own templates with any basic graphics program. Try to avoid concentric circles in your label design, though, as these look very bad if the label is slightly out of alignment.

using CD-Rs with a computer

When using a computer to edit your material prior to burning a CD-R, you have much more control over the process than you do when using stand-alone CD-R burners and DAT machines. Silencing the beginnings and ends of CDs and creating fades is very easy, although if your songs were recorded at different times, or in different studios, they may not sound consistent in either level or overall tone. Often, a little careful EQ (courtesy of software plug-ins) will improve matters, but don't overdo this, as you could make things worse. Listen in particular to the bass end of each song – for example, one song might have all of its bass energy bunched up at around 80-90Hz, while another might have an extended deep bass that goes right down to 40Hz or below. Your aim is to get them sounding more similar. For those tracks that have an extended bass but little focus, try rolling off the sub-bass and peaking up the 80Hz area slightly, while for the track with the bunched-up bass you could try adding a gentle 40Hz boost combined with a little cut at around 100-120Hz. You'll need to experiment with this, as I can't give you a definitive EQ setting, but it's always best to use cut rather than excessive boost to fix a problem, if possible.

At the mid point and high end, you can apply a gentle boost of between 12kHz and 15kHz to add a little air and presence to a mix without making it sound brash, but you should take care to use a wide Q setting. Cutting between 1kHz and 3kHz can help reduce harshness, while boxiness tends to occur between 150Hz and 400Hz, so use a little cut there if you have a problem.

In order to make a track sound louder when it's already normalised or peaking close to digital full scale, try using a software limiter. In most cases, you'll be able to increase the overall level by up to 6dB or even more before your ears begin to notice that the peaks have been processed. After processing, I tend to normalise the levels of individual songs where necessary, which brings their peak levels up to the maximum possible level without causing clipping, at which point I use the gain controls within my CD-burning software to lower the levels of any tracks that sound too loud, until the album sounds right. Normalising, or other level-matching changes, should always be the last thing that you carry out (other than limiting), as all EQ and dynamics processing causes some change in level.

Proper re-dithering to 16-bit resolution is also recommended as being the final step in the procedure, especially if you started out with 24-bit audio files. This doesn't make much difference when it comes to pop music with a limited dynamic range, but it can make fade-outs and reverb tails a little smoother. The science of dithering is rather beyond the scope of this book, but it's essentially a system of adding a very small amount of mathematically generated noise to a signal as it's reduced in bit depth, in order to preserve low-level fidelity at the expense of a minuscule increase in background hiss. Most dithering systems use a technique known as *noise shaping* to locate the added noise in a part of the spectrum at which human ears are at their least sensitive (usually above 15kHz).

CD-R-burning software

It's important that the CD-mastering software you use is designed to produce Red-Book-format CDs if you want to press commercial-quality

CDs from your master. The Red-Book specification simply means that the CD is produced to the same specification as a commercial CD, complete with all of the necessary timing subcode data. Red-Book CD-Rs have to be written in one session rather than in sections, just as with hardware CD recorders; but, unlike stand-alone recorders, CD-Rs can be burned faster than in real time (usually four or eight times as fast). Once the individual audio tracks have been edited and processed with editing software, the tracks are then loaded into the CD-burning software's playlist, where their running order may be changed as desired.

Macintosh users may want to look at Adaptec's Jam mastering software, as it's fully Red-Book compatible, it's very easy to use and it allows the user to adjust the level or stereo balance of any of the songs in the playlist. All gap lengths may be adjusted and auditioned independently, and there's also a provision to create crossfades between tracks, as well as fade-ins and fade-outs. Alternatively, some editing software packages also include similar CD-burning facilities as part of their main programs. One point to note, however, is that not all CD-burning software supports all CD-ROM writers, so you should contact your software's distributor or visit the manufacturer's web site in order to find a list of compatible drives before buying one.

It's also wise to confirm with the CD manufacturer that they can press CDs from your CD-R master. Let them know what CD-burning software you're using, just in case they know of any problems.

As with CD-Rs made on a hardware recorder, listen to the finished master all the way through – preferably using headphones, as this will show up small glitches and noises that loudspeakers may mask. Digital clicks can appear in even the best systems, although using good-quality digital interconnecting cables that are no longer than necessary will help to reduce the risk of these cropping up.

music and the internet

A lot of musicians have taken the opportunity to upload samples of their work onto the internet, either via a personal web site or via an MP3 site. MP3 describes a form of data compression used to make audio files small enough to transport over the internet, and this – like the systems used in DCC and MiniDisc – is achieved by discarding data that a designated algorithm judges to be inaudible. Typical MP3 files are around 10% of the size of uncompressed 16-bit audio files, although some encoding software allows you to choose between having the smallest file or the best audio quality. Different encoders produce different sound quality, so it's worth getting a good one. Because MP3 is so popular now, a number of software-editing packages come with good-quality MP3 encoding built into their specifications.

Once encoded, an MP3 file may be played via any software that includes MP3 playback facilities. If you don't have any such software, however, there are freeware and shareware programs with this facility available on the internet or on the cover disks of some computer magazines (but don't forget to check software obtained in this way for viruses before installing it onto your music system). As MP3 files are just like any other computer files, they can be copied, emailed and otherwise distributed just like any other computer file.

the future of home recording

As computers become more powerful, the need for DSP-assisted hardware will become less important, but it's pretty safe to assume that software designers will find something interesting to do with CPU power, no matter how much we have at our disposal. Virtual instruments and effects will become better as more power becomes available to drive them, and eventually we'll be able to forget about hardware synths, samplers and drum machines altogether (although, at the time of writing, hardware and software instruments look set to co-exist side by side for some time yet). Computer visionaries predict a time when all software will run on all computers and when, if we run out of processing power, we'll be able to ask for help from any other computer that's linked to ours, either via the internet, a local computer network or some yet-to-be-developed system. Perhaps one day we'll be able to call upon the computers in our toasters, TVs and microwave ovens to help us get just one more virtual synth up and running in a particularly busy composition, although I feel that this day is quite a way off yet!

In the foreseeable future, we can expect solid-state rather than disk storage, but I believe that, in the shorter term, digital tape, disk-based recording and even analogue tape will continue to remain viable for a number of years yet. I'm also expecting to see digital mixers appearing that can double as audio interfaces for computer-based music systems, with only a FireWire cable or something similar connecting the mixer to the computer. Many traditional musicians are still discouraged from using computer systems because of the mouse-and-keyboard user interface, so having a familiar hardware mixer would be a much more attractive proposition, from an ergonomic viewpoint, and of course it would free up those computer resources that are normally used to drive mixing, EQ and effects such as reverb.

The next big development in music recording is likely to be surround sound – home theatre systems already have it, so why not mix music for it? Mixing in surround is already supported by some sequencer software, but the monitoring requirements and mixing techniques needed are beyond the scope of this book. For the moment, stereo mixing is more important, as the audio CD remains a very common delivery platform, and anyone with a computer and suitable software can produce their own audio CDs. Surround sound requires a delivery format capable of holding much more data – a DVD player, for example – and at the time of writing DVD-authoring systems are still beyond the financial reach of most project-studio musicians.

DVD may also provide us with the opportunity to mix everything in a 24-bit/96kHz format. While 24-bit audio makes sense for classical and other demanding uses, it probably doesn't make much difference to the owner of a project studio, who's output is limited in quality by other factors, such as electronic noise from synthesisers, ambient noise picked up on microphone recordings and so on. Moving up to a sample rate of 96kHz is even less attractive when you consider that it halves the number of tracks, plug-ins and virtual instruments that can be used (compared to 24 bit/48kHz) while in return bringing about only a very subtle improvement, which can only be appreciated when using the very finest converters in conjunction with impeccable studio equipment in an acoustically ideal environment. Adopting 24-bit/96kHz resolution instead of the present-day 16-bit/44.1kHz CD format would mean that computer speeds and drive sizes would have to triple simply in order to allow us to stand still. Maybe one day we can be this generous with our resources, but my impression for the immediate future is that surround sound will attract more interest, because its audible effects are quite obvious.

the next step

Hopefully, this book has provided you with a useful insight into music recording, in terms of both the hardware options available and the basic techniques needed to obtain professional results. If you've got this far, and are creating music recordings of your own, I hope that you'll have developed an appetite for more knowledge on this subject. The other books in this series (see the front of the book for a full listing) are designed to provide a more in-depth look at specific areas of recording and music production, but they're also designed to overlap and interlock so that everything you learn is presented in the correct context rather than in isolation. Recording magazines also play an important part in keeping you up to date with new equipment, and they also provide interviews with record producers and musicians, practical guides to specific recording techniques and other informative features. No matter how much you learn, or how much recording experience you have, there's always something new to discover. It's a fascinating journey, and I hope that you enjoy making it, whether you end up making music for commercial reasons or purely for your own pleasure.

glossary

AC

Alternating Current. A dynamic electrical signal that regularly changes from positive to negative polarity. Audio signals are an example of alternating current, although the term more normally applies to mains electricity power supplies operating at a fixed frequency.

active

Circuit containing components that can amplify, such as valves, ICs, transistors or FETs. Circuits that work purely by resistive, capacitive, inductive or diodic action are classified as passive.

A-to-D converter

Device for converting analogue signals to a stream of digital numbers. The signal is sampled at regular intervals and the instantaneous level is represented as a binary number.

ADT

Automatic Double Tracking. A term used to describe the use of a short echo to simulate the effect of the same sound being recorded twice. (See Double Tracking.)

AES/EBU

Digital interfacing standard for transferring stereo audio data from one system to another. The connection standard is a balanced XLR, and regular mic cables may be used for short-distance communication, although specialised digital cable is recommended.

ambience

The perceived effect of the environment on a sound heard within that environment due to sound reflections and absorption from surfaces. Heavily reflective environments are said to be reverberant.

amp

Abbreviation of *ampere*, the standard unit of electrical current. Fuses are rated in amps. A current of one thousandth of an amp is one milliamp, or 1mA.

amplify

To increase the amplitude (magnitude) of an electrical signal.

amplitude

The level or magnitude of an electrical signal, expressed in volts.

analogue

A continuously varying electrical signal (unlike digital signals, which comprise a series of steps).

anechoic

Acoustic environment designed to absorb virtually all sound, producing no significant reflections.

attenuate

To reduce the level of an electrical signal.

audio

The area of technology related to sound recording, processing, amplification and reproduction.

aux send

A mix buss output designed specifically for driving external effects or foldback systems. (See Pre-Fade and Post-Fade.)

axis

Imaginary line depicting the primary direction of transmission or reception of an audio transducer.

back-up

Safety copy of tape or software.

balance

Ratio of the left and right channels in a stereo system.

balancing

Cabling system using two out-of-phase conductors within a common screen. When balanced equipment is connected on both ends of the cable, any interference affecting the cable is cancelled out, resulting in a cleaner signal. Most microphones used in recording are balanced.

band

A specific range of frequencies. In audio, this usually means a section of the audio spectrum.

bandwidth

The range of frequencies passed by an electronic circuit.

bias signal

A high-frequency signal which is recorded onto analogue tape along with the audio signal. This signal is inaudible but necessary for accurate recording.

binary

Numbering system comprising ones and zeros. Binary mathematics is the basis of virtually all computer operations.

bit

Short for *binary digit*. Describes the smallest piece of binary information, which may be either a one or a zero.

boost/cut control

Control which allows a range of frequencies to be either increased or decreased in level. In the centre position, the control has no effect.

bouncing

Process of mixing two or more tracks from a multitrack recorder and simultaneously recording the result back to another track.

buffer

Section of computer RAM used for the temporary storage of information. The term may also be used to describe an analogue circuit designed to isolate the effects on one circuit from another circuit connected to it. For example, a buffer circuit on the output of one device may be used to prevent the next piece of equipment in line from loading the output of the first device.

buss

An electrical signal path onto which other signals may be mixed. In a mixer or multitracker, different busses are provided to carry the stereo mix, the signals being mixed to tape, the aux sends and so on. The term "buss" is also applied to power cables that supply numerous destinations – for example, to the individual circuit boards inside a mixer.

byte

A piece of digital data comprising eight bits.

C-60

Cassette tape designed to provide a total of 60 minutes of playing time when used in a conventional cassette deck. When used in a multitracker, the maximum playing time will be reduced to 30 minutes, because the tape will be played in only one direction (ie it isn't turned over when it reaches the end). In some multitrackers, the tape speed is double that of a hi-fi machine in order to produce higher-quality sound. However, this halves the maximum playing time, which means that a C-60 tape will provide a maximum of 15 minutes of recording time.

cable

Insulated electrical conductor – for example, a power cord or signal lead.

Cannon connector

Proprietary brand of XLR connector.

capacitor

Electronic component comprising two spaced conductors coupled electrostatically. The space between the conductors may be air or some other non-conducting dielectric material.

capacitor microphone

A professional recording microphone that works by using small changes in electrical capacitance. Capacitor microphones require phantom power to operate, usually at 48V.

cardioid

A type of microphone pick-up pattern relating to a mic that picks up sounds from mainly one direction. These mics may also be known as *unidirectional*.

channel

The signal input path of a mixer or multitracker and its associated controls. MIDI systems also operate on one of 16 channels. (See the chapter on "Introducing MIDI".)

chase

The process whereby the slave device in a master/slave synchronisation system attempts to achieve sync with the master.

chorus

Effect using delay and pitch modulation to create the effect of two or more musicians playing the same part.

clipping

Type of distortion where the top of a waveform is truncated above a certain threshold. This usually occurs when a circuit is forced to handle a signal level higher than the maximum level that it was designed to take.

clock

Electronic circuit designed to generate precisely-spaced pulses for timing applications, such as analogue-to-digital conversion or to drive a digital processor.

clone

Exact copy. In digital recording, the term relates to a digital transfer of a tape or disk, where the data transferred is exactly identical to the original.

compander

Circuit with both compressor and expander stages, usually for use in a noise-reduction system.

compressor

Processor for reducing the dynamic range of an audio signal.

conductor

Material that presents little resistance to the flow of electrical current.

continuous controller

Control that provides smoothly variable control rather than obviously switched steps. Of course, in digital circuits and MIDI, all changes are made up of discrete steps, although the result is perceived as being continuous, provided that the changes between successive steps are small enough.

control voltage

A varying voltage used to control one or more parameters of a circuit.

CrO_2

Type of recording tape based on a chromium oxide compound. Also known as Type II. Most multitrackers are designed to give the best results with Type II tapes.

cut and paste

An editing term that originated with word processing. Describes the process of copying or moving data from one place to another.

cut-off frequency

The frequency at which the gain of an amplifier or filter falls by 3dB.

D-to-A converter

Circuit for converting a digitised signal back into an analogue signal. Also known as a DAC.

daisy chain

To connect two or more devices in series, where the output of one device feeds the input of the next device along, and so on.

damping

Control exercised by the output of an amp on a loudspeaker's attempt to overshoot. The damping factor is calculated as the load (speaker) impedance divided by the amp's output impedance.

DAT

Digital Audio Tape, used with DAT recorders.

data

Information stored in a digital (usually binary) form.

dB

Short for decibel. Used to express the relative levels of two electrical voltages, powers or sounds.

dBm

Reference level where 0dBm = 1mW into 600 ohms.

dB per octave

A measure of the slope of a filter circuit.

dBu

Same as dBv.

dBv

Reference level where 0dBv = 0.775V.

dBV

Reference level where 0dBv = 1V.

dbx

Type of tape noise-reduction system.

DC

Direct current.

decay

Time it takes for a reverberatory or echoing sound to fall in level by 60dB. Also used to describe the closing of an envelope-generating circuit.

desk

Alternative word for mixer or console.

depth

Amount by which one parameter is modulated by another – for example, vibrato or chorus depth.

detent

Mechanical "click" designed to indicate the centre of the travel of a rotary control, such as a pan pot of EQ cut/boost control.

dielectric

Insulating layer between the two conductors of a capacitor.

digital audio

Electronic device that works by representing electrical signals as a series of binary numbers.

digital delay

Digital processor for generating delay or echo effects.

digital reverb

Digital processor for recreating reverberation.

DIN connector

Type of multipin connector with several possible pin configurations. MIDI uses a five-pin, 180° DIN plug and socket.

disk drive

Mechanism for reading and writing computer floppy or hard disks. Fixed hard drives include a disk that cannot be removed.

display

Computer monitor or some form of alpha-numeric readout built from LCDs or LEDs.

distortion

Any measurable difference (other than in amplitude) between an input and an output signal.

dither

System of adding low-level noise to digital signals in order to produce smoother low-signal performance at the expense of a slight increase in background noise.

Dolby

Type of tape noise-reduction system. Dolby B, C and S are used in both hi-fi and semi-pro recording equipment, while Dolby SR and Dolby A are used only in professional applications.

double tracking

Process of recording the same performance twice onto two different tape tracks. When the two parts are played back, the effect of two people playing or singing together is created. Double tracking is often employed to thicken up the sound of weak vocals.

driver

Term used to describe the mechanical part of a loudspeaker. Also used to describe a piece of software that enables a hardware peripheral or internal card to interface with a computer.

dry signal

Sound source that has no added effect. Conversely, a sound treated with an effect, such as reverberation or echo, is often described as being wet.

ducking

Process of controlling the level of one audio signal with another.

dynamic microphone

Microphone that uses a moving coil in a magnetic field to generate an output signal

dynamic range

Range between the highest and lowest levels of a signal. This range is usually expressed in decibels.

echo

Effect created by repeating the original signal – often several times – after a short delay.

edit

To change recorded data or computer-stored digital data in some way.

effect

Device designed to add special effects to a sound. Examples include delay, reverb, pitch shifting, chorus, flanging, ADT, phasing and vibrato.

effects return

Additional mixer input designed to feed an effects unit back into a mix.

effects send

Mixer output designed to feed an external effects unit.

electret microphone

Type of microphone based on a permanently charged capacitor capsule.

envelope

Overall amplitude contour of an electrical waveform.

equaliser

Device used to selectively increase or decrease the level of specific parts of the audio spectrum relative to others.

erase

To remove data from a recording system and replace it with silence. Recordings may also be erased by recording new material in place of the original material.

expander

Audio processor designed to increase the dynamic range of a signal. Conceptually like a compressor in reverse.

expander module

Usually describes a MIDI sound module, although the term may also be used to describe an add-on used to provide a mixer with more channels.

fader

Slider control, as opposed to a rotary control.

ferric

Type of recording tape. Ferric tapes are usually the cheapest, but they don't produce such high-quality results as CrO_2 or Type II tapes.

filter

Circuit that amplifies or attenuates a specific band of frequencies.

FireWire

Computer connection protocol used to connect external devices, such as hard drives, scanners, digital cameras, audio interfaces and so on.

flanging

Delay effect using modulation and feedback to produce a sweeping sound.

foldback

Also known as cue. System for providing performers with a separate mix, which they can listen to while recording or overdubbing.

format

Process done to a computer disk before it can be used to store data. Formatting effectively creates "compartments" into which data can be stored.

frequency

Number of cycles of a repetitive waveform that occur each second.

frequency response

A measurement of the frequency range that can be accurately handled by a piece of electrical equipment, a microphone or a loudspeaker.

FSK

Frequency Shift Keying. A system for representing MIDI Clock pulses as bursts of audio tones that can be recorded onto tape.

FX

Slang term for effects.

gain

Amount by which a signal is amplified.

gate

Device for shutting off a signal when it falls below a specific threshold level.

glitch

Unwanted pop or click that gets recorded onto tape, often due to electrical interference from an outside source.

graphic equaliser

Equaliser that uses several faders, each of which provides cut or boost over a narrow range of frequencies.

ground

Electrical connection to earth.

ground loop

Wiring problem that causes unwanted hum to be added to an audio signal.

hard-disk recording

Process of recording digitised audio data onto a hard disk rather than onto tape.

harmonic

High-frequency component of a waveform at a multiple of the fundamental frequency.

harmonic distortion

Addition of harmonics not originally present in a signal.

HF

High Frequency.

high-pass filter

Filter that passes signals above a specified frequency and attenuates those that fall below it.

impedance

The AC resistance of a circuit.

inductor

Electrical component (usually some form of coil) that exhibits inductance. Inductors have a higher impedance at high frequencies than they have at low frequencies.

insert point

Connection socket that allows an external processor to be "inserted" in series with a signal.

insulator

Material with very high resistance that effectively prevents an electrical current from flowing.

interface

Device that converts one form of data or signal to another. For example, a MIDI interface allows MIDI information to be generated and read by a computer.

I/O

Input/Output.

ips

Inches per second.

jack plug

Common semi-pro recording and instrument audio connector. May be either mono or stereo.

jack socket

Receptacle for a jack plug.

keyboard

Musical interface based on the piano keyboard but electrical in operation. Also applies to a computer keyboard.

kHz

Multiples of 1,000Hz, or 1,000 cycles of a waveform per second.

kilo-ohm

1,000 ohms.

LCD

Liquid Crystal Display.

LED

Light-Emitting Diode – a type of solid-state lamp.

LFO

Low-Frequency Oscillator. Used as a control source rather than a sound source.

limiter

Device which prevents an audio signal from exceeding a set level. Signals below this level are unaffected.

logic

Type of circuitry used to process digital signals.

loop

Circuit where the output has a path back to the input.

low-pass filter

Circuit that passes signals below a set frequency and attenuates those above it.

mA

Milliamp (one thousandth of an amp).

mega

Abbreviation for 1,000,000 – for example, MHz (megahertz), MB (megabytes) and so on.

memory

Circuit used to store digital data.

metal

Type of tape formulation capable of producing very-high-quality recordings. Metal tape can only be used in machines specifically designed to take metal tape.

microprocessor

Chip at the heart of a desktop computer and other digital devices.

MIDI

Musical Instrument Digital Interface. (See the "MIDI Jargon" section at the end of this glossary for more MIDI terms.)

MiniDisc

Abbreviated to MD. This is a consumer stereo audio recording/playback format based around a small, rewritable digital disc. Data reduction is used so that a complete album will fit onto a disc that has around a quarter of the storage capacity of a regular audio CD. Multitrack machines which have been based on MD technology offer four or eight tracks of recording, but they have a very limited recording time (around 15 minutes, if all eight tracks are recorded).

modulate

To vary some aspect of a signal (or digital representation of a signal) by means of another signal or waveform.

monitor

In recording terms, this means to listen over loudspeakers or headphones.

mono

Single channel of audio information for reproduction over a single speaker. If multiple speakers are used, they all carry exactly the same signal.

multitimbral

Synthesiser or module capable of playing back two or more sounds simultaneously, each controlled by a separate MIDI channel. The majority of modern multitimbral instruments can produce either eight or 16 simultaneous parts.

multitrack

Process of recording a piece of music using a multitrack recording device so that different parts may be recorded at different times.

multitracker

Single piece of equipment which combines a multitrack tape recorder with a mixer. When spelled with a capital M, the term is a registered trademark of Fostex. The term Portastudio is also used generically by some people, but this is actually a trademark of the TEAC corporation. To my knowledge, there is no widely- used generic term for a cassette multitracker that doesn't rely on either of these brand names.

noise gate

See Gate.

(tape) noise reduction

Systems such as Dolby or dbx are specific examples of encode/decode noise-reduction systems, inasmuch as they process the signal during recording and then apply the opposite process on playback. The processing is designed to bring about a decrease in tape hiss, although it doesn't affect any hiss that may have been recorded as part of the original signal.

normalise (patchbay)

Term used to describe the process of wiring a socket so that the original signal path is unaffected unless a plug is inserted into the socket. Mixer insert points are normalised, as are some types of patchbay connection.

normalise (digital audio)

Process for increasing the level of a digital signal so that the highest signal peak is exactly at digital full scale.

octave

Range of frequencies where the upper limit is twice the lower frequency.

off line

Non-real-time process.

ohm

Unit of electrical resistance. A thousand ohms are expressed as one kilo-ohm (1kΩ), and 1,000,000 ohms are expressed as one mega-ohm (1mΩ).

Ohm's law

Formula relating resistance, voltage and current in a resistive circuit. I = V/R, where I is the current in amps, V is the voltage and R is resistance in ohms.

open circuit

Break in a circuit preventing the flow of current.

operating system

Basic "housekeeping" software used by a computer that allows it to run other software, communicate with peripherals and run a display.

oscillator

Electronic circuit that produces a repeating waveform.

overdub

To record onto a new track of a multitrack recorder while monitoring what has already been recorded on the other tracks.

overload

To exceed the limits designed into a circuit.

pad

Resistive circuit designed to reduce the level of a signal.

pan control

Control for moving a signal between the left and right stereo extremes.

parallel

Term used to describe two or more electrical components or systems arranged so that all of their inputs are connected together and all of their outputs are connected together.

parametric EQ

Bandpass equaliser providing independent control over cut/boost, frequency and bandwidth.

passive

Electrical circuit that contains no active (amplifying) components. For example, a resistive pad is a passive circuit.

patchbay

Panel-mounted connectors used to bring commonly-used inputs and outputs to a central location. Signal routing is changed by using patch leads.

patch lead

Short cable used in a patchbay.

phantom power

System for supplying 48V power to balanced capacitor and electret microphones via a standard microphone cable. The phantom power source may be a stand-alone unit, but is more often built into the mixing console or the mic pre-amp being used.

phase

Timing difference between two electrical waveforms, expressed in degrees. For instance, 360° represents a delay of one complete cycle.

phaser

Modulated delay effect which mixes a signal with a phase-shifted version of itself to produce a filtering effect.

phase shift

Change in phase of a signal relative to its original form, via time delay or some other electrical/electronic processing.

phasing

Studio effect created by adding a phase-shifted signal to a non-phase-shifted signal and then varying the amount of phase shift.

phono plug

Type of signal connector used on hi-fi and semi-pro recording equipment.

pitch

Frequency of a musical note.

post-fade

Aux signal derived from after a mixer's channel fader so that the aux send level reflects any adjustment made to the channel fader. Post-fade sends are generally used for feeding effects devices, and may be referred to as effects sends.

power supply

Converts mains electricity to the voltages required to power a piece of electronic equipment.

pre-fade

Aux signal derived from before the channel fader so that the aux send level is independent of the position of the channel fader. Pre-fade sends are often used for creating foldback or cue mixes, and may be referred to as foldback controls.

program change

MIDI command for changing synthesiser or effect programs.

punching in

Also known as "dropping in". Describes the action of putting a tape track into Record while the tape is in motion in order to replace a specific section of a recording.

punching out

Action of terminating a punch-in by switching the tape machine out of Record.

PZM

Pressure Zone Microphone, also known as a boundary microphone.

Q

Measure of the resonance of a filter circuit, defined as being the centre frequency divided by the bandwidth.

quantise

To divide information into equally spaced time divisions. For example, quantising MIDI data will place each note to the nearest 16th of a bar, or whatever quantisation resolution is selected.

RAM

Random Access Memory.

R-DAT

Rotary-head Digital Audio Tape machine.

real time

Process that takes place with no perceptible delay.

resistance

Opposition to the flow of electrical current, measured in ohms.

resonance

Degree to which a filter circuit or mechanical resonator emphasises a particular frequency. (See "Q".)

reverberation

Natural effect created when a sound bounces off nearby solid surfaces in an enclosed space.

sawtooth wave

Basic waveform containing both odd and even harmonics.

sample

Process of digitising a signal by measuring successive points along an analogue waveform. A sampler is a type of synthesiser that uses recorded sounds as its source, which are also called samples.

separation

Keeping sounds separate. In a studio where several musicians are playing together, each player's mic will tend to pick up some sound from the other instruments in the room. The lower the level of this unwanted spill, the better the separation.

sequencer (MIDI)

Device for recording, editing and replaying MIDI music compositions. May be computer based or a piece of stand-alone hardware.

short circuit

Term used to describe an accidental signal path between two points in a circuit not normally connected.

sine wave

Simplest of all waveforms, containing just the fundamental frequency and no harmonics.

single ended

Process that may be used in one stage, unlike double-ended systems, which require encoding at one stage and decoding at another.

signal

Any meaningful electrical information passing through an electronic system.

signal-to-noise ratio

Ratio of the maximum signal level to the circuit or tape noise, expressed in decibels.

SMPTE

Time code used in film soundtrack work, music and recording.

snapshot automation

System for automating mixers or plug-ins where static control settings (for the whole device) are saved as separate events, referred to as *snapshots*. These snapshots may then be made to change from one to another automatically at appropriate times during song playback.

S/PDIF

Standard digital interfacing system for transferring stereo audio data from one piece of equipment to another. The connection format is the RCA phono connector, but specialised digital cable should be used.

spill

Term used to describe unwanted sound leakage into microphones. For example, in a live situation, the drums and guitar amps will invariably spill into the vocal mics.

SPL

Sound Pressure Level.

square wave

Basic waveform containing only odd harmonics.

stereo

Two-channel system feeding left and right loudspeakers in an attempt to recreate the way in which we perceive sounds coming from different directions.

surround sound

System for recording and reproducing sound which uses four or more audio channels to recreate the illusion of sound coming from all directions rather than just from in front, as is the case with conventional stereo. Surround sound is currently popular for home theatre systems but is expected to extend to mainstream music in the near future.

sync

Synchronisation – a process for making two or more time-dependent devices play at exactly the same speed. Some systems, such as MIDI sync, ensure that sync'ed devices start and stop together.

synthesiser

Musical instrument able to generate a wide variety of musically-pitched sounds by electronic means.

track

Originally a tape-based term, track relates to the physical section of tape used to store individual parts of a recording. Tracks are parallel to each other, and are recorded and played back using a multisection head, which keeps them separate until they are mixed. The term has now been carried over to digital tape and hard-disk recording systems, although it's mainly conceptual in this context, inasmuch as the data isn't recorded on individual, parallel tracks.

transpose

To change the musical key or pitch of a note or sequence of notes.

unbalanced

Refers to a conventional audio connection that employs a single signal conductor surrounded by a screen.

unison

Term relating to two or more instruments or sounds playing the same notes at the same time.

valve

Active circuit component involving a heated cathode, a grid and an anode sealed in an evacuated glass tube. The device itself is also known as a tube.

VCA

Voltage-Controlled Amplifier.

VCF

Voltage-Controlled Filter.

VCO

Voltage-Controlled Oscillator.

velocity

Measure of how hard a note is played on a MIDI keyboard.

vibrato

Musical, low-frequency modulation of pitch.

volt

Unit of electrical potential energy.

wah

Filter sweep effect, originally developed for use in guitar pedals.

watt

Unit of electrical power.

waveform

Visual representation of an electrical signal.

white noise

Random electrical signal with equal average energy per hertz.

XLR

Type of pro-audio connector commonly used to carry balanced audio signals, including mic signals.

zero-crossing point

Point at which an AC waveform switches from positive voltage to negative voltage, and vice versa.

basic MIDI jargon

MIDI

Musical Instrument Digital Interface.

MIDI channel

The 16 channels over which MIDI information can be sent.

MIDI controller

MIDI message sent in response to the movement of certain physical controls on the master keyboard, or some other MIDI instrument.

MIDI merge

Device that combines two streams of MIDI data.

MIDI mode

MIDI information can be interpreted by the receiving MIDI instrument in a number of ways, the most common being polyphonically on a single MIDI channel (Poly/Omni Off mode). Omni mode enables a MIDI instrument to play all incoming data, regardless of channel.

MIDI module

Sound-generating device with no integral keyboard.

MIDI program change

Message used to change sound patches on a remote module or the effects patch on a MIDI effects unit.

MIDI sync

System of synchronising two or more pieces of compatible equipment using MIDI Clock, a tempo-related timing signal of 96 pulses per quarter note.

MTC

MIDI Time Code – a MIDI equivalent of SMPTE that uses the same time and frame parameters. Unlike SMPTE, however, MTC is incorporated into the MIDI data stream and can be passed down the same MIDI cable as other MIDI data.

multitimbral module

MIDI sound source capable of producing several different sounds at the same time and controlled on different MIDI channels.

note off

Message sent when key is released.

note on

MIDI message sent when a note is played (ie a key is pressed).

SPP

MIDI Song Position Pointer, a feature implemented by most modern sequencers and drum machines which locates the correct position within a song when syncing to MIDI Clock. If a sequencer is started halfway through a song and sync'ed to a drum machine via MIDI Clock, the drum machine will start at the right place in the song and keep in sync with the sequencer.

mixer jargon

aux returns

An aux return is, in effect, an additional line input channel, albeit one with fewer facilities than the main input channels. On smaller desks, they will be permanently routed to the stereo mix buss, while larger desks will provide the same routing arrangement as on the main input channels. Although these are included for use with effects, they can be used to add any line-level signal (such as that produced by a tape machine, CD player or MIDI instrument) to the mix.

aux sends

Mixers invariably incorporate both pre-fade and post-fade aux sends. Aux sends provide a means of setting up an independent mix of the channel signals, either for feeding effects or for providing a foldback mix. Pre-fade sends aren't affected by changes in the position of a channel fader, which makes them ideal for setting up foldback mixes. Post-fade sends are derived after the channel fader so that, if the channel fader is adjusted, the aux send level changes accordingly. This is necessary when adding effects such as echo or reverb, because it's normally desirable for the relative levels of the dry signal and the effect to remain constant.

in line

Term which means that the monitor channel controls are located in the same numbered strips as the input channels.

insert point

An insert point is simply a socket located at a point where the signal flow may be interrupted, allowing an external signal processor to be connected – for example, a compressor or a gate. Most consoles use TRS stereo jacks as insert points, which means that a Y-lead (with a stereo jack at one end and two mono jacks at the other) is needed to connect the external device. Alternatively, the insert points may be wired to a normalised patchbay. Insert points are usually provided in the input channels, the groups and at the main L/R stereo outputs.

mute

Most studio mixers have Mute buttons on their input channels that turn off both the channel signal and any post-fade aux (effects) sends. Pre-fade (foldback) sends are not normally affected.

PFL

Short for Pre-Fade Listen, a system that allows any selected channel or aux send/return to be heard in isolation over the studio monitors. Because PFL is pre-fade (ie monitored prior to the channel fader), the level is independent of the position of the channel fader. When a channel's PFL button is pressed, all of the other channels (on which the PFL button hasn't been pressed) are excluded from the monitor mix and, at the same time, the signal level of the channel being checked is displayed on one of the console's meters. PFL is generally used in this way to set up the input gain trims on each individual channel.

solo

Also isolates the channel in the monitor mix. However, unlike PFL, the signal is *post*-fader, which means that what you hear is the actual level of the signal in the mix. Most solo systems also retain the pan position of the signal being checked, which is why the term Solo In Place, or SIP, is also commonly used. On a studio console, the main stereo output feeding the master stereo recorder isn't interrupted when PFL, Solo or SIP is used.

split

Term which means that the monitor channels are physically separate from the input channels and are probably located in the master section, to the right of the console.

those numbers!

If you see a mixer described as a 24:8:24:2, that first number is the number of input channels. The second number (eight) means that the mixer has eight output groups. The third number tells us how many monitor channels the desk has – if it's an in-line desk, this will be the same as the number of input channels, while if it's a split console the number of monitor channels may be less than the number of inputs. Finally, the number two indicates that the main output is stereo.